CREATIVE SOLUTIONS FOR ORDINARY PROBLEMS

GİZEM ŞAHAN

42

ISBN Hardcover 978-625-98303-5-3

First Edition, May 2024.

Book design by C42C Publishing.
www.c42cpublishing.com
info@c42cpublishing.com
Publisher Certificate Nr: 76117

Author Email: gizemsahan@gizemsahan.com
Author Website: http://www.gizemsahan.com

Printed in the United States of America.

to my muse Robin
&
to my crazy cat Pusi Thor…

CONTENTS

WELCOME TO YOUR ADVENTURE!

Welcome to "Creative Solutions for Ordinary Problems," curious reader!

My name is Gizem Şahan, and I'm absolutely thrilled to guide you through this book. Think of life as coming with a blueprint. It doesn't, right? So, I drafted one. But here's the twist: this isn't just any typical self-help guide. It is far from that. Instead, it offers a thrilling journey through the highs and lows of daily existence, addressing an impressive 42 challenges directly and effectively.

Why 42, you ask? It's not just a random number; it's a nod to the brilliant Douglas Adams and his mind-bending iconic "answer to life, the universe, and everything!" Plus, it marks my 42nd year on this crazy, beautiful planet—the perfect time to explore the puzzle pieces of the human experience, right?

As you flip through these pages, don't think of it as just reading a book; you're embarking on an epic quest. Each chapter is a doorway to fresh ideas and out-of-the-box problem-solving, turning the mundane into something magical. Around here, we don't just tackle problems; we pull them apart like a magician pulls rabbits out of hats, always questioning with a cheeky, "Why not?" "What if?" and "How else?"

This book is your guide to navigating the wild cosmos of everyday life. We will turn each challenge into an opportunity for growth, and every problem into a moment to awaken your inner creative genius. It's about carving your own path, discovering your unique solutions, and posing the unique questions that only you dare to ask.

Picture yourself soaring through uncharted galaxies, where each star is a burning question waiting for you. This journey isn't just about finding solutions; it's about uncovering your ultimate question, the one that sets your soul on fire and lights your way through life's twists and turns. Whether it's about your purpose, your values, or your wildest dreams, exploring these questions will lead you to a deeper understanding of yourself and the world around you.

Every step of this adventure will challenge you, enlighten you, and make you think in ways you never have before. As Carl Sagan so eloquently said, "Somewhere, something incredible is waiting to be known." On this journey, that 'something incredible' might just be you—your everyday experiences, your insights, your dreams, and your untapped creative potential.

Your Invitation to Explore

From navigating digital overload to balancing personal relationships, each chapter dives into the nitty-gritty of modern life, serving up practical advice and mind-blowing insights. This book goes beyond just facing life's hurdles; it's about transforming how you view everything, sparking your curiosity, and learning to look at the world through a fresh lens.

So, bring your towel, lace up your boots, put on your thinking cap, and get ready to turn each page with bated breath! Let's tackle this adventure together, with curiosity as your North Star and creativity as your trusty sidekick.

Welcome to your adventure in the wonderful world of the everyday. Let the journey begin!

CHAPTER ZERO

DECODING LIFE WITH A DASH OF ENGINEERING, A PINCH OF HUMOR, AND A WHOLE LOT OF CREATIVITY, SCIENCE & COACHING

"In the beginning, there was nothing, which exploded." — Terry Pratchett

---

This book in your hands is more than just a collection of chapters; it's a part of my journey, my essence, my conversation with the world. As you embark on this journey with me, I'd like to share my story of how this book came to life and why its pages hold more than just words- they have a piece of my life, learning, and desire to make a difference.

I want to invite you deeper into my world—a world where an engineer's precision meets a coach's intuition, and corporate experience blends with a passion for personal growth.

The Spark in Izmir. My journey began in Izmir, the modern name for the city that once was known as Smyrna, a city as rich in history as in its zest for life. From a young age, I was a curious little thing. I was that kid—the one who dismantled toys and electronics just to see how they worked, the one who asked 'why' and 'how' more than any other word. That insatiable curiosity had me reading and writing by the tender age of three. (I know, right?)

Growing up, my world was a playground of curiosity—every question I asked opened doors to new worlds. As a young girl, I was fascinated by the intricate dance of life's little complexities, finding joy in the puzzle pieces of the everyday.

Engineering a Curious Mind & The Road Less Traveled. My journey isn't one of sudden revelations but of gradual discovery. From the disciplined halls of Science High School to the rigorous academics at Istanbul Technical University, my life was a quest for knowledge, not just to learn, but to understand.

While everyone else followed the well-trodden path, I found myself irresistibly drawn to the mysteries of the human mind and its untapped potential, setting the stage for this very book.

Studying business engineering, among the equations and theories, I found a language to understand the world's structure. But as I delved deeper, I realized that the most intriguing puzzles weren't in numbers or systems, but in people—their motivations, dreams, and fears—what keeps them up at night. My engineering background became more than a degree; it became the bedrock upon which I built my understanding of problem-solving — structured, analytical, yet inherently human.

From Backpacks to Boss Moves. Once I tossed my graduation cap into the air, I ditched the suit for a backpack and set off to wander around Europe. Think of it as my "not-yet-ready-for-a-desk-job" sabbatical. That year was a wild mix of freedom and "aha" moments that, much to my surprise, nudged me toward the business jungle. Trading in my backpack for high heels wasn't easy, but hey, the adventurer spirit didn't get left behind at baggage claim.

Over 10 years in corporate life, I worked with giants, learned from the best, and carved a niche at the intersection of innovation, business excellence, and human resources. My problem-solving skills deepened in the heart of corporate strategies and human ambitions. I discovered that behind every effective business strategy lies a powerful human story waiting to be told.

I witnessed firsthand the intricacies of human dynamics within professional settings. Where I saw challenges not just as business obstacles, but as opportunities for growth and innovation. It was here, in the bustling intersections of corporate strategies and human aspirations, that my perspective on problem-solving deepened. I learned that behind every successful business strategy, there's a human story waiting to be told. But even during corporate success, there was a voice inside me, whispering of unexplored paths and untold stories.

C42C: More Than Just a Name. In 2014, a brainwave struck me—why not channel this love for science into something bigger? Thus, C42C was born—not just as a catchy name, but as a testament to my love for science and creativity. C' for creativity, '42' for the answer to life, the universe, and everything (a cheeky nod to Douglas Adams), and 'C' again for coaching. C42C isn't just a company; it is a mission—to approach the world's puzzles with a blend of scientific rigor and creative flair.

Transitioning into coaching, I wasn't stepping away from business, but stepping deeper into the exploration of human potential. Coaching became my platform to blend analytical skills with personal insights. With over a decade of coaching, I have been working with high-achievers, entrepreneurs, engineers, and brilliant minds all over the world. What I've learned is that there are universal patterns that run through all our lives, and when we start to recognize them, we can unlock our full potential. These insights, born from engineering precision and the trenches of corporate life, are enriched by the empathetic touch of coaching, showing high-fliers and dreamers alike how to harness their inner scientists and creative genius to find solutions.

So, why this book, and why exactly now? Because in a world that often overlooks the magic of the mundane, I want to be your guide to finding it. "Creative Solutions for Ordinary Problems" isn't just a guide; this book is an interactive journey into the extraordinary side of the ordinary. It's where science meets storytelling, curiosity fuels creativity, and everyday problems become adventures. That's what it is all about. This is not your typical self-help book. It's a guidebook for life, a way of seeing the world that will change everything for you.

So, why should you care? Because if you're like me, you've probably faced a problem at some point and thought, "There has to be another way." And guess what? There is. This book is for anyone who's ever felt stuck, who's ever wanted more out of life, who's ever dreamed of turning the mundane into the magical.

Prepare to embark on a journey where no problem is too small, no question too quirky, and no idea too outlandish. As we turn each page together, I invite you to join me on this journey of discovery and transformation. Let's challenge the conventional, embrace the unconventional, and find joy in the journey of unraveling life's puzzles!

And the best part? You can dive in anywhere. Start at the beginning, the middle, or the end. It doesn't matter. Let the beginning, the end, and the middle be yours. Create your own story from these pages. What matters is that you're ready to embark on a journey of discovery, to challenge the status quo, and to make your everyday extraordinary.

Let's embark on this exploration together, not just to solve problems, but to discover stories—yours and mine.

Gizem Şahan
May, 2024.

CHAPTER 1
THE ART OF STARTING: WHY YOU'RE NOT LAZY, YOU'RE JUST PROGRAMMED THAT WAY

"You don't have to see the whole staircase; just take the first step." — Martin Luther King Jr.

Ah, procrastination- the ever-present shadow in our lives- is alluring and frustrating. Welcome to the paradoxical world of procrastination, where your brain—the most sophisticated organ in the known universe—excels at convincing you to "do it later."

Remember that time you planned to start your diet... next Monday? Or when you were about to begin your novel, right after you organized your entire bookshelf and color-coordinated your socks? Procrastination isn't just a thief of time; the charming burglar convinces you to help carry the TV out the door. That's the procrastination!

Last week, I decided to start exercising. I even bought new running shoes, which are currently under a pile of clothes... for 'easy access.' Sound familiar? It's the art of living in the tomorrow that never comes and the yesterday that's long gone.

Breaking Free from the Laziness Myth

Let's start with a confession straight from the trenches of time management gurus and productivity hackers: **you're not lazy**. No, you're far more fascinating than that. You're a biological being wired for instant gratification in a world that values long-term goals. Intrigued? Let's explore why you put off important tasks until tomorrow, what you could (and probably should) do today, and how you can rewire your brain to take action today.

Procrastination isn't about laziness. But sometimes, that important project you're supposed to work on gets sidelined by, well, everything else. You end up spiraling into a YouTube hole or obsessively checking emails. Why? Because procrastination is your brain's way of saying, "I'm scared, overwhelmed, or just not that interested."

Why Do We Procrastinate?

Procrastination isn't just a habit; it's a crafty beast with many faces. Fear of failure is its favorite mask, closely followed by the illusion of perfectionism. It slowly whispers, "What if you're not good enough?" and seduces you with the siren song of "I'll start right after this episode." or "You can start tomorrow."

But why do we wait? Why do we let the ticking clock drown out the quiet urgency of our unfinished tasks? Is it a fear of failure, or perhaps its sneaky cousin, a fear of success? Understanding the 'why' is like finding the cheat codes to beat the monster in a video game.

Here's a wake-up call: procrastination is not about time management either. It's about emotion management. Studies suggest that what we're really doing is avoiding discomfort. It's about the brain choosing immediate comfort over the stress of the not-yet-started, even when part of us screams to move forward.

The fear of screwing up, the dread of starting something big, and often, a misjudged perception of time—it's all about feelings.

So, if we can manage those feelings better, we can beat procrastination at its own game.

Did You Know? Procrastinators often have a distorted sense of time, perceiving future deadlines as far more distant than they are.

Wisdom from the Wise

Listen up, procrastinators! It's time for a reality check from the wise ones who came before us. Procrastination isn't a recent problem - it has existed since the beginning of time. The ancient Greek philosophers like Socrates and Aristotle talked about "akrasia" - that feeling when you know better but still choose the less optimal path. Sound familiar? It's the philosophical version of choosing Netflix over that nagging spreadsheet.

Even way back in the Victorian era, authors were already complaining about lazy, unmotivated youth. It's like every generation thinks they've got it all figured out, and the next one is just a bunch of slackers. But here's the thing: procrastination is part of being human. It's in our DNA.

Procrastination also raises significant philosophical questions about free will and self-control. Some of the greatest minds in history, like Augustine and Kant, have wrestled with these ideas of moral responsibility and the ethics of action versus inaction. It's not always easy to know what the right thing to do is, especially when procrastination is involved.

Jumping ahead to the Renaissance, Leonardo da Vinci, the ultimate master of starting projects but struggling to finish them, took 16 years to complete the Mona Lisa! His story teaches us that sometimes our quest for perfection can turn into our biggest enemy.

And who can forget the story of Victor Hugo, author of "Les Misérables", locking away his clothes to eliminate any distractions while he tackled his writing? This shows us that removing temptations and minimizing interruptions can be crucial in accomplishing tasks.

But it's not just historical figures who have struggled with procrastination - even modern-day successful individuals have dealt with it. Take Steve Jobs, the co-founder of Apple, for example. He famously said, "If you want to make an easy job seem mighty hard, just keep putting off doing it."

Tim Urban from Wait but Why openly shares his struggles with procrastination, helping others feel less alone in their time management challenges. So instead of feeling guilty about your procrastination tendencies, embrace them as a universal struggle that we all share. Let's turn to the advice and lessons from those who have come before us - they may just hold the key to our own personal success.

The Science of Procrastination and Motivation

Studies show that our tendency to procrastinate is connected to how we perceive our future selves. It's easy to burden our future self because it's not 'us' yet. It's like eating a donut today and leaving the treadmill for tomorrow's you. But in the future, you won't be a different person. They're just you, but slightly older and probably grumpier about having to do all the work.

Let's nerd out for a second. Think of your brain as running a legacy software program designed millennia ago, which sometimes crashes in today's fast-paced world, especially as deadlines loom.

Your brain has this little thing called the limbic system, essentially your emotional processor. It's in constant battle with your prefrontal cortex, the planner. This battle between the limbic system and the prefrontal cortex is at the heart of procrastination. When the emotional side wins (which it does a lot), you end up watching cat videos instead of doing your work. But understanding this can help you hack your brain's procrastination habit.

Meet Your Brain, the Master Procrastinator

The science behind why we procrastinate is fascinating. It all comes down to a battle between two parts of your brain - the prefrontal cortex and the limbic system. Think of your prefrontal cortex as the rational CEO of your brain, trying to plan and make smart decisions. And then there's the limbic system, the impulsive intern who's always looking for a good time, prioritizing immediate joy and the path of least resistance.

This battle between the prefrontal cortex and limbic system is at the heart of procrastination. Mundane or less appealing tasks trigger our limbic system to prioritize immediate pleasure over rational decision-making, tempting us to choose enjoyable or relaxing activities. Although the prefrontal cortex tries to focus on the long-term benefits of completing our tasks, it frequently loses out to our craving for instant gratification.

So, let's get into your brain!

The Limbic System - Your Feel-Good Friend:

This part of your brain is old, like a dinosaur old. It's not sophisticated, but it's powerful. It's the driving force behind our basic survival instincts - fight, flight, and, for our purposes, seeking pleasure.

Located deep within the brain, the limbic system is a network of structures including the amygdala, hippocampus, thalamus, hypothalamus, basal ganglia, and cingulate gyrus. This emotional powerhouse is crucial for regulating our feelings, memories, and how we respond to excitement or threats. It's what keeps us alive by prioritizing immediate emotional experiences and perceived dangers.

When you choose to binge-watch a series instead of working on that report, grab that snack, or scroll through social media, thank your limbic system for choosing comfort over productivity. It chooses immediate pleasure over long-term achievement because, in the wild, 'later' might never come.

The Role of Neurotransmitters

The limbic system's functioning is deeply tied to neurotransmitters like dopamine and serotonin:

Dopamine: Think of it as your brain's very own "feel-good" booster. It's all about rewarding us for behaviors that bring us joy, even if they're not productive. Dopamine is the driving force behind our desire to achieve and the pleasure of the reward. It's what makes us want to repeat actions that feel good. But here's the twist - when we face tasks that don't promise immediate joy, our dopamine levels drop, making those tasks less enticing. This is often why we put off what we need to do.

Serotonin: This neurotransmitter impacts mood, which can affect our perception of tasks. When our serotonin levels are low, we might feel anxious or down, making it tougher to get started on tasks. This lack of motivation and the increased perception of difficulty can lead us to procrastinate. Essentially, low serotonin can make everything seem more challenging and less appealing.

Limbic System Dominance in Procrastination

Procrastination kicks in when the limbic system, which is all about instant gratification, takes over from the prefrontal cortex (PFC) - our brain's planning and decision-making hub. This shift can happen when:

- The task doesn't offer immediate rewards.
- The task seems too complex or overwhelming, sparking a stress response that the limbic system wants to avoid.
- Negative past experiences with similar tasks, stored in the hippocampus, make us wary of starting.

In understanding these brain dynamics, we can better tackle procrastination and tap into our motivation and productivity.

Strategies to Mitigate the Limbic System's Influence

Say hello to mindfulness and awareness: Start noticing when your brain's ancient circuits kick in. This moment of awareness is golden. It's your chance to hit pause and let your brain's CEO, the PFC, step in and assess the situation.

Switch up the script: Look at a daunting task and flip the script. Instead of seeing it as a threat, view it as a challenge or a chance to grow. This little switch can tell your brain it's not in danger after all.

Take baby steps: Face your fears gradually. Each small exposure can teach your brain that the "threat" isn't so scary, reducing its alarm signals over time.

Change your routine: New, productive habits can actually rewire your brain's reward system. It's all about creating patterns that your brain starts to love.

The Prefrontal Cortex - The Struggling Manager

Meet the prefrontal cortex, the brain's shiny, new department. This is where all the high-level thinking happens—planning, decision-making, problem-solving, and keeping your emotions in check. It's the part of your brain that's looking out for you, making sure you don't make decisions you'll regret.

This brain region is all about executive function, helping you juggle conflicting thoughts, figure out what's right or wrong, and foresee the outcomes of your actions. Also, hold back on impulses that won't end well in polite company.

Setting a goal, like finishing a project by Friday, relies on your prefrontal cortex. But here's the twist: it gets tired. Ever heard of decision fatigue? It's real. Every decision, every act of resistance, chips away at your willpower.

Understanding that procrastination is your brain's way of

coping, not a personal failing, can change the game. We can work with our brains to get things done.

Cognitive Overload: The Modern Dilemma

Today's world is tough on the prefrontal cortex. Too much information, too many tasks, not enough sleep—all of these put stress on this brain region. And stress? It's like kryptonite to the prefrontal cortex, messing with your ability to make excellent decisions and leading you down the path of procrastination. That's because stress pushes your brain to rely on its more instinctive parts, like the amygdala, which is all about immediate reactions.

But here's where it gets interesting: our brains are built on habits. Keep putting off tasks, and your brain gets great at procrastinating. The silver lining? Thanks to neuroplasticity, we can teach our brains new tricks and healthier habits.

Boosting your prefrontal cortex's power is key to beating procrastination. Practices like mindfulness meditation, cognitive-behavioral techniques, and regular exercise can supercharge your brain's executive function. Breaking tasks into smaller steps helps your brain manage without freaking out, reducing the limbic system's panic response and making you more productive.

Feeling smarter yet? Procrastination is more than just a whimsical refusal to do tasks; it's deeply rooted in complex psychological theories—for example, *Ego Depletion Theory*, crafted by Roy Baumeister. Imagine your willpower as a muscle that gets worn out. Ever noticed craving that last slice of pizza more by the evening? That's *ego depletion* at play. Your self-control wears out as you make decisions throughout the day, which is why, by nightfall, procrastination often looks like the most attractive option on the menu.

Supporting this, many studies reveal that resisting temptations early on makes it tougher to stay disciplined later. This "depletion" effect makes starting or finishing tasks feel like climbing Everest, hence, procrastination.

Also, there is *Icek Ajzen's Theory of Planned Behavior*. This gem tells us our actions are tied to our intentions, shaped by our attitudes, the social vibe, and our control over the action. It's why we might ditch a task despite planning to nail it, thanks to our attitude towards it, its perceived toughness, or peer pressure.

Fascinating work by neuroscientists at MIT highlights the prefrontal cortex's role in planning and decision-making. When this brain region is off its game or tired, we opt for instant rewards. Hello again, procrastination!

From My Life to Yours: A Story of Overcoming

Diving into the brainy reasons behind procrastination is my jam, and yes, I'm a proud nerd. But don't fret; I'll keep the geek-out to a minimum moving forward.

Now, a bit about my saga. Picture this: me, frozen before my computer, staring down a project that could skyrocket my career. Yet, I hesitated, shackled by the comfort of the known, despite it holding me back. I conquered my procrastination in baby steps, starting with five-minute bursts of work, chipping away at mental walls until those minutes morphed into hours of productivity. It took me over a decade to publish a book—not this one, but five others I never did.

My demons? Fear of success and a quest for perfection. The eureka moment? Realizing that perfection is a myth. Nature isn't perfect, but it works beautifully. Tackling procrastination is about embracing imperfection and making incremental progress.

This book in your hands? It's solid proof that transformation is within reach. It's not about nailing it perfectly; it's about moving forward, one step at a time.

Apps: Use 'Forest' to keep your phone at bay while you work or 'Be Focused' to time your work sprints effectively.

Books: "The War of Art" by Steven Pressfield is a must-read book for tackling the resistance that often leads to procrastination.

Activity: Procrastination Power-Out

Today's mission is to combat procrastination through a series of targeted, engaging activities. This practical challenge boosts your productivity, clarifies priorities, and builds momentum in tackling tasks you've been delaying.

1. Morning Pep Talk: Start your day with a motivational pep talk. Stand in front of a mirror and affirm your capabilities and today's goals, emphasizing your commitment to making the day productive.

2. Clear and Immediate To-Do List: Write a list of tasks you've been procrastinating on, no matter how small or large. Prioritize this list based on deadlines and importance.

3. Pomodoro Technique: Identify a task you've been delaying. Break it down into small, manageable steps, and complete the first step right now. Implement the Pomodoro Technique for a day. Work on tasks for 25 minutes at a time, then take a 5-minute break. After four "pomodoros," take a longer break of 15-30 minutes. This method helps you concentrate without burning out.

4. Task Batching: Group similar minor tasks together. By completing all the tasks at once, you can reduce the time spent switching between them and ultimately increase your overall efficiency. So, why not streamline your work process and get more done in less time?

5. Accountability Partner: Pair up with a friend, family member, or coworker who wants to overcome procrastination. Share your task lists and check in with each other every hour to report progress and encourage adherence.

6. Visual Progress Tracking: Create a visual representation of your tasks and mark them off as you complete each one. Seeing your progress can provide a significant motivational boost.

7. Creative Activity: Engage in a short, creative activity unrelated to your tasks, like doodling, playing a musical instrument, or a quick walk outside. Creative breaks can refresh your mind and enhance problem-solving for subsequent tasks.

8. Reassess and Adjust: Evaluate your remaining tasks. If something takes longer than expected, break it into smaller, manageable parts or consider an alternative approach.

9. Reflection Session: Reflect on the tasks you completed and identify why you were putting them off. Understanding your procrastination triggers can help you address them more effectively in the future.

10. Relaxation Time: Reward yourself with a relaxing activity, like watching a favorite show, reading, or engaging in a hobby. This serves as a reward and sets a positive tone for future productivity.

Benefits: This exercise addresses procrastination directly by promoting a proactive mindset and offering tools for immediate and continuous productivity. It helps break the cycle of delay, offering a structure to manage time and tasks effectively.

Reflective Questions:

1. How did you feel after taking the initial step towards completing a delayed task?
2. What task did you find most satisfying to complete, and why?
3. How did the techniques used today help change your approach to procrastination?
4. What strategies can you deploy to prevent future procrastination?

Concluding Thoughts: Why Start Today? Because You Can.

Procrastination isn't just a bad habit; it's a deeply ingrained part of your neural architecture and evolutionary adaptations. Let's get real about beating procrastination. It boils down to mastering the start. It's about convincing yourself that the task at hand isn't a fire-breathing dragon but a friendly dog that just needs a little coaxing. It's about being smarter than your future self, who's probably a masterful procrastinator.

Think about it. You're not just putting off tasks; you're putting off your potential. Don't let procrastination be the sandbag weighing down your dreams. Remember, the road to someday leads to the town of nowhere. Start today.

Being human means we'll face procrastination. But it doesn't have to define us. We have the choice to act, to move beyond the fear and hesitation. That's the difference between leaders and followers, between doers and dreamers.

Choose one task that you've been putting off. Apply the strategies from this chapter, and just start, even for just 5 minutes. Notice how different it feels to approach it with this new mindset. You're not lazy—you're just about to get moving.

Choose a strategy from this chapter and put it into action today. Not tomorrow, not next week—today! Let this be your first win in mastering the art of starting. Begin small, but most importantly, begin now. Our quest for a more productive and fulfilling life starts with the decision made at this moment.

Lincoln's words echo through time, "You cannot escape the responsibility of tomorrow by evading it today." Imagine the possibilities if you tap into your full potential. Don't let procrastination dull the brilliance of your dreams.

CHAPTER 2

THE POWER OF ROUTINE & HABIT: ESTABLISH A TRANSFORMATIONAL DAILY ROUTINE

"Win the morning, win the day." - Tim Ferriss

Ever feel like your days are a scrambled mess of tasks, like a bad hair day, but for your to-do list? It's time to comb things out.

Routines are your life's stylists; they don't just organize your time—they maximize it. The power of a well-crafted routine is like having a GPS for your day—not only does it keep you on track, but it also ensures you reach your destination effectively and with less stress. Without a solid routine, you're just winging it, and let's be honest: winging it is for birds, not for professionals aiming for the sky.

Routines serve more than just keeping you busy. They are not about monotony; they are about momentum. A well-structured routine transforms chaos into order and anxiety into productivity. Routines are the secret ingredient to a successful life, automating excellence so you can focus on thriving, not just surviving.

Your habits enable you to have more mental space for creative and strategic thinking by automating decisions about when and how you perform the tasks.

Here's the deal: your life today is the sum of your habits. Your physical shape? A result of your habits. Your well-being? A result of your habits. What you repeatedly do (hello, habits!) ultimately forms the person you are, the things you believe, and the personality you portray. If you let bad habits take the wheel, get ready for a crash. If you steer your good habits, you're on your way to success.

Ready to craft a day that sets you up for success every single morning? Let's dive into creating routines that don't work but work wonders.

Wisdom from the Wise

Did you know Ludwig van Beethoven was super precise about his daily schedule? Ludwig van Beethoven, the mastermind of classical music, was as disciplined in his daily routine as he was passionate in his compositions. His morning coffee wasn't just a morning coffee. It was exactly 60 beans per cup, no more, no less. This precise routine helped him compose like a boss. Beethoven's structured daily rituals—meticulous walks, specific piano sitting arrangements, systematic note-taking—were his way of priming his environment and mind for genius to emerge. It's about creating a fertile ground for creativity through disciplined habits.

Meet the legendary Japanese novelist Haruki Murakami, whose secret to crafting mesmerizing novels lies in his iron-clad routine. Imagine waking up at 4 AM every day, diving into 5 to 6 hours of pure writing bliss. But Murakami doesn't stop there - he then shifts to physical activities, running or swimming, to keep his body as fit as his mind. By 9 PM, he wraps up his day, a disciplined practice that not only keeps him in peak physical condition but also hones his mental acuity, fueling his incredible literary output.

Then there's Ernest Hemingway, who wrote religiously each morning to capture the freshness of the early hours, his mind uncluttered by the day's distractions.

You might not be making bifocals or writing a novel every day, but who says you can't? Today's your chance to kick off something big, just like those historical legends did. Let's bring on our own epic starts!

Did You Know? Studies in behavioral psychology have shown that consistent routines can improve sleep quality, reduce stress, and increase overall life satisfaction. The practice of writing a reflective journal can improve cognitive processing, self-awareness, and emotional clarity.

The Science Behind Methodical Days

The science is clear: structured routines enhance mental health, boost creativity, and increase productivity. Our brains crave structure. By mapping out our days, we don't just save energy; we channel it toward what truly matters. My shift from a structured engineering role to the fluidity of coaching taught me one crucial lesson: routines are the scaffolding for success. They minimize decision fatigue, allowing us to channel our creativity and energy into higher pursuits. Let's embrace routines as liberators, not constraints, unlocking our potential with each streamlined day.

Your brain is a habit machine—it's constantly trying to save effort by automating everything it can. Whether tying your shoes or typing your password, if you've done it enough times, congratulations, it's a habit. Neurologically, this is all about the basal ganglia, the part of your brain that plays a key role in developing and maintaining habits. This isn't just handy for freeing up mental space—it's also your secret weapon for building better behaviors.

The science behind routines is compelling—from a neurological perspective, routines help to lower cognitive load, which means less mental clutter and more clarity. The more decisions we make throughout the day, the harder each one becomes, and the more depleted we feel. A solid routine decreases the number of decisions you need to make, preserving your brain power for what truly matters.

Habit Tracking Apps: Habitica or Done can motivate you to stick to your routines by turning your daily tasks into a fun, rewarding game. 'HabitShare' is a social spin on habit tracking because sometimes accountability is what you need.

Books: James Clear's "Atomic Habits" provides actionable advice on building good habits and breaking bad habits through routine adjustments.

Activity: Craft Your Perfect Day

1. Dream It: Take the first 15 minutes after you wake up to really picture your perfect day. Think of it as scripting your success from sunrise to sunset. What are you doing? Who's there with you? How incredible do you feel?

2. Map It Out: Jot down what your day usually looks like and then sketch out your dream day, inspired by your morning visualization. Highlight the shifts you need to make, whether it's adding something new, ditching a bad habit, or tweaking your schedule. Take a moment to review and commit to these changes.

3. Take Action: Pick one thing from your dream day and do it today. Maybe it's hitting the gym, carving out time to read, or working uninterrupted for a solid hour. By taking action, you're actively working towards creating your ideal day on a regular basis.

4. Repeat: Make it a habit to set aside time each morning to visualize and plan your dream day. As you continue this practice, you'll find that it becomes easier to identify and incorporate your talents into your everyday life. Keep tweaking and refining until every day feels like the best day of your life.

5. Share It: Don't keep your dream day to yourself! Share it with friends, family, and even colleagues. By vocalizing your dreams and goals, you not only hold yourself accountable but also inspire those around you to create their own ideal days.

6. Keep Growing: As you continue living out your dream day and incorporating your talents and passions, remember to keep growing and evolving. What may have been your dream day a year ago may look different now. Stay open to change and keep striving towards your ultimate goals and aspirations.

7. Reflect & Refine: Tonight, think about how today went with that new piece in your routine. Did it bring you joy or move you closer to your goals? What worked and what didn't?

8. Pay it Forward: As you achieve your dream day, don't forget to pay it forward by helping others do the same. Share your knowledge, insights, and experiences with others who may be struggling to find their own dream day. By lifting others up, you not only contribute to creating a more positive and fulfilled community, but also solidify your own dream day even further. 1

9. Live It: You've envisioned, planned, and committed. Now it's time to actually live out your dream day. As you go through each activity, be mindful of how it aligns with your talents and overall goals. Notice the difference in your level of joy and productivity compared to a regular day.

Benefits: By intentionally setting and adjusting your daily habits, you're crafting a life that not only looks good on paper but feels amazing to live.

Reflective Questions:

1. Which part of your current daily routine do you find most and least effective?
2. What's one habit that you know is holding you back? How can you make the smallest step towards changing it?
3. If you could add one habit to your daily routine that you believe would change your life, what would it be?

Concluding Thoughts: Reimagine Your Routines

We've explored how to harness the quiet power of routines to create days that support not just what you do, but who you are and who you want to become. Remember, your routine's actual power comes from its flexibility to grow with you and your dreams.

This week, take control and revamp a crucial part of your day. It might be launching your day with a morning routine that supercharges your energy or winding down with an evening ritual that grants you serene sleep. Embrace this change, track your steps, and see the ripple effect of this structured approach unfold into significant life shifts.

Consider habits as the unique code running your life's operating system. Ready to eliminate those glitches? Ready to take command of your days and ultimately your life? Let's stride into our next chapter with this momentum!

CHAPTER 3
THE MODERN TIMES DILEMMA: TOO MUCH TO DO, TOO LITTLE TIME

"Time management is an oxymoron. Time is beyond our control, and the clock keeps ticking regardless of how we lead our lives. Priority management is the answer to maximizing the time we have." — John C. Maxwell

You know that feeling on Sunday evening? You're looking at your calendar, and it's packed—looming deadlines, back-to-back meetings…Your heart races just thinking about it—wishing for a magical 25th hour. Well, we all have been there.

Time management is a bit like trying to catch smoke with a net. We all have the same 24 hours a day as Beyoncé, but somehow, it feels like she's got a secret stash of extra hours hidden somewhere. It's not about controlling time—that's impossible unless you're a Time Lord—but about managing yourself within the time you have.

The thing about time is, it's democratic. Time is the great equalizer: rich or poor, young or old, each of us is allotted the same daily allowance of 86,400 seconds. Yet, managing these seconds, minutes, and hours is more complex than just writing to-do lists and buying fancy planners (though, let's be honest, who doesn't love a good planner?). It's no longer just about having a good calendar app or a well-planned to-do list; it's about priorities, discipline, and the art of knowing what to do when to do it, and perhaps most importantly, what not to do.

In today's hyper-connected world, managing time isn't just a skill; it's a superpower. As the pace of life accelerates, the ability to juggle multiple demands without losing your sanity is more crucial than ever. This chapter will explore how modern life reshapes our understanding of time management, and how you can harness these changes to your advantage.

Wisdom from the Wise

The concept of time has captivated human imagination and necessity since ancient civilizations first observed the cycles of the sun and moon. In ancient Egypt, towering obelisks cast shadows that segmented the day, a primitive yet effective form of timekeeping. Fast-forward to medieval Europe, where mechanical clocks orchestrated the rhythm of daily life, primarily to call monks to prayer.

The Industrial Revolution marked a pivotal shift, as factory whistles and punch clocks orchestrated human labor with unprecedented precision. This historical journey through time management reveals an escalating obsession with efficiency, a crescendo that reaches its peak in today's digital age.

Dwight D. Eisenhower, who served as both the 34th President of the United States and a distinguished five-star general, used tools such as the Urgent/Important Matrix to make critical decisions during World War II. It's known today as the Eisenhower Box or Matrix. This matrix divides tasks into four categories based on urgency and importance, a method that can be particularly useful in clarifying which decisions need immediate attention and which can be planned for later or delegated.

The method highlights that not every decision requires the same amount of time and energy, teaching us to use our resources wisely. Influential leaders know how to cut through noise from CEOs to military generals and make decisions swiftly and effectively. This section explores techniques from high-stakes decision-makers, like using decision trees, the Eisenhower Matrix, and the principle of "strong opinions, weakly held" to navigate complex choices.

Consider the rigorous schedule of Amelia Earhart, who, while planning her flights around the world, also maintained commitments to her writing, public speaking, and fashion design. Her success depended heavily on her ability to manage priorities effectively.

Benjamin Franklin might be known for his electricity experiments, but his real superpower? Rock-solid routine. He meticulously planned his days, valuing each hour like a precious gemstone. His famous daily schedule wasn't just about doing things; it was about doing the right things at the right times, demonstrating the profound impact of routine on personal and professional productivity. Franklin's approach was holistic—balancing ambition with reflection and work with personal growth. His famous routine and philosophy, "Time is money," can be modernized to "Time is your life's currency—spend it wisely."

A time management expert, Laura Vanderkam, studies how successful people manage their time. In her book "168 Hours," she provides insights and practical advice on how to maximize the 168 hours available each week. She suggests that effectively prioritizing tasks leads to greater productivity.

Did You Know? The Pomodoro Technique, which was developed in the late 1980s, involves using a timer to divide work at intervals. These intervals are typically 25 minutes long and are followed by short breaks. This method is based on the idea that frequent breaks can improve mental agility. Studies show that regular breaks can increase overall productivity by up to 13%. It turns out that taking it easy can actually help you do more.

The Psychology of Perpetual Motion

Why do we feel the need to fill every moment with productivity? At its core, the drive can be traced back to a cocktail of psychological and sociological ingredients. Dopamine, the 'reward molecule,' plays a starring role, offering hits of satisfaction with each item checked off our to-do lists. But there's more. Social constructs of success push us to wear 'busyness' as a badge of honor, where being perpetually occupied is equated with importance and potential prosperity.

Let's dive deep into the brain science here: the prefrontal cortex —your executive function powerhouse—is the star of the show. When you improve your time management skills, you're essentially giving this part of your brain a killer workout. It becomes better at deciding, planning, and even resisting the urge to watch just one more episode on Netflix.

Time management used to be about managing tasks. Now, it's about managing distractions. The buzz of social media notifications and the constant flow of emails pull our attention in a thousand directions. Why does modern life make us feel like we're always behind, and how can we effectively prioritize in a world where everything seems urgent?

Our relationship with time is intriguingly complex. Psychologically, we tend to overestimate what we can achieve in a single day and underestimate what we can accomplish in a year—the classic 'planning fallacy.' Recognizing these mental traps is the first step toward true mastery over our schedules.

Our brains aren't just passive receivers of time's tyranny; they are active participants. Neuroscientific studies show that our prefrontal cortex, responsible for planning and decision-making, lights up with activity as we plan our days. However, this can lead to overload, a state of decision fatigue that impedes our ability to manage our time effectively.

Effective time management involves understanding cognitive load theory, which suggests that our brains have a limited capacity for simultaneous thought. By organizing tasks and setting priorities, we can optimize our cognitive resources to focus more effectively and reduce mental fatigue.

Researchers like David Eagleman have shown that our sense of time is flexible and influenced by attention, emotions, and even the amount of new information we process. For example, time seems to 'slow down' during a car accident because the brain records more detailed memories.

Laura Vanderkam, a time management guru, said: "Instead of saying 'I don't have time,' try saying 'it's not a priority,' and see how that feels." This shift in language can profoundly change how you view the importance of your activities.

Apps: Explore how tools like Todoist can automate reminders and keep you on track.

Books: Dive into "Deep Work" by Cal Newport to discover strategies for achieving focused success in a distracted world.

Activity: Master Your Minutes

Today's mission is to optimize your daily schedule by prioritizing tasks based on the importance and urgency, leading to more productive and fulfilling days.

1. Time Audit: Start your day by logging your activities and their durations. Use a time-tracking app or a notebook to capture accurately how you spend your time from morning to evening.

2. Prioritization Matrix: The Eisenhower Matrix is your friend here. It's a simple tool to categorize tasks by urgency and importance. Do what's urgent and important first. Schedule what's important but not urgent. Delegate what's urgent but not important. And for the love of productivity, eliminate what's neither.

Do: Tasks that are urgent and important.

Plan: Important, but not urgent tasks—schedule them.

Delegate: Urgent but not important—pass these on.

Eliminate: Neither urgent nor important—just let them go.

3. Plan Adjustments: Based on your prioritization, adjust tomorrow's schedule to focus more on 'important but not urgent' tasks. Minimize or delegate 'urgent but not important' tasks and eliminate distractions that fall into the 'neither' category.

4. Set Specific Goals: Now, for your priority tasks, set concrete, achievable goals for the next day. Make sure they're SMART—specific, measurable, achievable, relevant, and timely.

5. Reflection: Before you call it a day, reflect on the exercise. How did it feel to organize your tasks this way? What impact do you think these changes will have on your productivity?

Benefits: This exercise improves productivity and performance by helping you prioritize what truly matters, decreasing stress, and boosting satisfaction with how you use your own time. This isn't just about doing more; it's about doing what matters. By prioritizing effectively, you're setting yourself up for less stress and more wins, making every minute count.

Reflective Questions:

1. Reflect on an average day. What are you spending time on that isn't serving your goals?
2. How did the Pomodoro Technique affect your productivity?
3. What changes in your daily schedule could make this technique more effective for you?

4. How can you apply the Eisenhower Box to tomorrow's tasks?

Concluding Thoughts

Effective time management isn't about squeezing more into your day; it's about focusing on what truly matters. Remember, you can't save time; you can only spend it. So, spend it wisely. Better yet, live it wisely.

As we age, our routine becomes more predictable and the novel experiences that once caused the brain to take careful note become fewer. This reduction in new information leads to what psychologists call "time compression," where time seems to fly by faster as we get older. Research supports this, showing a 20% acceleration in perceived time from ages 20 to 60.

Practical Tip: To counteract this effect, intentionally introducing new experiences into your life can literally slow down your perception of time passing. This could be as simple as changing your commute route or as engaging as picking up a new skill or hobby every month. Such changes encourage the brain to process more information and thus slow down time perception.

This week, let's take on a thrilling challenge: face that big, scary task you've been avoiding, but with a twist. Break it down into bite-sized pieces and watch how your perspective transforms from "I can't" to "I've got this!" It's our moment to seize control of our time and, in doing so, master our lives! Ready to conquer?

As William Penn said, "Time is what we want most, but what we use worst." Let's change that! When we understand, respect, and get creative with our time, it becomes a canvas for us to paint our life's masterpiece instead of just slipping away like sand. Let's make time for our ally, not our enemy.

CHAPTER 4

UNLOCKING CREATIVITY: HOW TO SMASH THE BOX AND REINVENT THE WHEEL

"Creativity is intelligence having fun." — Albert Einstein

Imagine you're a painter standing before a blank canvas, or a writer staring at a blinking cursor on an empty page. The desire to create is there, palpable and urgent, but the inspiration just isn't flowing. That canvas stays blank; that document remains untitled. Welcome to the frustrating world of creative blocks, a realm where ideas are elusive, and inspiration seems like a distant memory. You sit down, ready to unleash a masterpiece, and... nothing. It's like your muse decided to take a vacation just when you needed her most.

Here's the straightforward truth: waiting for inspiration to strike is like waiting for a bus in a bus strike—it's not coming. You're staring at a blank screen, which might as well be laughing at you. It's maddening. But here's the kicker—creativity isn't about divine inspiration; it's about setting the stage, rolling up your sleeves, and getting your hands dirty. Let's get practical about sparking creativity, shall we?

Do you think your creativity is finite, like a gas tank running on fumes after a long journey? It's time to ditch that mindset. Creativity isn't a tank that depletes; it's a muscle, and like any other muscle in our body, it needs exercise to grow. Stuck in a rut? That's just your creativity craving a workout. Let's bust the myth that creativity is only for the chosen few and get everyone in the driver's seat.

Creative blocks don't discriminate. Whether you're a writer, artist, entrepreneur, musician, or anyone who relies on creative thinking in your personal or professional life, you've met this nemesis. It's like hitting a mental speed bump at full throttle. You want to move forward, but something invisible is holding you back. But what if we viewed these blocks not as barricades but as detours, guiding us toward new avenues of thought?

In this chapter, we dive deep into the shadowy corners of creative stagnation and, more importantly, how to break free from it. This chapter isn't merely about stepping out of the box; it's about smashing that box to smithereens and using the pieces as a launchpad. Let's ignite your creative sparks and make some fireworks!

"Art washes away from the soul the dust of everyday life." — Pablo Picasso

---

Wisdom from the Wise

Steve Jobs didn't just think differently; he made thinking differently a virtue. "Think different" was his motto. He connected calligraphy with technology and intuition with engineering. His ability to blend disciplines, to see the art in technology and the technology in art, revolutionized multiple industries. From him, we learn that if you want to be irreplaceable, you must be different.

Frida Kahlo, a maestro of emotion and color, turned personal agony into global admiration by using her canvas as a confession booth. Her story teaches us that the seeds of creativity grow best in the soils of sincerity and personal truth. She didn't just paint; she bared her soul, teaching us that true creativity often stems from raw, unfiltered honesty. Kahlo's work also reminds us that creativity usually thrives at the intersection of hardship and healing.

Picasso didn't just paint; he reinvented the canvas with every brushstroke. Each period, from the Blue Period to Cubism, was him showing off a new way to see the world. If Picasso taught us anything, it's that creativity is not a static trait but a dynamic process of continuous evolution and brave experimentation.

George Lois championed the idea that creativity is about connecting things. He believed creative people connect their experiences and synthesize new things. Creativity isn't about being the best; it's about being the most persistent. George Lois said best: "Creativity can solve almost any problem." The creative act, the act itself, can defeat habit by originality and overcome everything.

Did You Know? Psychological studies have found that people are more likely to reach peak creativity when slightly distracted, allowing their minds to make unique associations. Walking increases creativity. Stanford researchers found that when walking, a person's creativity increased by an average of 60%.

The Muses and the Modern Mind

In ancient Greece, the concept of creativity was intimately connected to the divine. Unlike today's internalized struggle with creative blocks, where the individual is often seen as solely responsible for generating and sustaining creativity, the Greeks looked to the muses for inspiration. This belief in divine muses as the source of all artistic and scientific inspiration provided not only a robust support system for creativity but also a way to understand and address the inevitable dry spells of artistic output.

The Greeks personified artistic inspiration through the muses, nine goddesses who each governed a specific artistic domain. This pantheon included:

- Calliope, the muse of *epic poetry*,
- Clio, the muse of *history*,
- Erato, the muse of *love poetry*,
- Euterpe, the muse of *music*,
- Melpomene, the muse of *tragedy*,
- Polyhymnia, the muse of *hymns*,
- Terpsichore, the muse of *dance*,
- Thalia, the muse of *comedy*, and
- Urania, the muse of *astronomy*.

These nine goddesses, daughters of Zeus and Mnemosyne (the goddess of memory), were thought to provide the spark for all forms of art and scientific endeavor. Each muse not only inspired but also guided the artists, poets, musicians, and thinkers of the time. This externalization of the source of creativity meant that artistic blocks, or periods of reduced creativity, were attributed to a muse's absence or inattention, not a personal shortcoming of the artist.

The Modern Creative Struggle: The Shift from Divine to Personal

In today's world, the creative struggle is deeply internalized, often perceived as a solitary journey fraught with personal challenges and self-doubt. This perspective marks a significant departure from historical views on creativity, which often attributed inspiration to external, often divine, sources. Modern creatives carry the entire weight of the creative process, from inception through execution, often viewing blocks and barriers as personal shortcomings rather than part of a natural ebb and flow.

This internalization of creativity affects individuals on multiple psychological levels, influencing how they perceive their abilities and worth.

Pressure to Perform: In the modern narrative, the artist is seen as a self-sufficient creator who must consistently produce innovative work. This shift puts immense pressure on individuals, making creative blocks feel like personal failures rather than moments of necessary rest or recalibration.

The Cult of Productivity: Modern culture often equates productivity with value, further intensifying the pressure on creatives to produce. This relentless push can lead to burnout, where the mind becomes fatigued and unable to generate new ideas effectively.

Fear of Inadequacy: Many creatives suffer from impostor syndrome, a pervasive feeling of self-doubt and fear of being exposed as a "fraud" despite evident success. This syndrome is exacerbated by the internalization of the creative process, as any failure or block can trigger deep-seated insecurities.

Perfectionism and Procrastination: The pressure to produce perfect work can lead to procrastination, where creatives delay starting or completing projects out of fear that the results will not meet high internal or external expectations. This cycle of procrastination can reinforce feelings of inadequacy and failure.

The Nature of Creativity

Forget the myth of the 'creative muse' that whispers in the ears of the chosen few. Creativity is a mental muscle that gets stronger with exercise. Neuroscience tells us it involves the default mode network, which is most active when you're daydreaming or letting your mind wander. That's right; creativity needs freedom, not pressure. Creativity isn't just about having occasional eureka moments; it's about cultivating a mindset that consistently questions, explores, and imagines.

Creativity isn't just for artists, musicians, or writers. It's the lifeblood of anyone who wants to succeed in the modern world. At its core, creativity is about problem-solving and innovation. Whether you're developing a marketing campaign, designing software, or planning your next career move, creativity is your ultimate toolkit for turning problems into showcases of your brilliance. It's like looking at the same thing as others, but seeing something totally different.

Breaking free from conventional thinking isn't a luxury—it's a survival skill. It's the difference between being a leader and being a follower.

Your brain loves efficiency; it craves the familiar. But creativity lives in the unfamiliar. It's about making new neural connections, firing up different parts of your brain to find solutions no one else sees. When you really get how creativity works—how it taps into divergent thinking to synaptic play—you begin to realize you can actually train your brain to be more creative. It's not magic; it's method.

Here's the science: your brain's a playground, not a warehouse. And creativity is not some mystical force; it's a brain function that can be nurtured and developed. Creative activities can improve mental health and reduce anxiety and stress because you are engaging the brain in unique and complex tasks. Neuroscientists have identified that creativity involves a complex interplay between the brain's executive functions and default mode networks. This means creativity can be cultivated by engaging both focused thought and daydreaming—a dance between structure and spontaneity.

Research shows that creativity involves several cognitive processes, such as divergent thinking, which generates many unique ideas, and convergent thinking, which is combining those ideas into the best result. Neurologically, creativity lights up multiple areas of the brain, not just one. This interplay highlights the complexity of stepping outside conventional thinking—it's about making new neural connections that defy old patterns.

Did You Know? Art therapy was established as a mental health profession in the 1940s, but the therapeutic use of art dates back to ancient times.

Think of creativity as brain alchemy—mixing old elements to forge new ideas. Neuroplasticity is the brain's secret weapon for creative power. Each time you challenge yourself with new experiences or learn something outside your comfort zone, your brain forms new neural connections. This isn't just brain gymnastics; it's constructing a highway system where ideas can travel faster and connect more freely.

Neuroscience shows us that when we're creative, different parts of our brain light up in symphony. It's not magic; it's mental agility, fostering connections that weren't there before. Every creative act strengthens these neural networks, making creativity not just an act but a habit. Art can be therapeutic. Studies have shown that both creating and viewing art can reduce cortisol levels (the stress hormone) and can help process trauma, leading to significant healing and mental well-being.

> Apps: Brainsparker for creativity prompts that encourage you to think outside the box and Oflow for creative prompts that push your thinking beyond the usual boundaries.

> Books for the Brave: Dive into "Outliers" by Malcolm Gladwell and explore how breaking norms are at the heart of extraordinary success. "The Creative Act" by Rick Rubin is a masterpiece about creativity. "Steal Like an Artist" by Austin Kleon.

Activity: Creative Exploration Day

Today's mission is to unleash and cultivate your creative potential through various mediums and activities, enhancing innovation and self-expression.

1. Morning Inspiration: Begin your day with a 10-minute meditation focused on opening your mind to creative possibilities. Visualize entering a space filled with inspiring art, ready to absorb and engage with new expressions.

2. Curated Playlist: Create or select a music playlist from different genres or cultures to set a stimulating backdrop for your day.

3. Local Art Tour: Visit a local art gallery, museum, or art installation in your community. If in-person visits aren't possible, explore virtual tours offered by world-renowned museums like the Louvre or MoMA.

4. Creative Sprint: Spend one hour on a creative activity without judgment or interruption. This could be sketching, writing poetry, crafting, or even brainstorming ideas for a new project.

5. No Judgment Zone: Create with the mindset that there are no mistakes, only experiments. Focus on the process of creation rather than the outcome.

6. Inspiration Walk: Take a walk in a stimulating environment, such as a park, a museum, or a busy urban area. Bring a notebook to jot down or sketch any ideas that come to you.

7. Cultural Exploration: Watch a foreign film or a play that offers insight into different cultural perspectives or historical contexts. Focus on understanding the themes, the use of visual symbolism, and character development.

8. Literary Arts: Read a poem or a short story from an acclaimed writer whose works you've never explored.

9. Evening Reflection and Creation: Use the evening to create something inspired by your day's experiences. This could be a sketch, a short poem, or a piece of creative writing.

10. Journaling: End your day by journaling about what you learned and felt during your artistic explorations. Note any new insights about art forms or artists and how they might influence your own creative expressions.

Benefits: This exercise opens new avenues for creative thinking and problem-solving, reduces stress, and boosts mental health by providing a productive outlet for emotions and thoughts.

Reflective Questions:

1. What did you notice about your emotional responses to different artworks? Which art form resonated with you most today and why?
2. How did engaging with art affect your mood and stress?
3. What are some areas in your life where you could benefit from thinking differently?

4. How can you incorporate more creativity into your daily life?

Concluding Thoughts

Here's the thing: if you want to unlock your creative potential and become a trailblazer in your field, you've got to be willing to take risks and challenge the status quo. It's not always easy, but trust me, it's worth it. So, are you ready to stop following trends and start setting them? Are you ready to unleash the innovative powerhouse within you and change the game?

Creativity is not just an action; it's a state of mind. Blocks often occur when we're stressed, fatigued, or trying too hard to be perfect. It's the brain's way of waving a white flag, asking for a different approach or a break. Creativity thrives on relaxation and subconscious processing. When we're relaxed, the brain makes unexpected connections – the bedrock of creativity.

This week, pick a project, any project. Now, I want you to take that project and flip it on its head. Tear it apart and put it back together in a completely new way. Think backward, upside down, inside out — whatever it takes to break free from your usual way of thinking.

Use the tools and strategies from this chapter as your blueprint for reinvention. Document every step of the process and pay attention to the outcomes. What new ideas emerged? How did it feel to extend your comfort zone and into the unknown?

I hope you are ready to stop playing it safe and start playing it smart. This isn't about little tweaks but monumental shifts in how you see and interact with the world around you. This is about taking a sledgehammer to the box you've been stuck in and smashing it to pieces. It's about becoming a person who doesn't just follow trends but sets them.

Let's disrupt the norm, shatter expectations, and unlock a world of possibilities. Your creative adventure starts now!

CHAPTER 5

FINDING 'THE ONE' IN THE MODERN AGE: NAVIGATING LOVE AND RELATIONSHIPS IN TODAY'S WORLD

"Bruce Wayne's parents get killed, and he goes to Tibet or whatever. Superman is an alien, and Spiderman had that radioactive spider. Me? I kissed a janitor in the school bathroom." — Rachel Hawkins

On a chilly evening in Victorian England, Eleanor clads in her finest silk gown, dips her quill into black ink, and begins to write a letter to a gentleman she recently met at a grand ball. Each word she crafts is deliberate, her script flowing elegantly across the parchment. Her heart flutters with anticipation, hoping her words will kindle a romance within the strict confines of societal expectations.

Across time and space, in a busy New York City café, Jay is swiping through dating profiles, pausing just long enough to check out potential matches. His experience, quick decisions and so many options—quite the opposite of Eleanor's way of doing things- deliberate and hopeful correspondence.

Even though they're from completely different times, Eleanor and Jay are both on the hunt for love. They navigate through their own worlds, shaped by their social norms and the tech at hand. This chapter is going to walk you through finding "the one" today, mixing old-school romance with the digital dating scene.

Brief History of Love and Relationships

Imagine a time when the game of love was less about swiping right and more about a left foot forward, right foot back—the dance of Victorian courtship. In this world, finding a soulmate was as much a matter of real estate and bank balances as it was about heart-racing attraction. Marriage? The ultimate game of social chess, with families plotting, moves to capture wealth, status, or power.

The way societies have approached romance and marriage provides a fascinating lens through which to view broader cultural and economic shifts. During the Victorian era, finding a partner was less about sparks flying and more about strategic alliances. Marriages were business deals designed to consolidate wealth, elevate social standing, or secure political leverage. Heartfelt love letters? Try negotiated dowries and estates instead.

Victorian courtship was a minefield of social etiquette. A young lady on the lookout for a husband had to be the epitome of grace, her dowry, her selling point. Men, on the other hand, had to formally seek permission just to show interest. Approved suitors could visit the lady's home, but only during approved hours and under the stern eye of family or chaperones. These visits were a chance to exchange polite banter, steal glances, and size up a shared future—all under strict supervision.

In this scheme, marriages were less about love and more about securing a good deal. Love, if it came at all, was a bonus, not the goal. The pressure to marry within one's class further underscored marriage as a tactical move rather than a heart-led choice. This system is locked in a rigid class hierarchy, leaving little room for personal choice—especially for women—seen more than as vessels of social capital than individuals with their own desires and dreams.

Did You Know? Studies show that relationships formed online are likely to be successful if communication moves from online to in-person relatively quickly.

Revolution of Hearts and Minds

Fast forward to the early 20th century, and you'll see a world buzzing with change. Women taking to the streets for their rights, global conflicts reshaping borders, and the Roaring Twenties flipping society on its head. This was a time when love started to shift from arranged courtships to dating based on personal connections and mutual sparks. Women were stepping into their power, and the idea of marrying for love, rather than social or economic advantage, began to take root.

Now, in the era of digital dating, we enjoy unprecedented freedom in our romantic pursuits. Love has broken free from all boundaries, with the next potential match, even from across the globe, just a swipe away. But, oh boy, does this freedom come with a twist! With endless choices at our fingertips, finding "the one" feels more daunting than ever, and the casual nature of modern dating leaves us questioning the depth of our connections.

Let's be real: dating in the modern world is like trying to navigate a maze blindfolded. One minute you think you've found a connection, and the next, you're left on "read" wondering what went wrong. It's a far cry from the days of Victorian courtship, where every interaction was scripted and every match was a strategic play.

But here's the thing: while the game may have changed, the goal remains the same. We all want to find that special someone, that a person who gets us on a level no one else does. And in a world where we have more options than ever before, it's easy to get caught up in the endless swiping and forget what really matters.

The Science of Modern Relationships

Gone are the days when relationships followed a predictable path. Now, it's a blend of texting, online dating, gaslighting and ghosting. It's less about finding 'the one' and more about understanding oneself and navigating the complex dynamics of modern love.

What does it take to make a relationship work in the digital age? It boils down to emotional intelligence, effective communication, and real compatibility. Studies show that the strongest relationships are built on shared values and open, honest conversations—not just shared hobbies or an initial spark.

Modern relationships are like trying to assemble IKEA furniture without instructions. You think it should be straightforward until you're left with an extra screw and a wobbly table. Love in the time of social media, ghosting, and swiping right can feel like a navigational nightmare in uncharted waters.

But here's the twist: the digital dating world isn't waiting for anyone. If you find yourself swiping endlessly without finding that genuine connection, or if the thought of diving into the dating pool feels like stepping into a vast unknown, consider this your guiding light.

This is the moment to embrace the digital tools at our disposal and set sail towards the love that lies ahead. The journey to find love has never been more exhilarating or complex, thanks to the digital revolution. Online dating, social media, and shifting societal norms have transformed the love landscape. But with new opportunities come new challenges to navigate and overcome.

Why Does Modern Dating Feel So Complicated?

The digital era has completely transformed the way we connect, giving us access to people we'd never meet in our usual circles. It's thrilling to have the entire world at your fingertips, but it comes with a downside: more options mean more confusion. With endless potential matches just a swipe away, finding someone truly special feels like searching for a needle in a haystack.

Dating today isn't just about meeting someone; it's about navigating a sea of digital profiles and making real connections in a world that values speed over depth. But don't worry—I'm here to help you cut through the noise, understand the new rules, and find someone who's as into you as you are into them.

The Science Behind Our Connections: Understanding Attachment Theory

Neuroscience has taken us on a journey into the heart of attachment, revealing the crucial role early experiences play in shaping our brains and how we connect. Secure attachments light up our brains, bolstering areas that help us manage emotions and understand others.

It turns out that the chemistry of our connections—driven by hormones like the bonding superstar oxytocin and the stress-related cortisol—directly influences our relationship dynamics. Oxytocin, often dubbed the 'love hormone,' strengthens bonds, and increases trust and loyalty in relationships. Conversely, high levels of cortisol, a stress hormone, are often found in individuals with insecure attachment styles, reflecting the chronic stress associated with unstable early relationships.

Our approach to relationships often reflects our deepest values and fears, such as the fear of being alone, the yearning for connection, and the quest for personal fulfillment. Nowadays, our relationships aren't just with other people but with technology too, which can either be a bridge or a barrier to making meaningful connections.

At the heart of understanding our relationships is attachment theory, a key concept in psychology that shows how our first bonds with caregivers influence our ability to form relationships later in life. Originated by John Bowlby and further developed by Mary Ainsworth, attachment theory explores how the dynamics between a child and their caregiver shape our feelings of security and our connections with others as adults.

John Bowlby, the pioneer of attachment theory, was deeply influenced by ethology, the study of animal behavior. He saw a clear parallel between children's attachment behaviors and the imprinting seen in birds and mammals, suggesting that children are naturally wired to form attachments with their caregivers as a means of survival.

Secure Attachment: Imagine this—children who consistently have caregivers who are right there when they need them end up feeling pretty great about themselves. They grow up feeling secure, valuing both closeness with others and their own independence. They basically see the world as a big, safe playground.

Anxious and Avoidant Attachments: Now, on the flip side, there are children whose caregivers were inconsistently responsive or consistently unresponsive, or maybe just not there emotionally. These kids developed either anxious or avoidant attachment styles.

Anxiously attached individuals often feel desperate for love to validate their self-worth. They cling to love like it's a lifeline to feeling worthy. In contrast, avoidantly attached individuals suppress their need for intimacy as a defense mechanism against potential rejection or pain. They might just push people away before they can get hurt. It's their way of protecting themselves.

Mary Ainsworth, a brilliant mind in developmental psychology, took John Bowlby's groundbreaking concepts to the next level. This method, known as the "Strange Situation," involves a series of introductions, separations, and reunions that reveal the nature of the attachment bond.

In a controlled environment, a child is briefly left alone or with a stranger and reunited with their caregiver. The child's behaviors are observed to determine if they exhibit secure, anxious, or avoidant attachment behaviors.

Ainsworth's studies were eye-opening. They showed that securely attached children show visible distress when their caregiver leaves, only to bounce back quickly once they return. On the flip side, anxiously attached kids are a whirlwind of distress, craving yet resisting comfort upon the caregiver's return. And then there are the avoidantly attached kids, who remain seemingly unfazed by the comings and goings of their caregiver.

Attachment Today: Navigating Modern Love's Turbulent Waters

In today's swipe-right culture, where options for romance flutter through our phones like butterflies in a meadow, understanding your attachment style could be your best bet at swiping right on a lasting match. For those securely attached, the dating app jungle is a playground. For the anxious and avoidant? It can feel like a labyrinth with moving walls.

If You Are Securely Attached: You're the relationship equivalent of a well-rooted tree. Storms may come, but you sway without breaking. You have confidence in your capacity to form meaningful connections and navigate through relationship challenges.

If You Are Anxiously Attached: You experience emotional turbulence, your state shifting with each text or missed call, much like a weathervane in a hurricane. Learning that silence isn't always a storm can be a game-changer.

If You Are Avoidantly Attached: Embracing independence might be your thing, but even lone wolves can benefit from the warmth of the pack.

Grasping the principles of attachment theory isn't just academic —it's a vital tool for enhancing our relationships and healing our emotional wounds. It's not about labeling yourself; it's about understanding your patterns in love and life to foster deeper, more resilient connections.

Let's explore additional psychological theories that shape our contemporary experience of love, emphasizing the role of technology and social changes in shaping romantic relationships today.

Embracing the Media Equation Theory: The Impact of Likes on Our Hearts

Ever felt a buzz of excitement from a text or a pang of pain from being ghosted? Welcome to love in the digital age, where our devices become extensions of our social lives. Byron Reeves and Clifford Nass's Media Equation Theory sheds light on our human-like interactions with technology, explaining the deep sting of being ghosted and the intensity of online connections that seem as real as those sparked in cozy coffee shops.

Our brains, it turns out, distinguish little between digital and face-to-face interactions, making every message feel like a meaningful social exchange. This insight helps us understand the phenomenon of digital heartache, which is just as sharp and real as traditional heartbreak.

The curated selves we encounter online often lead us down the rabbit hole of mismatched expectations. Recognizing this can arm us against potential disappointments and guide us toward more authentic engagements. So next time you find yourself swooning over a profile, remember, it's just the highlight reel.

Social Penetration Theory: Stripping Down to the Core

Think of human connections as an onion, and Social Penetration Theory by psychologists Irwin Altman and Dalmas Taylor shows us how peeling away each layer can bring us closer. This theory emphasizes the power of sharing bits about ourselves over time to build intimacy.

The digital era speeds up these disclosures, often leading us to share too much too soon. While this can fast-track intimacy, it might also bypass the natural rhythm of trust-building. Balancing openness and over-sharing is crucial in forging connections that last beyond the screens.

Cognitive Dissonance: The Lover's Quandary

Have you ever found yourself making excuses for a relationship that's clearly off track? Thank Leon Festinger's theory of Cognitive Dissonance for those mental gymnastics. This theory explains the discomfort we feel when our actions don't align with our beliefs, like staying in a lackluster relationship because, well, it's complicated.

In the maze of modern love, cognitive dissonance can lead us to make excuses rather than decisions. The key? Be honest with yourself about what you truly want and deserve in love. Recognizing this dissonance is the first step towards healthier, happier relationships.

A Call to Psychological Arms - Empowered Romance

Understanding these psychological theories isn't just academic—it's practical armor in the modern dating world. By applying insights from the Media Equation Theory, Social Penetration Theory, and Cognitive Dissonance, you can navigate the complexities of love with a more strategic eye.

Use these theories as your secret weapons. Analyze your online chats through the Media Equation, gradually open up to form deeper bonds, and stay loyal to your values, even when your heart and mind are in a tug-of-war.

As you step out, armed with psychological insights, remember that every swipe, text, and heart emoji is part of the broader narrative of your romantic journey. With this wisdom, you're not just getting through the dating maze but thriving in it, building connections that are as fulfilling as they are fun. After all, modern love might be complex, but with the right tools, you're more than ready to crack its code.

Alain de Botton said: "Intimacy is the capacity to be rather weird with someone - and finding that's ok with them." This quote captures the essence of modern love: finding someone with whom you can be open with and share not just your highlights but your shadows too and in that mutual vulnerability, finding the strength of true intimacy. Whether through the glow of a phone screen or the warmth of a shared gaze, may your journey in love be as richly rewarding as it is wonderfully surprising.

Handling modern relationships isn't about sticking to a rulebook but grooving to the beat of life's complexities. As Johann Wolfgang von Goethe put it, "We are shaped and fashioned by what we love." Let your relationships showcase the best version of yourself.

> Apps: Reputable dating apps like Bumble or Hinge that focus on creating meaningful connections.

> Books: "Modern Romance" by Aziz Ansari provides a comedic yet insightful exploration of how romance has changed with technology.

Activity: Modern Love Exploration Day

Today's mission is to explore and reflect on modern dating and relationship dynamics through engaging, thoughtful, and practical activities. This challenge aims to enhance your understanding of what you seek in a partner, the landscape of modern relationships, and effective communication strategies for dating in today's world.

1. Relationship Goals Assessment: Start your day by reflecting on your past relationships and current relationship goals. Reflect on what has worked and what hasn't, and determine your own definition of 'The One' based on your values and aspirations. It starts with understanding yourself. What are your values? What do you want from a relationship? Once you have a clear picture of who you are and what you're looking for, you can filter out the noise and focus on the connections that matter.

2. Vision Board Creation: Create a vision board representing your ideal relationship scenario. Include images and quotes that resonate with your vision of love, partnership, and what you find most important in a relationship.

3. Dating Trends Education: Spend some time researching current dating trends, methods, and statistics. Use resources like articles, podcasts, or documentaries to understand the broader landscape of modern dating, including the impact of technology on how we find and connect with potential partners.

4. Communication Styles Workshop: Engage in an online workshop or read about different communication styles and love languages. Understanding these can significantly improve how you express your needs and understand others in a romantic context.

5. Mock Dating Scenarios: If comfortable and possible, take part in mock dating scenarios with friends or through an online dating workshop. Practice your communication skills and be open and honest about your intentions and desires.

6. Dating Profile Review: Review and refine your online dating profiles. Ensure they align with your relationship goals and present you authentically. Ask a trusted friend to provide feedback on your profile from an outsider's perspective.

7. Feedback and Reflection: Reflect on the feedback received during mock dates or from your dating profile review. Consider adjustments to improve your approach to finding 'The One'.

8. Strategy Development for Meeting Potential Partners: Develop a strategy for meeting potential partners. Try including a mix of online and offline methods tailored to your lifestyle and preferences.

9. Relaxing Evening Routine: End your day with activities that relax and recharge you. This helps to digest the day's experiences positively.

10. Journaling on Love and Expectations: Write about the day's learnings in your journal-what you seek in a relationship and how you can actively work towards building a healthy, meaningful connection.

Benefits: This challenge aims to equip you with the tools to navigate the complex world of modern dating better, improve your communication skills, and align your dating strategies with your relationship goals.

Reflective Questions

1. How do your values and lifestyle influence your approach to finding a romantic partner?
2. What strategies can you implement to improve your dating experience?

Concluding Thoughts

Goethe had it right; it's not just about finding the right partner, but also about being the right partner. In the evolving dynamics of modern love, remember, the most consistent factor is you. Evolve, adapt, and love with courage.

But it's not just about knowing yourself; it's also about being emotionally intelligent. Can you express yourself clearly? Are you honest about your feelings and ready to tackle challenges together? It's not always easy, but it's the foundation of any strong relationship.

And let's not forget about compatibility. Sure, shared interests are great, but they're not everything. What's crucial are shared values and the desire to grow together. That's your anchor through every storm in a relationship.

Feeling adrift in today's dating scene? Hold up. Step back, dive deep into understanding yourself and your desires, and don't shy away from the work needed to forge a meaningful connection. It's challenging, but discovering that soul who truly gets you? Priceless.

Remember, navigating the complexities of modern love isn't about following a script or playing a game. It's about being true to yourself, being open to connection, and being willing to put in the effort to make it work. So go out there and start navigating that maze—your person is out there, waiting for you.

CHAPTER 6

KEEPING YOUR COOL: MANAGING STRESS IN A HIGH-PRESSURE WORLD

"It's not stress that kills us; it is our reaction to it." — Hans Selye

Mental health in today's world is like trying to keep a houseplant alive in a windowless room. It's possible, but it takes a lot of extra effort and creative solutions. In a society that glorifies being busy, taking care of your mind is like trying to meditate in the middle of a Metallica concert.

Every day, we're bombarded with stressors—deadlines, notifications, bills, you name it. The challenge isn't just to survive but to thrive, keeping our mental health intact and nourished. But how do we manage to keep our cool amidst this barrage?

Stress is like a modern-day dragon that we all battle—whether it's looming deadlines, overflowing inboxes, or juggling work-life balance. But what if I told you that stress, when harnessed correctly, can be transformed from a fire-breathing beast into a powerful ally?

This chapter is about flipping the script on stress and using it to fuel your productivity. Ready to turn what feels like kryptonite into your personal source of superpower?

Wisdom from the Wise

Over time and across different cultures, societies have created a wide range of techniques to handle stress and maintain mental balance. These practices reflect their times' prevailing philosophical, religious, and cultural contexts and offer us a tapestry of historical strategies for achieving personal tranquility.

Stoicism in Ancient Greece and Rome

Zeno of Citium founded Stoicism in the early 3rd century BC, and it gained popularity across Greece and the Roman Empire. This philosophy focused on personal ethics, drawing insights from its logical system and understanding of the natural world. The core of Stoic philosophy revolved around the idea that true happiness lies in embracing the present moment, not being driven by the fear of pain or the pursuit of pleasure. Instead, one should use their intellect to comprehend the world and fulfill their role in the grand scheme of nature.

Emotional Detachment: Stoics like Epictetus and Marcus Aurelius advocated for a detachment from emotions, not as a denial of feelings but to prevent emotions from dictating one's actions. They believed that by maintaining a calm rationality, one could achieve inner peace regardless of external circumstances.

Virtue as Happiness: For Stoics, virtue (the highest good) is intrinsically linked to one's emotional state. By living virtuously, aligning actions with nature, and practicing self-control, one could maintain serenity in the face of life's adversities.

Buddhist Meditation Practices

Originating in the Indian subcontinent with the teachings of Siddhartha Gautama (the Buddha) around the 5th to 4th century BCE, Buddhism encompasses a variety of traditions, beliefs, and spiritual practices primarily based on the Buddha's teachings. Meditation is a vital component of these teachings to achieve enlightenment and liberation from suffering.

Mindfulness and Awareness: Central to Buddhist practice is the concept of mindfulness, which involves being acutely aware of the present moment without emotional disturbance or judgment. This practice can lead to profound insights into the true nature of reality and oneself, resulting in decreased suffering and stress.

Compassion and Detachment: Buddhists are also taught to cultivate compassion towards all beings, tempering personal suffering by connecting individual experiences with the broader human condition. Simultaneously, detachment from desires and material concerns helps practitioners maintain mental focus and emotional balance.

Consider Theodore Roosevelt, America's cowboy president. Theodore Roosevelt was no stranger to stress, yet he channeled it through action, adventure, and relentless energy. His approach was straightforward: Use vigorous activity to manage stress and sharpen focus. He turned personal tragedy and physical challenges into catalysts for public service and individual achievement.

Think about the incredible pressure faced by astronauts like Chris Hadfield, who must manage stress in the confined and isolated environment of space. Hadfield used techniques such as visualization, focused training, and controlled breathing to manage stress, demonstrating the power of preparedness and mental resilience.

Did You Know? Endocrinologist Hans Selye popularized the term "stress" as it relates to life's pressures in the 1950s after borrowing it from physics.

Science of Managing Stress

Stress isn't just a feeling; it's a physiological response. Originally meant to help us escape predators, a hostile email can now trigger the "fight-or-flight" response. Chronic stress can mess with everything from your digestion to your brain chemistry. It's like having an overzealous security system in your body—it means well, but sometimes it goes off when there's no actual threat. Your body says, "Hey, I'm geared up for a challenge, are you?"

It's a biological fire alarm, a call to action.

However, not all stress is bad. There's a sweet spot where stress actually enhances performance—welcome to the world of 'eustress,' or beneficial stress.

The key lies in understanding the Yerkes-Dodson Law, which shows us that performance increases with physiological or mental arousal (stress), but only up to a point. The law shows that a certain amount of stress sharpens your focus and energizes your drive. Too little? Snoozeville. Too much? Burnout city. The trick is keeping the balance—just enough to invigorate, not enough to hinder.

Stress, the Transactional Model, and You

Let's strip down the science and get honest about stress. Imagine stress as that unrelenting, nosy neighbor constantly peering over your fence, ensuring you're not having too much fun without some challenge.

Now, how do you handle this neighbor? Maybe you've tried ignoring them, or perhaps you've confronted them directly. This is where Richard Lazarus and Susan Folkman's Transactional Model of Stress and Coping comes into play. Think of it as your guidebook to handling that pesky neighbor in a way that doesn't end with you losing your cool.

Appraisal: Where Stress Gets Personal

Stress isn't just about what happens to you; it's about how you interpret what happens to you. This model starts with the concept of appraisal, which is a fancy way of asking, "What does this mean to me?"

Primary Appraisal: This is your first reaction. Is this stressor (let's say, your overflowing inbox) a threat, a challenge, or a minor annoyance? This determines whether you even need to whip out your coping toolbox.

Secondary Appraisal: Now it's time to assess your resources. Do you have what it takes to tackle this challenge? Can you delegate some tasks or buckle down and handle them yourself? It's about gauging your capacity to deal.

Think of appraisal as checking the weather before you head out. It's about preparation and perception, helping you choose the right gear for the day's challenges.

The Dynamic Dance of Stress and Coping

Once you've sized up your stress, it's time to deal with it. Lazarus and Folkman break it down into two key strategies, and choosing wisely can make all the difference.

Problem-Focused Coping: This is about taking action to change the situation causing the stress. It's practical and proactive—like building a higher fence to block out that nosy neighbor.

Emotion-Focused Coping: Sometimes you can't change the situation. Maybe the fence is as high as city ordinances allow. Now, it's about managing your feelings about the problem. This could mean learning to laugh it off, practicing meditation, or venting to a friend.

What's truly incredible about the Transactional Model is its recognition of the fluid dance of stress and coping. Our assessments and strategies evolve as conditions change—today's dragon may be tomorrow's lizard. This model empowers us, suggesting that mastering stress isn't about wielding a mightier sword but about being nimble at adapting our tactics, refining our perceptions, and sometimes simply changing the game.

The implications of this model ripple across our lives, influencing everything from therapy rooms to corporate offices. It teaches us that the mastery of stress lies in our hands. We learn not just to endure but to thrive, using our insights to transform challenges into opportunities for growth and learning.

Let us heed the words of Marcus Aurelius, who might as well have been a proponent of the Transactional Model: "You have power over your mind—not outside events. Realize this, and you will find strength."

Through the lens of this model, managing stress becomes an empowering journey of self-discovery and proactive engagement. It's not just about surviving the storm—it's about learning to dance in the rain.

Apps: 'Calm'—because sometimes, you need a pocket-sized peace negotiator.

Books: "Why Zebras Don't Get Ulcers" by Robert Sapolsky offers an in-depth look at stress and its management.

Activity: Stress-buster Sprint

Today's mission is to equip you with practical, immediate stress-relief techniques. This exercise aims to help you identify stress triggers, apply quick relief strategies, and cultivate a mindset that enhances your resilience against daily stressors.

1. Kickstart with Mindfulness: Jump into your day with 10 minutes of mindfulness meditation. Focus on your breathing—it's like a coffee for your soul, calming your brain and setting a positive tone for what's ahead.

2. Set Your Victory Goal: Post-meditation, declare your daily stress victory goal. Maybe it's staying Zen in chaos, breezing through traffic without an eye twitch, or embracing curveballs with elegance.

3. Stress Detective Work: As you roll through your morning, play detective on your stress. Spot those sneaky stress moments and jot them in a notebook or on your phone. Capture the what, the feels, and your knee-jerk reactions.

4. Ninja Moves for Stress: Whip out those quick stress-smash moves—deep breaths, stretch it out, or take a quick lap. Spot which moves delivers that sweet stress relief and makes a note. When faced with a stressful situation, take a few deep breaths to calm your mind and body and try to replace negative thoughts with positive affirmations. This simple exercise can do wonders for reducing stress levels.

5. Your Stress Relief Jam: Dive into a stress-relief activity that makes your soul sing. Be it yoga, a sweat session, or getting artsy —choose your flavor of joy and distraction.

6. Lunchtime Zen Eats: Fuel up with a lunch that's tasty for your taste buds and soothing for your soul. Think omega-3-rich goodies, lush greens, and nuts for that Zen vibe.

7. Evening Wind Down: As the day wraps, revisit your stress notes. Pinpoint your top stress culprits and the MVP stress relief tactics of the day. Lack of sleep can make you more susceptible to stress. Prioritize getting enough hours of quality sleep each night.

8. Strategize Like a Boss: Armed with today's intel, sketch out a badass plan for a typical day. Weave in regular chill breaks and quick fixes for surprise stress ambushes.

Benefits: You're taking the driver's seat in managing your stress all day long. By tracking down stress triggers and trialing on-the-go relief methods, you'll get the lowdown on what works uniquely for you, crafting your own custom-fit stress mastery playbook.

Reflective Questions:

1. What are the top three stressors in your life currently, and what steps can you take to mitigate them? What's one stressor you can transform from a foe to a friend this week?
2. When has stress unexpectedly improved your performance or focus?
3. Which part of the day did you feel most stressed, and what quick relief method helped you the most?
4. How can you integrate the most effective stress-relief techniques into your everyday routine to manage stress better?

Concluding Thoughts

Alright, listen up! It's time to take control of your stress and make it work for you. Stress is an inevitable part of life, but it doesn't have to control you. You have the power to cope with it through creativity, resilience, and proactive engagement. Recognize when stress is beneficial and when it diminishes your effectiveness. Harness the energy of stress; don't let it harness you.

It's all about shifting your perspective. Instead of seeing stress as an enemy, embrace it as a catalyst for growth and innovation. When you do that, you unlock your potential to lead a more fulfilling and balanced life. Know your triggers, set boundaries, keep moving, and practice mindfulness.

But here's the thing: it's not enough to just know this. You have to take action. Start small, build on your successes, and keep going. Remember, managing stress is a continuous journey, and it's always evolving. When you can manage stress well, it can propel you to the heights of productivity and focus. So, this week, I want you to tackle your stress head-on. Choose one strategy from this chapter—whether it's setting boundaries, starting a meditation practice, or getting physically active—and make it a part of your daily routine.

As Karen Salmansohn said, "It's okay not to be okay as long as you are not giving up." And if you need support, don't be afraid to ask for it. Your mental health is your top priority, so take care of it no matter what. Don't give up, even if you're not okay right now. Every effort you make is worth it. It's time to make stress a part of your success story. You've got this!

CHAPTER 7
PERFECTLY IMPERFECT: BREAKING THE CHAINS OF PERFECTIONISM

"At its root, perfectionism isn't really about a deep love of being meticulous. It's about fear. Fear of making a mistake. Fear of disappointing others. Fear of failure. Fear of success."
— Michael Law

Does the pursuit of perfection leave you feeling stuck, unsatisfied, or perpetually stressed? You're not alone. I remember a time when I was like a chef who never served a dish because it could always use a pinch more salt. It was a relentless pursuit of the culinary masterpiece, where the kitchen was spotless, but the dining table remained empty. It took me a while to realize that sometimes, 'good enough' is a feast.

Living with perfectionism is like being in an art gallery where the paintings are never quite ready for the public. There's always a stroke to be added, a color to be adjusted. Perfectionism is like constantly painting and repainting a masterpiece, never quite satisfied with the shades or strokes. It's an endless art project where the canvas is never quite ready for the gallery.

But what if the true masterpiece is in the layers, the changes, the evolution of the work? This chapter is about breaking free from that trap and learning to embrace 'good enough.'

"Perfectionism is the belief that something is broken — you. So, you dress up your brokenness with degrees, achievements, accolades, pieces of paper, none of which can fix what you think you are fixing." — Edith Eger

---

Wisdom from the Wise

Many exceptional achievements are the result of trial and error, rather than flawless execution. By examining the lives of successful entrepreneurs, artists, and scientists who embraced imperfection, we'll see how letting go of perfection can lead to not just success but also greater happiness. Embracing imperfection can open doors to new possibilities and experiences and free us from the shackles of self-imposed standards.

Tal Ben-Shahar, a psychologist and author known for his work on positive psychology, advocates for the concept of 'optimalism.' This approach is about striving for the best outcome possible and recognizing that perfection is not always attainable or necessary. It's about maintaining a healthy acceptance of imperfection and understanding that sometimes, 'good enough' is indeed good enough.

Understanding Perfectionism

Why are some of us compelled to aim for perfection in everything we do? Psychological theories suggest it's often tied to self-esteem, fear of failure, or external expectations. But here's the good news: understanding these underlying reasons is your first step toward overcoming the need to be perfect. Many have successfully embarked on this journey, and you can, too.

Perfectionism isn't just about high standards; it's a complex dance of fear, control, and self-imposed pressure. It's like setting up a mental obstacle course where the finish line keeps moving. The challenge isn't just crossing it; it's realizing you designed it.

Perfectionism is rooted in a blend of fear—fear of judgment, failure, and not meeting expectations (often our own). It's a shield and a burden, protecting us from criticism but also preventing us from truly experiencing the joy of completion and the growth that comes from mistakes.

Underlying perfectionism is often a fear of vulnerability, believing that anything less than perfect is equivalent to failure. This mindset turns every endeavor into a high-stakes game, where self-worth is on the line with every action.

"Have no fear of perfection—you'll never reach it." - Salvador Dalí

Perfectionism is a complex trait influenced by personality and environment. It involves relentless striving for flawlessness, setting high-performance standards, and being overly critical of oneself. However, it's essential to differentiate between adaptive perfectionism, which can enhance achievement by setting high standards and motivating continuous improvement, and maladaptive perfectionism, which can impair it and lead to significant stress by setting unrealistic standards and causing excessive self-criticism.

Studies reveal that maladaptive perfectionism is linked to various psychological issues, including anxiety, depression, and burnout. Cognitive-behavioral frameworks offer insight into how perfectionist tendencies develop and persist, often tied to fears of failure and judgment.

Creative Insights

Prioritize tasks and set realistic goals. Set *good enough* goals. It's about redefining success from 'flawless' to 'accomplished.' Celebrate the finished, not just the perfect. Differentiate between 'must be perfect' and 'good is good enough.' Not every task requires a gold-medal performance.

Implement 'timed challenges' in your projects. For example, set a timer for 30 minutes and see how much you can accomplish on a task within that time frame. Create with constraints. For instance, limit your time or materials on a project. It's a surprising way to sidestep perfectionism—when you can't overthink, you create more freely. By limiting the time you spend on a task, you force a conclusion, preventing endless revisions and encouraging you to focus on the most important aspects of the task.

Celebrate small wins and progress. Break down tasks into smaller bits and give yourself a pat on the back for finishing each one. It's about enjoying the milestones, not just the finish line.

Practice the art of *'done.'* Implement a *'done day.'* Once a week, whatever you've completed by the end of the day is enough. It's about learning to let go and appreciate progress over perfection. Completing a task is a victory. Allow yourself to feel accomplishment without the post-completion analysis. For example, you could designate a specific day of the week as your 'done day,' at the end of that day. Take a moment to reflect on what you've accomplished and celebrate your small wins.

Have a *'wabi-sabi'* day—embrace the beauty in imperfection. In Japanese culture, wabi-sabi is an aesthetic principle that cherishes the beauty of imperfection, impermanence, and incompleteness. Whether it's art, writing, or another activity, the focus is on the natural, the raw, the real. It's about appreciating the beauty in the imperfect brushstrokes of a painting or the cracks in a ceramic bowl and understanding that imperfection is a natural part of life.

Learn from children or pets. Their unapologetic, joyous, and uninhibited approach to life is a lesson in valuing the moment over the masterpiece.

Connect with fellow 'recovering perfectionists.' Share experiences and strategies. Realizing you're not alone in this struggle can be a powerful catalyst for change.

Apps: 'Fabulous' for habit tracking and building routines prioritizing well-being over perfection. Project management tools like Trello or Asana can help you track progress without getting bogged down in details.

Books: "The Gifts of Imperfection" by Brené Brown encourages embracing authenticity over perfection.

Activity: Perfectionism Detox Day

Today, our mission is to work actively on understanding and dealing with perfectionism in our lives. This challenge has fun exercises that make you think and take action. They help you understand the importance of 'good enough' and let go of perfectionism's stress and limitations. Let's say you begin by setting a 'good enough' goal for the day and seeing how it feels to let go of perfection in that part of your life.

1. Journaling on Perfectionism: Start the day by journaling about how perfectionism appears in your life. Figure out the areas where your high standards might be stressing you out or holding you back, like work projects, personal relationships, or self-expectations.

2. Educational Insight: Learn about the psychological impacts of perfectionism. Use resources like articles, books, or podcasts to understand the balance between healthy striving and detrimental perfectionism.

3. Imperfection Exercises: Engage in activities where perfection is not the goal, such as drawing with your non-dominant hand, cooking a new recipe without measuring precisely, or writing a short story quickly without editing. Get creative and express yourself. Don't worry about being perfect. Engage in spontaneous creativity. Draw with your non-dominant hand, cook a new recipe without measuring precisely, or write a short story quickly without editing. Let go of the outcome and savor the process. Embrace the unpredictable and unpolished outcome.

4. Feedback Reflection: After each activity, reflect on how it felt to allow imperfections. Note any anxiety or liberation you experienced and what you learned about your need for control or perfection.

5. Setting Realistic Goals: Revisit your current goals and revise them to be more realistic. Incorporate achievable standards that emphasize progress over perfection.

6. Failure Embracing Exercise: Challenge yourself to try something you might fail at, such as a complex puzzle or a new sport. Focus on the effort and learning, not the outcome. Adopt a learner's mindset. View every task as an opportunity to learn and grow rather than as a verdict on your abilities.

7. Sharing Session: If comfortable, share experiences of your day's activities with friends, family, or online forums. Discuss how embracing imperfection felt and the reactions it provoked in you and others.

8. Community Stories: Read or listen to stories of people who have successfully overcome perfectionism. Note any strategies or perspectives that could be useful for you.

9. Reflective Journaling: End the day by reflecting on the exercises and insights. Consider how reducing perfectionism could impact your life positively.

Benefits: This day-long challenge helps to dismantle the barriers that perfectionism can create in your life. By consciously practicing imperfection and reflecting on the outcomes, you can reduce anxiety, improve productivity, and enhance your overall well-being.

Reflective Questions:

1. How has perfectionism affected your personal and professional life?
2. What did you find most challenging about allowing imperfections today?
3. How can you begin to adopt a mindset of 'good enough' in your everyday tasks?

Concluding Thoughts

It's time to get real about this whole perfectionism thing. We're all out here killing ourselves, trying to be flawless, but guess what? It's a trap! And it's time to break free.

Perfectionism isn't about having high standards. It's about having unrealistic standards that nobody could ever meet. It's like running on a treadmill that never stops - you're exhausted, but you're not getting anywhere.

So, here's what I want you to do this week. Pick one area of your life where your perfectionism is holding you back. Maybe it's that project you've been working on forever because it's never quite "perfect." Maybe it's your fitness routine that you keep putting off because you don't have the "perfect" plan.

Whatever it is, I want you to approach it differently this week. Embrace the idea of "good enough." Remember, done is better than perfect. Progress is better than perfection. And here's the thing: when you let go of perfectionism, you're not lowering your standards. You're setting yourself free to achieve more. You're giving yourself permission to move forward, to take action, to make things happen.

So, repeat after me: "I am perfectly imperfect, and that's okay." Let that be your mantra this week.

Chase excellence, but invite imperfection along for the ride. It's what makes life interesting!

Are you ready to stop chasing perfection and start achieving more? Embrace your imperfections, take action, and watch yourself soar. You've got this!

CHAPTER 8

THE ART OF SAYING NO: SETTING PERSONAL BOUNDARIES

"Daring to set boundaries is about having the courage to love ourselves, even when we risk disappointing others." — Brené Brown

---

Learning to say no is a powerful skill that can dramatically improve your life, empowering you to control your time, energy, and priorities. In a world that often demands constant availability and acquiescence, setting personal boundaries is not just essential; it's a declaration of self-worth and respect for your values.

This chapter delves into the art of effectively and confidently saying no, guiding you toward empowerment and self-respect. Are you ready to master the art of saying no and set boundaries that honor your needs and aspirations?

"Some of us think holding on makes us strong, but sometimes it is letting go." — Hermann Hesse

---

Wisdom from the Wise

When Rosa Parks refused to give up her seat didn't just contribute to the Civil Rights Movement; it also marked a monumental example of 'saying no' as a form of personal and political stand against *injustice*, resonating through history as a powerful act of defiance and self-respect.

Maya Angelou, the amazing poet and civil rights activist, always said it's crucial to say no to things that don't serve your soul. Her philosophy was that every person has the right to say no without explaining themselves, a testament to the power of personal boundaries. Angelou's life and work exemplify how respecting oneself commands respect from others, fostering healthier, more fulfilling relationships. Remember, setting boundaries is not just about you; it's also about creating a healthier dynamic with others where everyone's needs and boundaries are respected.

Warren Buffet famously said, "The difference between successful people and really successful people is that really successful people say no to almost everything." These wise words guide many to prioritize and focus effectively in their personal and professional lives.

Did You Know? When you say no, reinforce your decision with a positive statement to soften the refusal and maintain good relationships. For example, "I can't join you for dinner because I have other commitments, but let's catch up another time soon!"

The Psychology of Saying No

Saying no can be a challenge for many people because of the fear of being rejected, getting into conflicts, or feeling like they are missing out. However, the ability to say no is closely tied to self-esteem and can significantly impact one's mental health and interpersonal relationships. Understanding the psychological barriers to saying no can help you overcome them and embrace the benefits of setting clear boundaries.

Psychological research highlights that people with clear boundaries tend to have higher self-esteem and less anxiety and depression. Boundaries help manage emotional energy and protect one's sense of self. They are not just a defense mechanism, but proactive assertions of one's needs and desires. Neurological studies show that setting and respecting boundaries can lead to a more balanced life and healthier interpersonal dynamics.

> Apps: 'Todoist' allows you to manage your tasks and visualize your schedule, making it easier to say no when your plate is full.

> Books: Greg McKeown's "Essentialism: The Disciplined Pursuit of Less" advocates making more selective choices about where to spend energy and time.

Activity: The Power of No Day

Today's mission is to empower yourself by setting clear boundaries and prioritizing your needs and goals. This will increase your self-respect and time management.

1. Understanding Boundaries: Start the day by learning about the importance of boundaries. Read articles or watch videos that explain different types of boundaries (emotional, physical, intellectual) and their significance in personal and professional contexts. Also, familiarize yourself with the concept of 'boundary violations'- situations where your boundaries are being crossed—which can help you identify areas where you need to set clearer boundaries.

2. Self-Assessment: Think about areas where you feel drained or uncomfortable. These feelings are often indicators that boundaries need to be set. Identify situations where you usually say yes but wish you had said no.

3. Define Your Boundaries: Clearly define what you need from various relationships and interactions to feel respected and whole. Create a 'Boundary Map' for different areas of your life. Outline what you are comfortable with, what you are not, and why.

Don't forget, setting boundaries isn't about being selfish or uncaring; Consider the feelings and needs of others while setting your limits and find a balance that works for everyone.

4. Practice Saying No: Like any skill, the ability to say no improves with practice. Start with small, low-stakes situations and gradually work up to more significant boundaries. This gradual escalation will build your confidence and comfort level.

Throughout the day, consciously make decisions to decline requests that do not align with your priorities or that would overextend you. Practice polite but firm refusal techniques. Be clear, assertive, and respectful. Just a reminder, being assertive doesn't mean you have to be aggressive or rude. It's all about communicating your needs and boundaries clearly and respectfully.

5. Role-Playing: Engage a friend, family member, or your coach in a role-playing exercise to practice saying no. Discuss different scenarios and rehearse your responses.

6. Implement Boundaries: Apply your new boundary-setting skills in real interactions. This could be as simple as saying no to an unplanned commitment, asking a friend to stop discussing a topic that makes you uncomfortable, or turning off your phone during personal time.

Keep in mind, that setting boundaries isn't just about saying no, but also knowing when to say yes. Be open to opportunities that align with your values and goals and that you can take on.

7. Reflect on Feelings: After each instance of saying no, jot down how you felt immediately afterward and later in the day. Were there any feelings of guilt, relief, or empowerment? Just think about your feelings to understand why you react the way you do when setting boundaries and saying no. It'll be a game-changer for future interactions.

8. Adjustment Planning: Plan adjustments for future boundary settings based on your review. Consider different phrasing, timing, or methods of conveying your needs. Also, anticipate and prepare for common challenges you may face in setting boundaries and saying no, such as guilt, fear of conflict, or pressure from others. Here are some strategies to overcome these challenges: [strategies].

9. Relaxation Time: Engage in a relaxing activity that you enjoy and that respects your boundaries, such as reading, taking a bath, or meditating.

10. Reflection and Planning for the Future: Reflect on the day's lessons about boundaries. Consider the benefits gained from saying no, like having more time for important tasks or feeling less stressed. Plan how you will continue to practice and reinforce these skills regularly, ensuring they become a natural part of your interactions. This commitment to self-improvement is a testament to your dedication and resilience.

Benefits: This exercise strengthens your ability to protect your time, energy, and emotional well-being. It empowers you to navigate your social and professional worlds more confidently and healthily, opening a world of possibilities for personal growth and fulfillment.

Reflective Questions

1. What are the typical situations or requests you find most challenging to say no to?
2. How can you more effectively communicate your boundaries to others?
3. What boundary was the most difficult to enforce today, and what made it challenging?
4. How did it feel to communicate your boundaries? What reactions did you encounter?

Concluding Thoughts

Mastering the art of saying no is essential for anyone looking to lead a balanced and fulfilling life. If you're the kind of person who's always saying yes to everything, you're probably feeling stretched thin, overwhelmed, and not living the life you really want. Am I right?

Here's the truth: saying no is not about being selfish or mean. It's about setting boundaries and prioritizing what truly matters to you. It's about taking control of your life and making decisions that align with your values and goals.

So, here's your challenge for this week: pick one area where you're always saying yes, even when you don't want to. Maybe it's taking on extra projects at work, or agreeing to social plans when you'd rather have some alone time. Whatever it is, practice saying no.

I know it might feel uncomfortable at first, but trust me - when you start setting those boundaries, you'll be amazed at how much more time and energy you have for the things that really light you up.

Remember, you are in charge of your life. You get to decide what you care about and where you focus your energy. When you master the art of saying no, you're not just taking care of yourself - you're also improving your relationships and showing up as the best version of yourself.

So, are you ready to embrace the power of no? Let's do this together! Take that first step, set those boundaries, and watch how your life transforms.

CHAPTER 9

THE TIGHTROPE WALKER: BALANCING WORK AND LIFE

"Imagine life as a game in which you are juggling some five balls in the air. You name them—work, family, health, friends, and spirit—and you're keeping all of these in the air. You will soon understand that work is a rubber ball. If you drop it, it will bounce back. But the other four balls—family, health, friends, and spirit—are made of glass." — Brian Dyson, former CEO of Coca-Cola Enterprises

---

Balancing work and personal life is like trying to juggle flaming torches while riding a unicycle. It's a skillful act, but one wrong move can lead to a spectacular disaster. Remember the time you tried to cook dinner while on a conference call and ended up seasoning your report with salt and your pasta with statistics?

Let's face it—the mishaps of trying to balance work and life can be comically relatable. Picture the disastrous teleconference interruptions by pets or children or the valiant attempts to work out in between emails. There's a sitcom-worthy episode in our daily struggles that serves as a reminder: you're not alone in this circus act.

The work-life balance isn't just a buzzword; it's a daily challenge.

Millions of us step onto this line daily, a balancing pole in one hand (coffee, obviously) and a smartphone in the other, inching our way between professional ambitions and personal commitments. In a world where 'busy' is a status symbol, it's easy to fall into the trap of measuring our worth by how full our calendars are. But being busy isn't the same as being productive; just like running in circles, it isn't the same as making progress.

Wisdom from the Wise

Imagine if Julius Caesar had Zoom meetings or Cleopatra used Google Calendar to manage her empire. Sounds ridiculous, right? But believe it or not, our ancient forebears faced their own versions of work-life balance dilemmas.

Historically, philosophers like Aristotle spoke of "eudaimonia," or the state of living well, which modern psychology translates into concepts of well-being and work-life balance. But how do we achieve this in a world that demands our attention around the clock?

The quest for balance is as old as civilization itself. In ancient Greece, the concept of eudaimonia was not merely about happiness but about achieving excellence through balance and moderation. Ancient Romans advocated "Otium cum dignitate" (leisure with dignity), reflecting a time when balance was not only cherished but expected among the elite.

They knew the importance of downtime, often spending afternoons in public baths or at the theater. Fast-forward to the Industrial Revolution, when the concept of a "weekend" emerged as a necessary break from factory life.

Our ancestors might not have had psychology degrees, but they had keen insights into human behavior. Aristotle's concept of eudaimonia, flourishing through balanced living, echoes today's psychological theories. Modern studies underscore this, suggesting that balance isn't just nice to have; it's essential for psychological resilience and productivity. Understanding these historical contexts allows us to apply ancient wisdom to modern-day stress management and well-being.

Did You Know? Psychologist Wayne Oates coined the term "workaholic" in the late 1960s to emphasize how workplace culture has evolved to recognize the dangers of overworking.

Let's dive into some historical daily routines that might just be your ticket to modern balance. Benjamin Franklin meticulously planned his day in 13-week blocks, each with a specific virtue to cultivate. Imagine applying a similar structure to our modern tasks and goals. What if you dedicated weeks to creativity, learning, or fitness, much like Franklin's virtues? These practices from the past can inspire innovative approaches to our contemporary schedules.

Consider Charles Darwin, who, after his morning walk and a solid block of work, would take a break for lunch and a quick nap—every day without fail. This routine wasn't just about sticking to habits but respecting the natural rhythm of his mind and body's productivity and rest cycles. Similarly, Winston Churchill, known for leading Britain during some of its darkest hours, maintained a strict regimen of afternoon naps and early evening relaxation, believing it doubled his daily productivity.

Albert Einstein famously had periods of intense work followed by times of rest and music, particularly violin playing, which he claimed helped him solve complex problems during moments of relaxation.

Let's draw lessons from their routines:

Einstein's Musical Breaks: Incorporate music or art into your breaks to stimulate different brain areas and foster creative connections.

Darwin's Walks: Like Darwin, take regular walks to clear your mind and reset your cognitive engines. Research shows us that walking increases creativity and problem-solving abilities by up to 60%.

The Brain at Work: Understanding Our Inner Mechanics

This is our brainy section—where we put on our lab coats and peer through the microscope at the science behind work-life balance. It's not all neurotransmitters and neural pathways; it's about understanding how these elements influence our everyday lives and how we can practically use this science to craft a happier, more balanced existence.

Psychologically, the struggle for balance is rooted in our desire for achievement and fulfillment. We're torn between making a living and making a life. Stress, burnout, and a haunting feeling of missing out loom large when we tip too far in either direction. Understanding our deep-seated needs and values is the key to finding equilibrium.

Today, psychological research underscores its importance, with studies showing that a good work-life balance improves productivity and personal happiness. Theories like the "Conservation of Resources" suggest that individuals strive to acquire, retain, and protect their resources—and time is one of the most valuable.

According to a study conducted by Stanford University, productivity per hour significantly decreases when the workweek exceeds 50 hours, and it drops to a point where working over 55 hours becomes futile.

Our brains aren't designed to be in constant "go" mode; instead, they thrive on cycles of stress and recovery, much like the muscle-building process in athletes. This is grounded in the science of neuroplasticity, where our brain changes and adapts through growth and reorganization. Think of it as a CPU; to maintain optimum performance, it needs to cool down after being heavily used. Our brains need "off time" to process, recharge, and come back stronger. For example, sleep researchers emphasize the critical role of deep REM sleep in consolidating memories and rejuvenating the brain, which is crucial for maintaining cognitive sharpness and emotional balance.

Apps: 'Trello' for organizing tasks and projects and 'Headspace' for meditation and stress management.

Books: "Thrive" by Arianna Huffington, which advocates for a broader definition of success that includes well-being, wisdom, and wonder.

Activity: Balancing Work and Life Day

Today's mission is to dedicate a day to mastering the art of balancing work and life, the very essence that drives innovation, learning, and personal growth.

1. Turning Morning Madness into Morning Gladness: Most of us treat mornings like a cold plunge—it's shocking, unpleasant, and we want to get it over with as quickly as possible. However, research shows that a morning routine can set the tone for the day. Instead of the cold plunge, think of it as a warm-up session for the Olympics of daily life. Start simple: a favorite song as an alarm, a minute of stretching, and a breakfast that doesn't involve just coffee shots. It's about making the morning less about madness and more about the method.

2. The Commute - From Stress Lane to Zen Lane: The average person spends about 27 minutes commuting. That's 27 minutes of potential Zen or, for most, a symphony of honks and frustrations. Here's a tip: transform your commute with audiobooks or podcasts that intrigue you. Suddenly, you're not just commuting; you're escaping into a world of stories or learning—your car becomes a classroom, your train a theater.

3. At Work - Beyond the Cubicle: Once at work, the cubicle or desk awaits—often a shrine to monotony. Let's dress it up! Uplift your workspace with items that spark joy: photos, quirky gadgets, or a plant (preferably one that survives neglect). Next, try using the Pomodoro Technique—work hard for short bursts, then take quick breaks. Not only does this boost productivity, but it also keeps burnout at bay.

4. Lunch Break—A Midday Retreat: Often, we waste our

lunchtime scrolling through our phones. Flip the script: take an actual break. Take a walk outside, chat with coworkers about non-work topics, or eat a lunch that doesn't look like a sad sandwich. Use this time to recharge; consider it a pit stop in a Formula 1 race.

5. Conquering Afternoon Slumps: The afternoon slump is like the boss level in video games—tough to beat but not impossible. Arm yourself with a healthy snack, a quick walk, or a power nap. Yes, a nap! Many cultures embrace the rejuvenating power of the afternoon siesta—why not you?

6. The 5 PM Freedom and Beyond: As the clock strikes five, don't just rush out the door. Plan an after-work activity that excites you: a hobby class, a workout, or a casual meet-up with friends. This isn't just about filling time; it's about enriching your life beyond the office.

7. Here's a Fun Tactic: Create a 'not-to-do' list. It's as important as your to-do list. Write down activities that drain your time and energy without contributing to your well-being or productivity. Start by setting boundaries. Decide when you'll stop answering work emails or calls each day. Treat your personal time with the same respect you give your work time. It's about quality, not just quantity.

8. Role-shifting Exercise: At the end of your workday, change your clothes, take a short walk, or do something that symbolically marks the shift from work to personal time. This exercise helps you mentally compartmentalize your day.

9. Try micro-adventures: Create an 'unscheduled' calendar that includes non-work activities first. Schedule your hobbies, family time, and relaxation before fitting into work commitments. Inject mini, achievable adventures into your week. It could be a new restaurant, a short hike, or a creative workshop. These activities break the monotony and rejuvenate the spirit.

10. A Curiosity Recap: End the day by journaling about your experiences. Which activities expanded your mind? What new interests may have been sparked? Write any follow-up actions you'd like to take to continue exploring these new areas. Learn to say 'yes' to the right things. It's not about doing more, but about doing more of what matters. Do what makes you happy and helps you chill out.

11. Stargazing Reflection: If possible, end your day with some stargazing. Reflect on the vastness of the universe and the endless possibilities for learning and discovery. It's a fitting metaphor for the boundless nature of human curiosity.

Benefits: This structured approach to balancing work and life helps to enhance focus during work hours and increases personal time quality, reducing stress and improving overall life satisfaction.

Reflective Questions:

1. How effective are your current boundaries between work and personal life, and what steps can you take to strengthen them?
2. What part of the day did you find most challenging, and how can you improve it?
3. Which activity helped you feel most balanced, and why?
4. How can you use what you learned today to have a better work-life balance in the long run?

Concluding Thoughts

Work-life balance isn't a mythical land. Nope, it's about the choices YOU make every single day.

Listen up, because this is important: sometimes, your work is gonna take the lead. Other times, your personal life needs to be front and center. And guess what? That's totally okay! Forget about perfect balance - it's all about finding a harmonious imbalance that works for YOU.

Here's the deal: balancing work and life isn't about splitting your time down the middle. It's about making sure you've got quality in both areas. When you have a fulfilling day off, you might just find that your best work happens afterward. And when you're not constantly stressing about work? That's when the most amazing personal moments can happen.

This balancing act looks different for everyone, and that's how it should be. What works for your best friend or your co-worker might not work for you, and vice versa. The goal is to find YOUR rhythm, where work and life aren't battling it out, but actually making each other better.

As Heather Schuck said, "You will never feel truly satisfied by work until you are satisfied by life." Let that sink in for a minute. Your work matters, but so do YOU.

So, how do you create this balance? It's not about waiting for it to magically appear. You've gotta make it happen, one small change at a time. Take your daily grind and turn it into your Daily Grand! It doesn't require huge, sweeping changes - just little tweaks infused with creativity and a healthy dose of humor.

When you start looking at your daily routines in a new light, you'll be amazed at how your mood, productivity, and overall satisfaction skyrocket. So, let this be your wake-up call to start transforming the mundane into the marvelous. You've got this!

CHAPTER 10
EFFECTIVE COMMUNICATION: MASTERING THE ART OF PERSUASION

"The most important thing in communication is hearing what isn't said." — Peter Drucker

---

Communicating effectively today is tough—it's like trying to recite Shakespeare in the middle of a bustling flash mob. Everyone's moving, nobody's listening, and you have about 280 characters to make your point.

Welcome to the age of emojis, tweets, and eight-second attention spans!

The challenge lies in our brain's wiring. It craves novelty, processes visuals faster than text, and loves stories. Modern communication isn't just about sharing information; it's about packaging it in a way that's as catchy as a pop song chorus.

Whether trying to convince your boss, sway a client, or charm a crowd, the difference between 'meh' and 'wow' hinges on your communication chops. This isn't about talking more; it's about talking right. Buckle up because we're about to make you impossible to ignore.

Wisdom from the Wise

Aristotle wasn't just a philosopher; he was a master rhetorician. His principles of ethos, pathos, and logos (credibility, emotion, and logic) are more than ancient Greek ideals; they're the bedrock of effective persuasion. His big three—*ethos, pathos, and logos*—are about establishing trust, stirring emotions, and appealing to logic. This trio is your best bet for getting your audience nodding along instead of nodding off. Let's get Aristotelian and turn your speech into something that sticks.

Joe Navarro, a former FBI counterintelligence officer and an expert on body language, teaches how non-verbal communication can reveal thoughts and intentions. His books and seminars offer deep insights into how understanding body language can enhance interpersonal communication and security practices.

In her book *We Need to Talk*, award-winning journalist Celeste Headlee advocates effective communication. She provides modern techniques for improving conversational competence, emphasizing listening and simplicity.

Did You Know? A fitting metaphor doesn't just speak to us; it sets off fireworks in our brains, lighting up more areas than literal language ever could. Our brains process visuals 60,000 times faster than text, and 90% of the information we take in is visual. In the digital age, visuals aren't just an add-on; they're at the heart of how we effectively communicate. That's why a picture really is worth a thousand words!

The Dynamics of Effective Communication

In the digital era, our attention spans are shorter than a goldfish's (which is actually a myth, but you get the point). We live in an age where attention is the new currency, but inflation is rampant. Messages are brief, attention spans are shorter, and the competition for eyes and ears is fierce. How do you shine a spotlight on your message in a world that's constantly switching stages?

Effective communication is more than a skill; it's an art form. At its heart, it's about clarity, empathy, and understanding. Persuasion isn't about manipulation; it's about articulating your thoughts in a way that resonates, influences, and engages others. This chapter unpacks the psychological tools and linguistic strategies that can elevate your communication game from mundane to masterful.

Words are your brain's programming language. Neuro-linguistic programming (NLP) isn't just geek speak; it's essential in understanding how language patterns can prime brains for positive responses. Every word you speak or write triggers your audience's mental and emotional response. NLP shows that specific language patterns can influence listeners' thoughts and feelings. It's about crafting your words, not just to hit the ear but to stick in the mind.

Storytelling remains an essential aspect of communication, with narratives being 22 times more memorable than facts alone. The brain's wiring favors stories over disconnected information, making storytelling a powerful tool to engage audiences. Everyone loves a good story, so tell one. Whether tweeting, posting, or emailing, frame your message as a story. Who is the hero? What's the conflict? What's the resolution? This isn't just chatting; it's strategic storytelling. Make your audience care, make them curious, and they'll follow you through to the last word.

> Apps: 'Orai' will coach you through your speeches like a personal trainer for your vocal cords.

> Books: "Influence: The Psychology of Persuasion" by Robert Cialdini. It's a must-read for anyone who wants to master the art of influencing others effectively.

Activity: Conversational Mastery

Today's mission is to enhance our interpersonal abilities and forge deeper relationships. How can we achieve this? By engaging in meaningful conversations with enthusiasm and purpose. Are you ready to speak so people don't just listen but lean in? Here's how to master the art of conversation:

1. Active Listening Bootcamp: Practice active listening today. In every conversation, focus entirely on the other person, avoiding the urge to think about your response while they are speaking. Reflect on what they say and respond thoughtfully. Show you're all in with nods and smiles.

2. Open-Ended Quests: Ditch the yes/no questions. Get curious. Ask questions that open up a real dialogue, where sharing just flows. Here's your challenge: strike up a conversation with someone new every day this week. It could be with a co-worker, a cashier at the store, or even the person sitting next to you on the bus. Ask open-ended questions and really listen to their responses. You may be surprised by what you learn and how it can impact your perspective.

3. Empathetic Engagement: Empathize with the speaker, understanding their feelings and viewpoints without immediately offering advice or judgment.

4. Feedback Request: At the end of one conversation, be bold and ask how you did. Did they feel heard? It's gold for knowing where you can level up.

5. Reflect and Write: End the day with some journal time. How did switching up your style change the game? Did changing your approach affect the depth and quality of your interactions?

Benefits: This exercise cultivates better listening skills, empathy, and the ability to connect with others—key ingredients for winning at life and work.

Reflective Questions:

1. How well do you really listen, and what steps can you take to improve that skill? How did active listening affect your conversations today?
2. What new insights did you gain about the people you communicated with?

3. Think of a recent communication failure. What could have been said differently?

Concluding Thoughts

Alright, it's time to wrap this up. Effective communication combines clarity, empathy, and well-structured arguments. Here's the deal: mastering communication in today's digital age is no walk in the park. It's like being a jazz musician, constantly improvising and finding the right rhythm. But here's the thing: it's not just about being heard; it's about creating a balance between speaking and listening.

This week, I want you to challenge yourself. Turn every important conversation into an opportunity to practice these principles. Pay attention to how people respond and engage with you, and take note of where you need to improve.

Remember, the best communicators aren't born; they're made. It's not just about making a point; it's about making a difference. Your communication skills are like a Jedi's force. When you master them, you can move mountains—or at least change minds.

So, here's your mission: strive to be more than just a speaker. Be a communicator who resonates, connects, and engages with their audience. Are you ready to light up the room with your words? Let's do this!

CHAPTER 11

EMBRACE MINIMALISM: DECLUTTER YOUR SPACE, DECLUTTER YOUR MIND

"Simplicity is the ultimate sophistication." — Leonardo da Vinci

Imagine a space that breathes tranquility and a mind free from the fog of clutter. Minimalism isn't just about having fewer possessions; it's about liberating yourself from the chaos to focus on what truly matters.

Clutter isn't just the stack of unopened mail on your kitchen table or that closet filled with things you might use "someday." It's also the myriad of unfinished tasks, unresolved issues, and unused ideas cluttering your mind.

In this chapter, we explore minimalist philosophy and guide you through decluttering your environment and mind for a clearer, more focused life.

Ready to strip away the excess and uncover the essentials? Let's begin the journey towards minimalism.

Did You Know? One strategy adopted by many successful individuals worldwide to combat decision fatigue is to wear the same outfit consistently. Including Steve Jobs and his iconic black turtleneck and jeans.

Wisdom from the Wise

Marie Kondo, the famous tidying expert and author, has changed the game for millions with her KonMari Method™. Her cool way of decluttering and organizing does more than just tidy up spaces - it also boosts mental clarity and happiness.

Imagine hanging out for a day with Marie Kondo, a tidying wizard who believes in more than just sorting your closet; it's about finding what truly makes you happy. Her approach goes deeper than just keeping things clean - it's about really appreciating what you have and making better choices in life. It's like a metaphor for mental health: hold on to the thoughts that bring you joy and purpose and let go of the stuff that doesn't do you any good anymore.

Albert Einstein had a cluttered desk, and he thought it showed how busy his mind was. But when it came to his work, he was all for keeping things tidy and organized. He believed having a balanced, neat space around you is super important. It's all about having that organized vibe to help focus your thoughts and boost your productivity.

Dieter Rams, a pioneer in the design world, famously advocated for the principle of "less, but better." His work teaches us that minimalism isn't about deprivation; it's about achieving better quality through simplicity and careful curation. In George Lois's words, "You need the passion to create, but you need to evaluate your creations with brutal honesty, and you need the guts to cut what doesn't work." Just like cutting non-essential elements enhances creativity in design, removing clutter enhances focus in life.

The Psychology of Decluttering

Minimalism isn't just about owning fewer possessions. It's about freeing yourself from the clutter of too many things and too many decisions, allowing you to focus on what truly matters.

Clutter isn't just physical. It's psychological, too. Studies show that clutter can significantly affect our anxiety levels, sleep, and ability to focus. Engaging in decluttering can result in a calmer and happier state of mind, illustrating the powerful connection between our environment and mental health. Having a messy environment can lead to cognitive overload and hinder our working memory.

The 90/90 rule asks two questions about each item. Have you used this in the last 90 days? Will you use it in the next 90 days? If the answer to both is no, it might be time to let it go. This rule helps remove the ambiguity from decluttering decisions, making the process more straightforward and less emotional.

To avoid re-cluttering, adopt the **"one in, one out"** policy. For every new item you bring into your space, one old item should go. This practice helps maintain a balanced and intentional environment.

> Apps: 'Tody' for managing cleaning tasks effectively, ensuring your space remains decluttered. 'Calm' is for guided meditations that help clear mental clutter and foster a minimalist mindset.

> Books: "Goodbye, Things" by Fumio Sasaki explores personal insights and practical tips for living minimally and focusing on what truly matters.

Activity: Minimalist Day Challenge

Today's mission is to explore and integrate minimalist principles into your daily life to simplify your environment, reduce stress, and enhance your focus on what truly matters. This engaging exercise is designed to reduce clutter and distractions, fostering a sense of calm and efficiency in your personal and professional life.

1. Physical Declutter: Set a timer for 30 minutes and tackle a physical area you use daily—perhaps your desk, a drawer, or your digital desktop. Remove anything that doesn't serve a purpose or bring you joy. (Sort, organize, and remove unnecessary items.)

2. Mental Clutter: Take another 30 minutes to write down any lingering tasks or commitments you've been avoiding. Decide which to prioritize, reschedule, or cancel. (List tasks, assess their relevance, and clear out mental clutter.)

3. Essentials Only: Limit yourself to using only the most essential items for your morning routine. This might include simplifying your breakfast choices, using fewer beauty or grooming products, or choosing an outfit with fewer accessories.

4. Needs Versus Wants: Reflect on each item's necessity. Ask yourself, "Does this item add value to my life? Is it essential for my daily functioning or well-being?"

3. Digital Declutter: Dedicate 30 minutes to clean up your digital workspace. Unsubscribe from unnecessary emails, uninstall apps you haven't used in the past month, and clear out old files and photos that no longer serve a purpose.

4. Mindfulness Pause: After each decluttering session, take a few minutes to observe how the cleaner space affects your mood and mental clarity.

5. Focused Work Block: Dedicate a solid two-hour block to the most important task of your day. Turn off all notifications and other potential distractions. This is about doing one thing well rather than multi-tasking.

6. Nature Walk: Take a walk in a natural setting, leaving your phone behind. Focus on the surrounding environment, observing the sights, sounds, and smells without the urge to capture or share the experience digitally.

7. Minimal Entertainment: Spend your evening engaged in a simple, relaxing activity that doesn't involve technology. You could try meditating, journaling, or drawing.

8. Plan for Less: Reflect on your day and identify areas where you can implement more minimalist practices regularly. You can implement a 7-day no-buy challenge for non-essential items. During this period, focus on appreciating and using what you already own. For necessary purchases, practice thoughtful buying by asking yourself several questions to determine the item's long-term value and necessity. Consider planning your next day with fewer tasks, aiming for quality over quantity.

9. Reflection: End your day by reflecting on the process in your journal. How did decluttering affect your productivity and stress levels? What other areas could benefit from this exercise?

10. Plan for Sustainability: Make a weekly plan to tackle other areas that need decluttering, spreading the task to remain manageable. At the end of each week, review your progress. Evaluate how living with less has impacted your lifestyle, challenges, and any additional adjustments needed.

Benefits: This exercise helps you experience the benefits of a minimalist lifestyle, including decreased stress, increased productivity, and a greater appreciation for the simple things in life. It fosters a greater appreciation for what you have and reduces the urge for constant consumption. A decluttered space can boost focus and productivity while also providing a sense of calm and control.

Reflective Questions:

1. How has reducing physical and digital clutter affected your daily routine and mental clarity?
2. What was the most challenging part of adopting a minimalist approach today?
3. How did simplifying different aspects of your day affect your stress levels and overall happiness?

Concluding Thoughts

Embracing minimalism is not just about having fewer possessions—it's about making more room for joy, fulfillment, and growth. And I've got a simple way for you to get started: The Minimalist Day Challenge.

Here's the deal. Minimalism isn't a one-and-done thing. It's a daily practice of choosing less so that you can experience more. And with every single step you take towards simplifying your life, you'll feel lighter and more at ease. So here's your challenge for this week: pick one area of your life or your home, and get rid of the unnecessary stuff. Just one area. And pay attention to how it makes you feel.

Because let me tell you, decluttering is so damn liberating. It frees up space physically and mentally. It gets rid of the cognitive clutter that drains your energy and creativity every single day. When you choose simplicity, you're choosing clarity. And with clarity, you can create a life that's deliberate and fulfilling.

So let me ask you this: are you ready to declutter your space and your mind? Are you ready to embrace a minimalist lifestyle that brings you more peace and focus? If your answer is yes, then let's do this together. Let's get rid of the excess and uncover what truly matters.

Remember, as Joshua Becker said, "The first step in crafting the life you want is to get rid of everything you don't." It's time to take that first step. Embrace minimalism, and watch how it transforms your world.

CHAPTER 12
OUTWITTING THE IMPOSTOR: A CLEVER GUIDE TO CLAIMING YOUR WORTH

"The exaggerated esteem in which my lifework is held makes me very ill at ease. I feel compelled to think of myself as an involuntary swindler." — Albert Einstein

Living with impostor syndrome is like being a secret agent in your own life—always undercover, never quite believing you've earned your place. It's the mental equivalent of sneaking into a concert and then spending the entire show wondering when you'll get caught. Spoiler alert: You had a ticket all along!

Imagine you're at an awards ceremony, mistaken for a celebrity, and now you're on stage, Oscar in hand, delivering a speech. That's impostor syndrome—the feeling of being a fraud despite evidence of success. You're the star of the show, but part of you is waiting for security to escort you off stage. Plot twist: You belong here more than you think.

Impostor syndrome is when you constantly doubt yourself, even though you're totally crushing it. It's like this constant fear of being exposed as a "fraud". This chapter helps you identify those emotions and figure out how to deal with them.

Wisdom from the Wise

Impostor syndrome is widespread among high-achievers who struggle to accept their accomplishments. Strategies to mitigate these feelings include acknowledging and owning successes, understanding the commonness of these feelings, and talking about them with trusted peers.

Albert Einstein, known worldwide for his brilliance, had moments of doubt and imposter syndrome, describing himself as an "involuntary swindler" who believed his work was not worthy of the recognition it garnered.

Even a celebrated poet and author, Maya Angelou, confessed to feeling like an impostor despite her vast literary achievements. She once said, "I have written eleven books, but each time I think, 'Uh oh, they're going to find out now. I've run a game on everybody, and they're going to find me out.'" Angelou's experience highlights that impostor syndrome does not discriminate by success level; it is a shared human experience.

Did You Know? Suzanne Imes and Pauline Rose Clance, psychologists, during the 1970s initially created the term "impostor syndrome."

Science of the Impostor Syndrome

At its heart, impostor syndrome is a clash between perception and reality. It's a psychological heist, where your confidence is the hostage. This inner critic questions and undermines your successes, attributing them to external factors - luck, timing, or just fooling others. At its core, imposter syndrome is about self-perception - it's a distorted view of our capabilities and achievements.

Impostor syndrome is the brain's way of keeping you in a perpetual state of suspense, like a thriller where you're both the hero and the skeptic. It's a narrative full of plot holes, where your achievements are attributed to everything but your own talent and hard work.

Apps: 'Moodfit' to track and improve your mood, which can be beneficial in managing feelings of impostor syndrome.

Books: Valerie Young's "The Secret Thoughts of Successful Women" delves into why so many accomplished women feel like they are faking it and how to thrive despite it.

Activity: Impostor Syndrome Breakdown

Today's mission is to confront and diminish the feelings of impostor syndrome through a series of reflective and proactive exercises designed to be completed over a single day. This exercise aims to boost your self-confidence, recognize your achievements, and challenge the self-doubt that hinders your growth.

1. Identify Feelings: Start the day by journaling about recent moments you felt like an impostor. Describe the situations, your thoughts, and how those thoughts made you feel. Play detective with your doubts. Challenge negative thoughts. Each time you think, "I can't do this," counter it with, "Why not me?" It's about rewiring your response to doubt.

2. Reality Check: For each noted feeling, challenge its validity. Write evidence that counters the impostor syndrome, such as past successes, positive feedback from others, or skills you've developed that contributed to your achievements. Talk back to the impostor. When it says, "You can't," retort with, "I already did." Sometimes, a witty comeback is the best defense.

3. List Your Lifelong Accomplishments: Compile an 'Achievement Archive.' Think of it as your personal hall of fame, a collection of victories, kudos, and successes. List your five greatest accomplishments and the skills or qualities that helped you succeed. It's hard to argue with a room full of trophies.

Reflect on this list whenever you feel doubts about your abilities. Go ahead and add even more to it, if you feel like it.

4. Positive Affirmations: Create a list of affirmations

focusing on your capabilities and worth. Examples might include, "I am competent, skilled, and knowledgeable," or "I earned my position through hard work and dedication." Celebrate your growth. Every challenge you've faced and overcome is a testament to your capability. Remember, even diamonds start under pressure.

5. Visualization Exercise: Spend a few minutes visualizing a recent success. Recall in detail how you accomplished that success, overcame challenges, and received recognition.

6. Speak Up About Your Feelings: You'll be surprised by how many people share your experience. It's not admitting weakness; it's uncovering a shared human experience. Many successful people feel the same way, showing that impostor syndrome affects everyone, but can be overcome.

Talk to a mentor or peer about your feelings of impostor syndrome. Ask for their honest feedback about your performance and contributions. Share experiences and discuss times you have felt like an impostor. Understanding that others have similar feelings can normalize your experiences and reduce feelings of isolation.

7. Skill Inventory: Make a comprehensive list of all your skills and the projects or tasks where you have successfully applied them. To see your strengths, take the Clifton Strengths online talent assessment.

8. Teach or Mentor Others: Nothing reaffirms your competence, like helping someone else grow. Feeling like an imposter is hard when you see your knowledge benefiting others.

9. Host an 'Imposter Syndrome Banishing' Party: Gather friends or colleagues to share doubts and boost each other's confidence. It's like group therapy, but with snacks and laughter. Laughter can be a powerful tool to diminish those doubting voices.

10. Learning Commitment: Choose one skill to enhance. Research a short online course or tutorial you can start today to bolster your confidence in this area. Seek stories of triumph over doubt. Seek mentors and role models. They've likely danced with their own imposter fears and can provide guidance and perspective. Explore biographies, podcasts, and talks by people you admire. Spoiler: Many had their own battles with impostor feelings.

11. Success Journal: Keep an achievement journal and document your successes, big or small. You'll have a weapon to fight back when the imposter monster rears its head. For today, note all the exercises you completed and any insights or positive feelings that arose from them.

12. Planning Forward: Set a weekly goal to add entries to this diary, focusing on small and large successes and the steps you took to achieve them.

Benefits: This exercise empowers you to combat impostor syndrome by validating your accomplishments and worth. It encourages a healthier self-perception and builds a supportive foundation for ongoing personal and professional development.

Reflective Questions:

1. How did it feel to confront and record your feelings of impostor syndrome directly?
2. What accomplishments are you most proud of, and what does this say about your abilities?
3. What was the most challenging part of today's exercises, and what was the most rewarding?

Concluding Thoughts

It's time to get real about impostor syndrome. You know that nagging voice in your head that tells you, "You're not good enough, smart enough, or deserving of your success?" Every time that voice whispers, "You just got lucky," gather evidence to the contrary. Be your own Sherlock Holmes of self-worth.

Well, I'm here to tell you that the voice is a liar, and it's time to shut it down. But here's the thing: silencing self-doubt is just the beginning. To truly overcome impostor syndrome, you need to accept and embrace yourself, flaws and all. It's about recognizing your talents and owning your achievements like the boss you are.

Embrace new challenges. Each new endeavor is an opportunity to prove to yourself, yet again, that you're capable and competent. No more hiding behind masks or capes, pretending to be someone you're not. It's time to step into the spotlight and claim your place center stage. You've earned it, and you deserve it. "Fake it till you make it" doesn't apply here. Instead, "Face it till you ace it." Acknowledge your fears, then conquer them with the undeniable evidence of your own competence and worth.

Now, I know what you might be thinking: "But Gizem, I don't feel like I belong here. I feel like a fraud." Well, guess what? That's normal. Even the most successful people have those moments of doubt. Take Tina Fey, for example. She once said, "The beauty of the impostor syndrome is that you vacillate between extreme egomania and a complete feeling of: 'I'm a fraud! Oh God, they're on to me!'" But she didn't let that stop her from becoming one of the most influential comedians of our time.

So, here's my challenge to you: embrace the duality of impostor syndrome with humor and grace. Recognize that everyone is just improvising in this crazy show called Life. And most importantly, remember that you are worthy, capable, and deserving of all the success that comes your way.

It's time to outwit the impostor and claim your worth!

CHAPTER 13
CHARTING THE UNKNOWN: DECISION-MAKING IN THE FOG OF UNCERTAINTY

"The only thing that makes life possible is permanent, intolerable uncertainty; not knowing what comes next." — Ursula K. Le Guin

Decision-making in uncertainty is like being a captain navigating through fog. You can barely see beyond the bow of your ship, yet you must make choices that steer your course. It's a thrilling, sometimes daunting, it's challenging, often dizzying, but also an inevitable part of life. It's the difference between being a leaf in the wind and the wind itself.

Every day, you're bombarded with decisions. What to eat, where to work, who to spend time with; these choices directly shape your life's trajectory. But what if you could make better decisions faster and with more confidence? What if you weren't just reacting to what life throws at you, but actively designing your destiny with each choice you make?

This chapter isn't just about improving how you decide—it's about transforming you into a master decision-maker.

Wisdom from the Wise

Take Socrates, the ancient wisdom guru famous for his "I know that I know nothing" approach. His style of hitting you with question after question to untangle complex ideas set the stage for Western philosophy.

Imagine zooming to the edge of space in something, part plane, part rocket. For Richard Branson, the founder of Virgin Galactic, stepping into the unknown isn't just a challenge; it's pretty much an invitation to smash some boundaries and rethink what's doable. Branson's whole career vibe is about diving headfirst into new industries and unknown territories, showing us how getting cozy with uncertainty can lead to some wild achievements and adventures.

Then there's Kathryn Schulz, a journalist and author who totally gets the perks of being wrong. In her book *Being Wrong*, she digs into how some of the sharpest minds thrive by being chilled with not having all the answers.

According to Daniel Kahneman, we should be cautious of relying on fast and intuitive thinking when faced with decisions that demand careful consideration. At the same time, Richard Thaler's work on nudge theory suggests that the way choices are presented can have a significant influence on the outcomes of decisions, highlighting the influential role of context in decision-making.

Why Decision Quality is Your Superpower?

Decisions are the building blocks of your life. The quality of your decisions creates the quality of your life. It's that simple—and that complex. Understanding the mechanics of good decision-making can be as transformative as any skill you ever gain. This section unpacks why smart decisions are your gateway to a more prosperous and fulfilled life.

Let's break down what happens in your brain when you make decisions. Neuroscience shows us that decision-making involves a complex interplay between intuition and logic. You can refine your decisions' speed and quality by enhancing certain cognitive functions —like attention, reasoning, and flexibility. This isn't about trusting your gut over your head; it's about aligning both to work together.

While uncertainty can trigger stress and anxiety, it also significantly enhances creativity and mental agility. When faced with unknowns, the human brain is wired to look for creative solutions, a survival mechanism that has propelled human innovation.

Research shows that embracing new experiences can increase cognitive flexibility, helping you adapt to new situations more effectively and promoting mental growth. Individuals who regularly face unpredictable situations tend to exhibit enhanced problem-solving skills and increased adaptability.

Paul Arden points out, "Without the unpredictable, creative work is merely mediocre." Let's embrace the comfort of uncertainty and the excitement of learning new things.

> Apps: 'Lucidchart' for visual decision-making using flowcharts or decision trees that can help map out potential outcomes and their impacts.

> Books: Daniel Kahneman's "Thinking, Fast and Slow" offers profound insights into the different systems of thought that drive our decisions. Malcolm Gladwell's "Blink" gives insights into the power of thinking without thinking.

Activity: The Uncertainty Challenge

Today's challenge pushes you out of your comfort zone and into the unpredictable to become comfortable with uncertainty and use it as a catalyst for growth and creativity. This exercise isn't just about physical exploration, but about opening your mindset to new experiences and spontaneous interactions.

1. Study Decision-Making Theories: Begin your day by exploring various decision-making models and theories, such as probabilistic thinking, the OODA loop (Observe, Orient, Decide,

Act), and scenario planning. Focus on understanding how these models can help navigate uncertainty.

2. Journaling for Clarity: Write about a recent situation where you had to decide in uncertainty. Reflect on what you did, what you could have done differently, and how theoretical models might have aided your process.

3. Challenge the Known: Choose a routine task and perform it differently or introduce an unexpected change to your routine. For example, hold your toothbrush with a non-dominant hand or drink your coffee in a different mug—so simple yet different. Reflect on how it feels to step out of your comfort zone.

4. Scenario Planning: Create several "what-if" scenarios for your current decision. Outline possible outcomes for each scenario, assessing potential risks and benefits. This helps visualize different paths and their likely impacts on your decision.

5. Risk Assessment Matrix: Develop a risk assessment matrix for a critical decision. Break down potential risks by how likely they are to happen and how much impact they could have, then strategize on how to tackle them.

6. Random Exploration: Go to a part of your town you've never visited. Take no map, no plan. Just walk and observe what you find.

7. Conversation with Strangers: Strike up a conversation with someone you don't know. Ask them something you genuinely want to know about them.

8. Pros and Cons Analysis: Conduct a detailed pros and cons analysis for a more considerable pending decision. It is important to consider not only the quick wins of outcomes but also the long-term implications of each alternative.

9. Develop a Decision-Making Framework: Based on today's exercises and feedback, develop a personal decision-making framework incorporating elements from the models you've learned about. Tailor this framework to your specific needs and decision-making style.

10. Reflective Walk or Meditation: Take a reflective walk or engage in meditation, focusing on how you felt throughout the day while making decisions in uncertainty. Consider the mental and emotional challenges and how you addressed them.

11. Relaxation and Visualization: End your day with a relaxation technique you prefer, followed by a visualization exercise where you imagine successfully navigating a major uncertain scenario using your new skills.

Benefits: This exercise strengthens your decision-making skills in uncertain conditions, reduces anxiety about the unknown, and prepares you for more effective leadership and personal growth. It cultivates flexibility and creativity, critical skills in an ever-changing world. It challenges cognitive biases, opens new ways of thinking, and leads to creative ideas and solutions.

Reflective Questions:

1. Reflect on a recent hard decision: what tools could have helped you make a better choice?
2. How did you feel during these activities? What was uncomfortable, and what was exhilarating?
3. What decision-making model did you find most helpful during today's exercises?
4. What did these experiences teach you about handling uncertainty in your daily life?

Did You Know? The phenomenon of decision fatigue shows that people tend to make poorer choices after a long decision-making session. That's why it is better to tackle essential decisions first thing in the morning.

Concluding Thoughts

Listen up, because this is important. Today, you took a chance and stepped into unfamiliar territory. Maybe it scared the hell out of you, or maybe it lit a fire inside you. The point is, you did it. You faced uncertainty head-on. And let me tell you something—having fear is not the issue. It's what you do with that fear that counts.

What is your life like right now? It's the direct result of the choices you've made. Every single decision, big or small, has led you to this moment. And if you want to take control of your life, it starts with making better decisions.

So here's what I want you to do this week. Think of one decision you've been avoiding. You know the one. It's been nagging at you, keeping you up at night. Well, it's time to face it. Use the tools you've learned—figure out what really matters to you. Don't overwhelm yourself with too many options. Make the decision, and then reflect on how it went. Because every tough choice you make is a step toward becoming the master of your own destiny.

But here's the thing—it's not just about making faster decisions. It's about making smarter ones. It's about turning your decision-making skills into your secret weapon. Don't forget, one decision at a time! So I ask you—are you ready to step up? Are you ready to make the choices that will shape the future you want?

CHAPTER 14
EMBRACE CURIOSITY: THE ENDLESS PURSUIT OF KNOWLEDGE

"Be curious. Read widely. Try new things. I think what people call intelligence boils down to curiosity." — Aaron Swartz

Why do children seem so alive? Simple. Curiosity. It's the spark behind every magnificent invention, every inspiring piece of art, and every life well-lived.

Curiosity isn't just about asking questions; it's about daring to challenge every "why," embracing the discomfort of not knowing, and turning the mundane into the miraculous.

For many of us, curiosity fades as we age, stifled by routine, fear, or societal expectations. But what if curiosity isn't just a whimsical luxury? What if it's a powerful tool for transforming your mind and life?

I want you to remember one thing: curiosity didn't kill the cat; it gave the cat nine lives. In this chapter, we'll explore why curiosity matters and how to reawaken it within yourself.

The Courage to Ask Why

Imagine the last time you felt truly curious—that childlike sense of wonder that made the world feel fresh, joyful, and full of possibility. When was it? Last week? Last year? Longer still?

Why? It's the favorite question of every toddler, the bane of many parents, and the fundamental tool of the great innovators. Today, we dive back into this three-letter powerhouse that you might have forgotten is at your disposal. It's not just a question; it's a way of engaging with the world.

As you blinked the sleep from your eyes this morning, what was the first thing that ran through your mind? Did you groan about the day or were you busy calculating how much longer you could stay in bed? Now, imagine if your first thought was a question driven by genuine curiosity instead. What might today bring? What can I discover?

"I have no special talents. I am only passionately curious." — Albert Einstein

---

A Tale of Two Minds

Think of a young Albert Einstein encountering a compass for the first time. This wasn't just a tool for him; it was a gateway to the invisible forces that shape our world. That childlike wonder didn't fade as he grew; it expanded into questions that changed the very fabric of physics. Your inner Einstein is ready to explore, too—every question you ask can lead to your own small or big revelations.

Then there's Leonardo da Vinci, who saw art in anatomy and engineering in art. His relentless questioning not only filled journals but also revolutionized numerous fields.

Let's also talk about Richard Feynman, a Nobel Prize-winning physicist famous for his endless curiosity. Instead of just sticking to his own field like others did, Feynman's adventurous spirit took him from quantum mechanics to biology. This curiosity didn't just keep him entertained; it helped him develop new, fun ways to teach physics that we still use today.

Jill Tarter, an astronomer and the former director of the SETI (Search for Extraterrestrial Intelligence) Institute, is all about curiosity. She's spent her career chasing the big question: Are we the only ones out here? Her work not only pushed forward what we know about the universe but also got more people excited about the stars.

But why talk about these giants? Because they were once like us, staring at the ceiling and deciding what to think about when they woke up. They chose curiosity.

Did You Know? Nikola Tesla envisioned his inventions in such precise detail within his mind that he could effectively 'run experiments' in his imagination, often leading to insights that would bypass years of physical experimentation.

The Power of Curiosity

Curiosity is the spark that ignites innovation, fuels discovery and breathes meaning into our lives. It's a fundamental human trait, hard-wired into our DNA. Studies show that curiosity activates reward circuits in the brain, releases dopamine, and stimulates the growth of new neurons. It's not just pleasurable—it's essential for cognitive vitality and lifelong learning.

Throughout history, curiosity has propelled humanity forward. It led Galileo to point his telescope skyward, Edison to tinker tirelessly, and Marie Curie to unravel the secrets of radioactivity. In our own lives, curiosity can be just as revolutionary. It opens doors to new passions, deeper relationships, and a richer understanding of ourselves and the world.

Your Brain on Curiosity

What happens in our brains when we let curiosity lead us? Dopamine floods our system, which feels fantastic. Dopamine—the 'reward chemical'—isn't just about pleasure; it's about motivation and focus. It stimulates our neurons to actively engage with the puzzles and mysteries of life. According to George Lois, creativity isn't finding a thing but making something out of it after it is found. And guess what leads you to 'find' things? Curiosity.

Neurologically, curiosity is like a superfood for the brain. When we're curious, our brains enter a heightened state, more ready to learn and retain information. One study found that curiosity essentially "primes" the brain, putting it in an optimal state to absorb and remember new knowledge.

Psychologically, curiosity is linked to greater well-being and life satisfaction. Curious people tend to have lower stress levels, more positive emotions, and a greater sense of purpose. They cultivate resilience and adaptability by continually seeking new experiences and perspectives.

Paul Arden once said, "It's not how good you are; it's how good you want to be." Curiosity is about wanting—to know, understand, and explore. It's what turns a mundane walk down the street into a detective mission, where every window, passerby, and stray cat has a story.

Barriers to Curiosity

So, if curiosity is so beneficial, why do many of us experience it less than we age? Common barriers include:

Fear of the unknown: Curiosity requires venturing into unfamiliar territory, which can be intimidating.

Societal pressures: As we age, societal expectations can push us toward conformity and risk avoidance.

The comfort of routine: It's easy to fall into the groove of familiarity, but growth happens outside our comfort zones.

Overcoming these barriers starts with awareness. Recognize

when fear, pressure, or routine are holding you back. Then challenge yourself to take small steps into the unknown.

Apps: 'Curiosity' app that provides a variety of informative articles, videos, and infographics across different topics to spark your interest daily.

Books: "A Curious Mind: The Secret to a Bigger Life" by Brian Grazer and Charles Fishman explores how curiosity has been a driving force in the film producer's career and personal life, offering insights into how others can leverage curiosity.

Activity: A Day of Curiosity

Today's mission is to cultivate a deeper sense of curiosity through a series of fun and engaging activities designed to expand your knowledge and challenge your perspectives, all within one day. This exercise stimulates intellectual curiosity and encourages exploring new ideas and experiences. Try to rekindle your sense of wonder and curiosity about the world around you.

1. Question Jar: Begin the day by creating a 'question jar'. Write any random questions that come to mind on slips of paper—questions about everyday phenomena, historical events, scientific concepts, or anything you're curious about. Throughout the day, pull out a question to research and explore.

2. Curiosity Walk: Go for a 30-minute walk in your neighborhood or a nearby park. Approach this walk with the eyes of a traveler in a foreign land. Notice the details in the environment you usually overlook—the textures of buildings, the colors of leaves, the patterns of shadows, and the sounds of life bustling around you.

3. Question Everything: Carry a small notebook and jot down every question that comes to your mind about objects, people, and activities you observe throughout your day. Why is the stoplight red, yellow, and green? Who decided on the standard height of a mailbox? What journey did my coffee take to reach my cup?

4. Learn One New Thing: Choose one question from your

notebook and spend 20 minutes researching the answer. If the subject intrigues you, delve deeper into it, allowing your curiosity to guide your exploration.

5. New Skill Workshop: Take part in a workshop or online class to learn a new skill utterly foreign to you. This could be anything from coding to pottery to a new language. The key is to engage with something entirely new.

6. Reflection on Learning: Reflect on the learning process. What did you find challenging? What surprised you about this new skill?

7. Curiosity Conversations: Start conversations with friends or strangers about their hobbies, jobs, or passions. Ask open-ended questions to understand what excites and motivates them. This not only builds your knowledge but also strengthens your social connections.

8. Journal Your Discoveries: Spend 10 minutes writing about your experiences in the evening. What surprised you the most? Did anything shift in the way you view your daily environment? Reflect on how these activities affected your mood and intellectual engagement.

9. Curiosity Action Plan: Based on today's experiences, draft a plan to continue integrating curiosity into your daily life. Set goals for learning new things and exploring unfamiliar topics.

Benefits: The benefits of embracing curiosity include enhanced adaptability, improved social relationships, and increased professional success. Engaging in this activity promotes intellectual growth and mental agility by pushing you to explore and engage with the world in new and varied ways. It renews appreciation for the complexities and beauties of everyday life, combating the mundane routines that dull our senses.

Reflective Questions:

1. What are you most curious about right now, and what steps can you take to explore this curiosity?
2. What surprised you most on your curiosity walk?

3. How can you integrate a curiosity-driven approach into your daily routine?

Concluding Thoughts

Curiosity fuels learning and personal growth, leading to a more fulfilling and insightful life.

Today is just the beginning, and every single question you ask opens up a whole new world of possibilities. And let me tell you something, curiosity ain't just for kids. It's the secret sauce that keeps life exciting no matter how old you are.

So here's what you're gonna do. You're gonna grab life by the horns and embrace every opportunity to question, explore, and learn. You're gonna stay curious and let yourself be blown away by all the incredible things around you.

And who knows? You might just discover something about yourself that you never even knew existed.

CHAPTER 15
TRANSITIONING CAREERS: NAVIGATING THE CHALLENGES OF CHANGING CAREER PATHS

"Choose a job you love, and you will never have to work a day in your life." — Confucius

---

You wake up every morning, and there it is—feeling like you're in the wrong story. Are you stuck in a job that no longer excites you? You're not alone.

Embarking on a career change is like deciding to jump out of a plane you've been flying for years—except this time, you're not the pilot; you're skydiving. It's thrilling, a little terrifying, and a surefire way to feel alive. You're swapping your well-worn pilot's seat for a parachute packed with hopes, dreams, and a touch of audacity.

If your current career isn't making you jump out of bed each morning, maybe it's time to consider a switch. Changing careers isn't just about new opportunities; it's about rediscovering your passions and aligning your work with your evolving life. Let's ditch the fear, embrace the excitement, and plan.

This chapter will guide you through transitioning careers smoothly and successfully, showing you how to do it with confidence and strategic planning.

Wisdom from the Wise

Vera Wang, a figure synonymous with luxury bridal wear, didn't begin her career in fashion design until she was 40 years old. After a successful stint in journalism, including being a senior fashion editor at Vogue, Wang encountered a personal need (a wedding dress) and transformed it into a global brand. Her story is a powerful example of how skills from one career can translate into another and how personal passion can drive professional reinvention.

Consider the career of Sheryl Sandberg, who strategically advanced through various roles by leveraging her skills and building solid networks before becoming Facebook's COO. She emphasizes the importance of taking risks and leaning into challenges, especially when feeling complacent. Her advice encourages professionals to embrace uncertainty as a catalyst for growth and her proactive approach to career development is a powerful model for anyone looking to climb the professional ladder.

Consider the stories of people who have successfully changed careers: a former lawyer becomes a thriving entrepreneur, or a burnt-out tech executive becomes a fulfilled non-profit leader. These stories aren't just motivational; they're blueprints for how to pivot with purpose.

Did You Know? Career changes are increasingly common in the modern workforce, with studies showing that the average professional will change careers 5-7 times during their life.

Understanding the Dynamics of Career Transition

Career transitions? They're the job equivalent of a wardrobe change in a superhero movie. One minute you're Clark Kent, the next, you're Superman, but without the cape or the clear instructions. It's more than just changing jobs; it's like swapping genres, from a drama to an action-packed adventure.

Career transitions and periods of unemployment are more than just professional challenges; they're emotional rollercoasters. The uncertainty can be paralyzing, the rejection disheartening, and the silence from job applications deafening.

These periods test not only our professional resilience but also our personal identity and self-worth. There's the fear of the unknown, the sting of rejection, and the daunting task of reinventing yourself professionally. It's a journey through a landscape constantly shifting under your feet. It requires us to reevaluate our skills, rethink our goals, and rewrite our career narratives.

I always tell my clients that without proper planning and strategic execution, the journey can be overwhelming, leading to stress and missed opportunities. Career transitions are more than just job changes; they involve transforming your lifestyle, identity, networks, and, often, your skill sets. Such changes require a strategic approach that includes psychological preparation, market research, and network development.

Changing careers is about leveraging everything you've learned so far to enhance your professional journey, not starting from scratch.

The Psychology of Career Change

The key to a successful career change is understanding how our brains handle new challenges. Neuroscience tells us that our brains are adaptable, capable of learning, and growing well into adulthood.

This plasticity means you can rewire your brain to thrive in a new environment with the right strategies and habits. Therefore, career transitions can significantly impact your psychological well-being. Studies in occupational psychology suggest that preparation, resilience, and adaptive coping strategies are crucial for that successful transition.

Recent research in neuroplasticity and career adaptability,

published in the Journal of Applied Psychology in 2024, highlights that individuals who engage in regular mental flexibility exercises experience a 40% quicker adaptation to new roles or industries.

Develop resilience by adopting a growth mindset, which views challenges as opportunities for growth rather than obstacles. Regularly engage in activities that push your boundaries, such as public speaking, leading projects, or learning new technologies.

This proactive approach not only builds resilience but also enhances self-efficacy and confidence in facing career transitions. Also; incorporate cognitive flexibility exercises into your routine, such as problem-solving under constraints or engaging in strategic games like chess. These activities enhance your ability to cope with change and uncertainty, making you more adaptable in shifting career landscapes.

Understanding the psychological stages of career transition can help you manage stress and build a new professional identity more effectively.

The work we do often influences our sense of self. A change or pause in a career can trigger a profound existential crisis, leaving us questioning our skills, choices, and future. It's a fight between self-doubt and resilience, testing our mental and emotional strength.

Transitioning careers taps into deep layers of our psyche. It challenges our notions of stability and success, often stirring fears and uncertainties. However, it also presents an opportunity for growth, fulfillment, and realizing latent aspirations.

Future of Work

By 2030, nearly 375 million people—around 14% of the global workforce—might need to switch careers because of how fast technology, like AI and automation, is changing the game. Think about it. That's a massive shift, almost like moving from working on farms to factories, but it's all happening much faster now. So, what are you going to do about it? Sit back or jump in?

First, understand this isn't just about losing jobs to robots. Nope, it's also about new opportunities popping up in places we can't even predict yet. Jobs that demand not just tech smarts but also creativity, emotional intelligence, and a knack for navigating complex problems—skills that machines can't replicate. According to industry leaders, about 82% believe that retraining and boosting your skill set is a massive part of the solution.

So, if you're feeling overwhelmed by the digital revolution, here's your action plan: Get curious and stay agile. Immerse yourself in learning skills that match the future of tech. Whether AI, machine learning, big data, or enhancing your soft skills like leadership and communication, there's a course or a workshop with your name on it. Remember, the future belongs to those who prepare for it today.

Embrace this shift with an open mind and an action-ready attitude. Because when the ground moves under your feet, you don't have to fall. You can dance. Let's get moving!

The 2024 Global Freelancer Insights report indicates that the freelance economy is not only growing but diversifying, allowing professionals to engage in cross-industry opportunities that were not previously accessible. According to a 2024 report by the Global Gig Economy Data Hub, nearly 35% of the global workforce is engaged in freelance or contract work, with projections suggesting an increase to 50% by 2030.

Consider leveraging freelance opportunities as a strategic step in your career transition. Platforms like Upwork and Freelancer can provide flexible work options while you explore new industries, allowing you to gain relevant experience and build a portfolio that attracts full-time opportunities.

Identify projects that allow you to apply existing skills in new contexts or industries. This approach provides flexibility and income during transitions while building a diverse portfolio that demonstrates your capability to adapt and innovate.

Apps: LinkedIn for networking and industry insights; Coursera or Udemy for skill development.

Books: "What Color Is Your Parachute?" by Richard N. Bolles offers practical tools and tips for job hunters and career changers.

Activity: Career Leap Sprint

Today's mission is to boost your career development through a series of strategic, practical tasks completed over a week. This dynamic exercise enhances your professional visibility, expands your network, and pinpoints new career opportunities.

1. Career Goals Clarification: Start with a 15-minute session where you clearly define your short-term and long-term career goals. What position are you aiming for next? What skills do you need to develop to get there?

2. Skill Gap Analysis: Quickly review your current skills versus those required for your next career step. Identify one critical skill gap that you can address today.

3. LinkedIn Update and Connection: Update your LinkedIn profile with recent achievements, a new profile picture, or an engaging summary. Then, spend an hour connecting with new professionals in your field, especially those who work in roles or companies of interest. Personalize your connection requests with a note about why you're reaching out.

4. Industry Engagement: Post an article, comment on posts relevant to your field, or share your insight on a trending topic in your industry on social media.

5. Online Mini-Course: Enroll in a short online course or workshop that addresses the skill gap you identified earlier. Complete the course or make significant progress if it's longer.

6. Practical Application: Apply what you've learned immediately in a small project or by adjusting a current work task to include your new skill.

7. Attend a Local or Virtual Event: Take part in a webinar, workshop, or networking event related to your field. Make it a point to engage actively: ask questions, offer answers, or volunteer information about a project you're passionate about.

8. Follow-up Bonding: Once the event is over, remember to reach out to at least three people you connected with and send them a thank-you message or a LinkedIn connection request. It would be great if you could mention something specific you talked about during the event.

9. Reflective Journaling: End your day by reflecting on your activities and their potential impact on your career. Which actions felt most productive? What new insights or connections did you gain?

10. Action Plan for Next Days: Based on today's momentum, create an action plan and schedule follow-up activities, further learning, or another networking event in your calendar.

Benefits: This focused day of career-oriented actions will significantly enhance your professional profile and network, potentially opening doors to new opportunities. It boosts your active engagement in your career progression, combining immediate actions with long-term planning.

Reflective Questions:

1. What are the driving factors behind your desire to change careers?
2. What steps can you take this week to explore an alternative career path that interests you?
3. Which of today's activities do you see having the most impact on your career in the long run?
4. How will you continue to build on the connections and skills developed today?

Concluding Thoughts

Let me make this clear: you can't just wait for the ideal opportunity to magically appear. You need to take action and make it happen. That's right, you heard me. It's time to take control of your career and start taking action.

The good news is, you've got what it takes. You've been learning, growing, and preparing for this moment. All you need now is the courage to take that first step. Deciding to switch careers ain't easy, but with the right mindset and preparation, it can be the most rewarding choice you'll ever make.

What are you waiting for? Start putting together a plan. Figure out what you want, and what you need to do to get there, and then start taking action. Every single day, do something that moves you closer to your goal.

And when things get tough (and they will), remember this: you're not built for the easy road. You're built for the challenges, the obstacles, and the triumphs. John A. Shedd wisely said: "A ship in the harbor is safe, but that is not what ships are built for." You're built to navigate the high seas of your career, to chart your own course, and to chase your dreams.

So, are you ready to make the leap? Are you ready to upgrade your career and start living the life you've always wanted? Let's make a plan, take action, and then let's do this!

CHAPTER 16

UNLOCK YOUR GUT GENIUS: MASTERING THE ART OF INTUITIVE INTELLIGENCE

"The intuitive mind is a sacred gift and the rational mind is a faithful servant." — Albert Einstein

---

Ever had a "gut feeling" about a decision, something beyond logic? Intuition isn't just mystical; it's a practical tool that can improve our decision-making, creativity, and understanding of the world.

Your gut instincts are a powerhouse of intelligence you're probably under-using.

Why? Because you've been taught to value facts over your inner wisdom. This chapter is about harnessing that quiet voice inside you that whispers before you even have a chance to think.

We will explore the concept of intuitive intelligence—your "gut genius" that taps into the subconscious mind to guide you through life's complexities. Ready to unlock and master intuitive intelligence?

Let's explore your inner wisdom!

Wisdom from the Wise

History is dripping with stories of geniuses who trusted their gut. Think of great military leaders, visionary artists, and pioneering scientists—they all had a knack for following their instincts. From Steve Jobs to Marie Curie, their most significant breakthroughs often came from a deep trust in their intuitive intelligence. This isn't old news; it is timeless wisdom.

Albert Einstein is often celebrated for his scientific genius, but few realize how much he valued intuition alongside empirical evidence. He famously said, "The only real valuable thing is intuition." Einstein's breakthroughs in physics were not just products of calculations and experiments, but also his deep intuitive understanding of the universe's mysteries.

Steve Jobs, co-founder of Apple Inc., is another modern icon who harnessed the power of intuition. Jobs said, "Have the courage to follow your heart and intuition. They somehow already know what you truly want to become." His approach to designing technology was not just about technical specifications but about creating user experiences that felt intuitively right. As a result, Apple became the most valuable company in the world.

Then there's Leonardo da Vinci, a polymath whose intuitive grasp of art, science, engineering, and anatomy propelled him far beyond his contemporaries. Da Vinci's notebooks are brimming with insights that only centuries later would science confirm, showing that his intuitive intelligence was as formidable as his observational skills.

Nikola Tesla, a pioneer in electricity and magnetism, greatly valued intuition in his scientific discoveries and innovations. He believed that his intuition was a powerful tool for tapping into hidden knowledge and bringing forth groundbreaking ideas.

Intuition is not just reserved for the geniuses of history; it is a universal gift that we all possess. It is our inner knowing, our subconscious mind at work, guiding us towards the best decisions and solutions. But somewhere along the way, we have been conditioned to rely solely on logic and reason, dismissing the power of our intuition.

Listen to the Mavericks. From tech entrepreneurs to creative directors, the people who change the world know how to listen to their inner voice. From Elon Musk revolutionizing space travel with SpaceX to Jony Ive redefining design at Apple, these leaders demonstrate the power of trusting one's inner voice. They make decisions that defy logic because their gut tells them something logic can't.

Did You Know? The "gut feeling" is not just a metaphor, but a real physiological phenomenon. The enteric nervous system can sense environmental threats and relay that information to the brain before the conscious mind has a chance to process the information.

Your Gut Genius is the Real Deal

Your gut and your brain are directly connected by a nerve called the vagus, one of the longest nerves in the human body. This nerve transmits signals in both directions and is part of the "gut-brain axis," which allows for continuous communication between the gastrointestinal and central nervous systems.

The enteric nervous system, also known as the "second brain," is a complex system of approximately 100 million neurons in the gut wall. It governs the function of the gastrointestinal system independently, but is influenced by and communicates with the brain.

Research has shown that the gut microbiome, which is made up of trillions of bacteria and other microorganisms, may have an impact on mood and behavior. Certain probiotics referred to as "psychobiotics" have been discovered to have the potential to ease symptoms of depression and anxiety. Also, fermented foods that are rich in probiotics, such as yogurt, kefir, sauerkraut, and kombucha, can enhance gut health and, potentially, intuitive abilities by increasing the diversity and health of gut flora. Let's take good care of our gut genius; it is incredible!

What Exactly Is Intuitive Intelligence?

Forget the mystical fluff. Intuitive intelligence is your mind's cut-through-the-noise, get-to-the-point, incredibly efficient way of understanding the world. Your brain can digest the data it receives from your experiences, emotions, and perceptions—then arrive at conclusions faster than you can say "conscious reasoning." It's the kind of smart that feels like instinct because it almost works behind the scenes.

Let's get technical, but not boring. Your brain has this fantastic area called the subconscious, which processes information way faster than your conscious mind can handle. It pulls from past experiences, emotional memories, and learned patterns to inform you in real-time, resulting in what we call gut feelings. Neuroscience has shown that this isn't just quick thinking—it's fast and smart thinking. It's your brain on its best day, every day if you let it.

Apps for Mindfulness: Use 'Headspace' or 'Calm' to practice daily mindfulness, which sharpens intuition.

Journaling for Insight: Keep a decision journal to note your intuitive choices. Note the outcomes and your thought process.

Activity: Intuition Activation Day

Today's mission is to focus on recognizing, trusting, and enhancing your intuitive intelligence. This challenge involves engaging in exercises that help you tap into and strengthen your 'gut feelings', improving your decision-making and problem-solving skills through the power of intuition.

1. Mindfulness Meditation: Begin your day with a meditation focused on grounding and centering yourself. Use techniques that enhance sensory awareness, such as focusing on sounds, smells, or tactile sensations, to heighten your attunement to the present moment.

2. Journaling on Intuition: Post meditation, spend some time journaling about times when you've experienced intuitive solid feelings. Note what those feelings were, how you responded, and the outcomes of following (or not following) your intuition.

3. Blind Decision-Making: Engage in simple exercises where you must make choices based on little to no logical information— relying solely on your gut feelings. This could be as simple as choosing between two meals, selecting a book to read based on the cover or choosing a walking path randomly.

4. Body Scan for Emotional Feedback: Conduct a body scan to identify how different thoughts or decisions affect your physical state. Notice where in your body you feel tension or ease when contemplating other options.

5. Intuition Walks: Take a walk without a predetermined route, allowing your intuition to guide your direction. Be mindful of the impulses that guide your turns and stops.

6. Creative Free Flow: Engage in a creative activity like single-line drawing, painting, writing, or playing music with no planned outcome. Allow your intuition to guide your actions, focusing on the process rather than the product.

7. Reflective Review: Reflect on the day's exercises and identify which activities most effectively tapped into your intuition. Consider how using intuition felt different from more analytical decision-making processes.

8. Discussion with Others: Discuss your experiences with a friend or mentor if possible. Share insights about when intuition was beneficial and explore situations where it might be precious.

9. Integration Journaling: Spend the evening integrating what you've learned about your intuitive capabilities. Outline ways to incorporate intuition more effectively into your daily decision-making processes.

10. Relaxation Techniques: Wind down with the relaxation techniques you enjoy, such as yoga, deep breathing, or listening to soothing music, to help assimilate the day's lessons and relax your mind.

Benefits: This challenge enhances your ability to trust and use your intuitive intelligence, a key skill that complements analytical thinking and enriches your life choices. It can lead to quicker and more effective decision-making, especially in complex or uncertain situations.

Reflective Questions:

1. What did you learn about your intuitive responses during today's activities?
2. How can you better integrate intuition into your daily routines to enhance decision-making?

Concluding Thoughts

When it comes to decision-making, many of us tend to rely solely on logic and rational thinking. We weigh the pros and cons, consider all potential outcomes, and try to make the most sensible choice. However, sometimes we may find ourselves struggling with a decision despite having all the information at hand.

This is where intuitive intelligence comes in. It's that gut feeling or inner voice that guides us toward a decision or action with no need for all the logical reasoning. And contrary to popular belief, it's not some mystical force or magical power. Intuitive intelligence, or 'gut genius,' is a crucial aspect of human cognition that complements analytical thinking. It's actually a combination of our past experiences, emotions, and instincts that help us make quick, instinctive decisions.

"Intuition is a very powerful thing, more powerful than intellect." — Steve Jobs

As we wrap up this chapter, make sure you don't just understand your intuitive intelligence, but actually start living by it. It's time to turn your gut into your ultimate guide. Now, I'm not talking about taking wild, unrealistic leaps of faith. I'm talking about making smarter, faster, and more aligned decisions that reflect the incredible intelligence you hold within. You know that decision you've been agonizing over? Forget the endless list of pros and cons. What does your gut say? Listen to it. Follow it. See where it leads you.

This is your moment to document this experience. Was your intuition correct? What did it feel like to trust it? This isn't just another chapter to read; this is your call to revolutionize the way you think by trusting the way you feel.

Are you ready to unlock your gut genius? Are you ready to master the art of intuitive intelligence? It's time to tap into that inner wisdom and let it guide you to incredible places. Your gut has been waiting for this moment—and so have you. Let's do this together!

CHAPTER 17

OVERCOMING STAGNATION: STRATEGIES FOR BREAKING THROUGH PLATEAUS IN CAREER AND CREATIVITY

"If you're not moving forward, you're falling back." — Sam Waterson

---

Ever feel like you're running on a treadmill—lots of effort, but going nowhere? Whether it's in your career or your creative pursuits, hitting a plateau can be frustrating and disheartening. But here's the good news: you're not doomed to stay there. Overcoming this plateau is essential not only for career advancement but also for personal fulfillment.

Stagnation often occurs to avoid criticism. Criticism can feel like being told your baby is ugly. It stings, whether it's about your work, your ideas, or even your cooking. It's like you've painted a masterpiece, only for someone to point out that the sky looks a bit off. Ouch. This chapter is about identifying the signs of stagnation and implementing strategies to overcome them, ensuring you continue to grow and succeed.

Wisdom from the Wise

Here's the truth—criticism is your gateway to greatness. As Aristotle famously said, "Criticism is something we can avoid easily by saying nothing, doing nothing, and being nothing." But if you're someone who strives to make a difference, to be more, and to do more, then criticism isn't just inevitable; it's essential.

Think of criticism as a coach, not a critic. It's here to push you, not to pull you down. Every piece of feedback is an opportunity to learn and to improve. The goal isn't to avoid criticism but to leverage it. It's a tool designed to sharpen your skills and clarify your path.

Charles Darwin experienced long periods of data collection, analysis, and seemingly mundane research before arriving at the groundbreaking theory of natural selection. His ability to persevere through years of detailed study, overcoming periods of doubt and frustration, exemplifies how significant breakthroughs often come from pushing through stagnation.

Did You Know? Psychological studies suggest that setting specific, challenging goals increases performance by up to 250% compared to simple task completion or vague goals.

Understanding Stagnation

Stagnation is a sneaky beast. It cloaks itself in the guise of routine, making you believe that you're just "settling in" when, in reality, you're sinking into complacency. It's that comforting lull that numbs you into believing that "good enough" is fine, but deep down, you know it's not. Today, let's uncover why stagnation takes hold and how it quietly drains the zest from your career and creativity.

Stagnation often results from a combination of external constraints and internal barriers, such as fear of failure, lack of motivation, or inadequate challenges. If not addressed, stagnation can psychologically lead to reduced job satisfaction, decreased creativity, and even burnout.

Comfort Zone or Comfort Trap?

Stagnation is born in comfort zones—and then the comfort zone becomes too comfortable. It loves the familiar, the safe, and the unchallenging. It's human nature to seek safety and familiarity, but when these instincts go unchallenged, they can lead to a state of static existence. Unfortunately, stagnation is the product of sticking to what's familiar and safe, avoiding risks that could lead to growth.

In careers, this means doing just enough to get by, recycling old ideas instead of seeking new challenges, or shying away from opportunities that could lead to significant advancements. It manifests as a lack of innovation for creative minds—repeating what works without exploring what else could work.

Red Flags of Stagnation

Career Stagnation: You might feel like you're no longer moving forward. Promotions stop coming, learning curves flatten, and work starts feeling like clockwork—predictable and uninspiring. It's more than climbing the corporate ladder; it's about feeling your potential is not being fully utilized or recognized.

Creative Stagnation: For those in creative fields, stagnation means finding yourself repeating the same themes and methods because they worked before. It's the comfort of the known that stifles the thrill of discovery and the satisfaction of breaking new ground. It's sticking to the same palette because it's sold well, not because it still excites you.

Lost Spark: You don't wake up excited about work anymore. Projects that used to make your heart race now barely raise your pulse.

Slipping Standards: A noticeable dip in the quality and quantity of what you produce. You're doing less and caring less about the outcome.

Innovation Aversion: You resist changes and new ideas, clinging to the outdated mantra of "if it ain't broke, don't fix it," even when innovation could bring significant improvements.

Wasted Potential: Deep down, you feel underutilized, knowing you have much more to offer.

Escaping the Stagnation Trap

Realizing you're stuck is the first step toward getting unstuck. The journey out of stagnation involves seeking new challenges, embracing risks, and continuously setting fresh goals. Upcoming sections will develop actionable strategies to reignite your passion and propel you forward.

Research in motivation theory and career development suggests that stagnation can occur when there is a lack of balance between one's skills and the level of difficulty in their tasks or career path. The concept of flow, as introduced by psychologist Mihaly Csikszentmihalyi, emphasizes the crucial role of achieving a harmonious balance between skill level and task difficulty in sustaining engagement and deriving satisfaction. Learning Platforms: Use online resources like LinkedIn Learning, MasterClass, or Skillshare to learn new skills or deepen existing expertise.

Apps: "MindMeister" to create mind maps to visualize ideas, solve problems, and stimulate creative thinking.

Books: Mindset: "The New Psychology of Success" by Carol S. Dweck explores how a growth mindset leads to greater success and personal fulfillment.

Activity: Breakthrough Day

Today's mission is to overcome feelings of stagnation and propel you past plateaus in your career and creative endeavors. This challenge is all about using practical, scientific, and creative methods to level up your growth, innovation, drive, and productivity.

1. Self-Assessment: Begin your day by assessing areas where you feel stagnant. Identify specific aspects of your career or creative pursuits where progress seems to have slowed or stopped.

2. Inspirational Input: Consume content that inspires you. This could be a podcast, a TED Talk, or reading about individuals who have successfully overcome similar challenges. Focus on stories that provide practical insights and motivational takeaways.

3. Creative Freewriting: Spend 30 minutes on a freewriting exercise. Choose a prompt that challenges you to think outside your usual patterns. The goal is to unlock new ideas and perspectives.

4. Cognitive Flexibility Tasks: Engage in tasks that require you to think differently, such as solving puzzles or brain teasers that are not typical for you. This helps to enhance your cognitive flexibility and can spur creative thinking.

5. Goal Revision and Strategy Session: Revisit your long-term goals and the strategies you've been using to achieve them. Revise your plans to incorporate alternative approaches based on your morning's insights and inspiration.

6. Skill Enhancement: Identify skills that will help you overcome plateaus. Dedicate time to learning a new skill or improving an existing one through online courses or practical exercises.

7. Networking for New Perspectives: Reach out to mentors, peers, or new contacts to discuss overcoming professional or creative stagnation. These conversations can provide fresh insights and renewed motivation.

8. Feedback Session: If possible, present your revised goals and strategies to someone you trust for feedback. Use this feedback to refine your approach further.

9. Reflective Journaling: Spend the evening reflecting on the day's activities—Journal about new ideas, feelings, and the actionable steps you have planned to overcome stagnation.

Benefits: This challenge will push you to expand your comfort zone and reinvigorate your personal and professional growth approach. By addressing stagnation head-on, you can re-energize your career and creative pursuits, leading to significant breakthroughs.

Reflective Questions

1. What aspects of your current role feel the most stagnant?
2. What was the most surprising insight you gained today about your stagnation?
3. What new skills or projects could inject excitement and challenge into your daily routine?

Concluding Thoughts

Getting unstuck isn't about finding a quick fix, but changing how you approach your work and creativity.

Overcoming stagnation requires a proactive approach to seeking new challenges, continuous learning, and expanding networks. By embracing challenges and continually seeking growth, you can transform periods of stagnation into stepping stones to success.

Identify one area where you feel stagnant and choose one strategy from this chapter to address it. Go ahead and take that first step now, whether it's setting a new goal, starting a course, or searching for fresh experiences.

Embracing a growth mindset and regular self-reflection can help realign your career trajectory and reignite passion in your work. Just a reminder, you can't make progress without doing something.

Are you ready to break free from stagnation and rediscover passion şin your work? With the right mindset and strategies, every plateau can become a launchpad. Let's embrace these strategies and start a new chapter in your professional life.

CHAPTER 18
THE QUEST FOR MEANING: FINDING YOUR PASSION AND PURPOSE

"What is the most important thing you could be working on in the world right now? And if you're not working on that, why aren't you?" — Aaron Swartz

---

Have you ever felt like there's something you were just meant to do, but you can't quite put your finger on it?

Imagine waking up one morning, feeling the weight of routine pressing down on you. Despite having a stable job and a comfortable life, there's a gnawing sense that something vital is missing—something that makes life worth living beyond the daily grind.

This is a common crisis many of us face, often expressed as a quest for deeper meaning.

This chapter is about discovering that path—the one that aligns perfectly with who you are, what you love, and your true calling. It's time to stop sleepwalking through life and start living with intention.

Your true calling is out there waiting for you, but it's not just going to fall into your lap. You've got to go out there and claim it!

Wisdom from the Wise

In the realm of psychology, Abraham Maslow's Hierarchy of Needs provides a modern framework for understanding this quest. At the pyramid's peak lies self-actualization—achieving one's full potential for creativity, independence, understanding, and acceptance. Maslow posited that only after satisfying more basic needs could individuals explore personal growth and fulfillment.

Viktor Frankl's logotherapy posits that the primary drive in human beings is not pleasure (as Freud suggested) or power (as Adler suggested), but the pursuit of what he called 'meaning.' According to Frankl, life has meaning under all circumstances, even the most miserable ones, and it's our responsibility to find it.

These historical and psychological views inform us that the journey to finding one's passion and purpose is both universal and uniquely personal. They pave the way for exploring how contemporary thinkers like Viktor Frankl, who survived the Holocaust by clinging to his purpose, have further defined the importance of meaning in our lives.

Leonardo da Vinci wasn't just a master painter and inventor; he was also a prolific journal keeper. His journals were filled with sketches, ideas, observations, and reflections on his work. His notebooks are legendary, not just for their artistic brilliance, but for their reflections on mistakes, lessons learned, and areas of curiosity. Da Vinci's practice of detailed documentation and reflection was not just a way to record ideas but a tool for intellectual exploration and personal growth - his secret sauce to sustaining genius and continuous improvement. Da Vinci's life teaches us that self-reflection fuels creativity—it's about asking relentless questions and relentlessly seeking answers.

Marie Curie's career is a prime example of someone following their true calling. Her unwavering dedication to physics and chemistry led to groundbreaking discoveries, including the theory of radioactivity and the isolation of radioactive isotopes. Her passion for science not only fulfilled her but also made significant contributions to the world.

Florence Nightingale, the pioneer of modern nursing, found her purpose in improving hospital conditions and reforming nursing practices. Her dedication transformed medical care and provided a model for future generations about the impact of a purpose-driven life.

Elizabeth Gilbert, author of "Big Magic," suggested that curiosity, rather than passion, can be a more accessible guide when exploring potential callings. She advocates following your curiosity and letting it lead you to your passion.

Discovering Meaning: Insights from Ancient Wisdom to Modern Philosophy

Since ancient times, the pursuit of meaning has been at the core of human existence. The Greeks advocated for 'arete,' or the realization of one's fullest potential, often achieved through personal virtue and excellence in all endeavors. This historical perspective underscores that the quest for purpose is not a modern phenomenon but a timeless challenge.

In our relentless pursuit of passion and purpose, we embark on a journey echoing the footsteps of giants—philosophers who dared to ponder life's deepest mysteries.

Let's rocket back in time and explore the transformative ideas from two towering figures in philosophy: Marcus Aurelius and Jean-Paul Sartre. Their contrasting yet complementary insights provide a powerful framework for anyone on the hunt for their true passion and purpose.

Marcus Aurelius: The Stoic Guide to Inner Peace

Imagine being an emperor of Rome, the most powerful man in the known world, and still finding the time and mental space to write a diary about personal growth and virtue. That's Marcus Aurelius, a stoic philosopher whose work "Meditations" provides critical lessons on resilience, self-control, and understanding what we can and cannot change.

• Stoicism in Action: Aurelius teaches us the art of focusing our energy solely on what's within our control. He believed that peace comes not from external achievements but from doing our best with what we control, and letting go of the rest.

• Apply It Like This: Each morning, ask yourself, "What's in my control today?" Focus your efforts here and practice letting go of what isn't. This mindset is crucial when discovering your passion because it keeps you centered amidst the chaos of expectations and societal pressures.

Jean-Paul Sartre: Existentialism and the Power of Choice

Fast forward nearly two thousand years to Jean-Paul Sartre, a French philosopher who flips the script with his assertion that "existence precedes essence." This means we're thrown into the world first and then must define ourselves through our choices. It's a liberating, if daunting, way to look at life and our purpose in it.

• Freedom to Define Ourselves: Sartre's existentialism empowers us with the freedom to shape our lives and identities through the choices we make. He argues that we are not defined by pre-set narratives or roles; instead, we create our essence through our actions.

• Embrace Your Freedom: Reflect on the choices you're making: Are they truly yours, or are they influenced by others? Every day, try to make choices that align more closely with your authentic self. This practice helps to actively craft the person you want to be, rather than passively falling into roles that don't fit.

Integrating Historical Insights into Modern Life

Marcus Aurelius and Jean-Paul Sartre may seem worlds apart, but their philosophies can be combined for a powerful approach to finding and living your passion. Aurelius grounds us with his focus on virtue and acceptance, while Sartre sets us free to forge our paths through bold choices.

Start your day with a Stoic reflection to focus on what you can control. End your day with an existential review of the choices you made. Were they authentic? Did they align with your true self? This combination of Stoic calm and existential boldness can guide you to discover and live your passion in a way that is both grounded and liberating.

Remember, finding your passion isn't about uncovering a hidden secret—it's about creating it through your everyday choices. Use the wisdom of Aurelius to keep you steady and the freedom espoused by Sartre to boldly go after what sets your soul on fire.

Your Brain on Passion: It's Electric!

Imagine your brain doing a happy dance—that's pretty much what happens when you engage in something you're passionate about. Neuroscience shows us that when we do what we love, specific areas of our brain light up like a Christmas tree.

• Neurological Fireworks: Areas like the dopamine pathways (think of dopamine as your personal feel-good neurotransmitter) activate, which makes you feel joy and pleasure. This isn't just about feeling good at the moment; it's your brain reinforcing behaviors that it wants you to repeat.

• Emotional Resonance: Meanwhile, your limbic system, which is central to emotion processing, gets in on the action, too. This part of your brain responding strongly to passion-filled activities explains why they're so satisfying and why they stick to our memories.

This brain activity isn't just random; it's a sophisticated system designed to guide you toward what fulfills you. It's like your brain's way of saying, "Yes, more of this, please!"

Why Motivation Isn't Just About Willpower

Let's switch gears to psychology—specifically, Self-Determination Theory (SDT), which might just change how you think about motivation. It's not just about pushing yourself harder; it's about meeting your deep psychological needs.

Autonomy: Feeling in control of your actions is huge. When you choose what you're doing, engagement skyrockets. It's the difference between being told to go to a party and wanting to go. The choice fuels your drive.

Competence: This is about getting good at what you do. There's a real thrill in mastering a skill, whether it's cooking, coding, or climbing. As you get better, your desire to keep going gets stronger.

Relatedness: We're social creatures, and connecting with others through activities makes those activities more rewarding. Whether it's joining a book club, playing on a sports team, or volunteering, feeling connected ups the motivation.

Putting It All Together: How to Light Your Fire

Understanding the neuroscience and psychology of passion means you can better navigate your way to a fulfilling life. Here's how you can use this knowledge to stoke your inner flames:

Tune Into Your Joy: Start noticing which activities make you lose track of time, make you feel excited, or leave you wanting more. These are clues to what your brain and body want more of.

Fulfill Your Needs: Actively seek ways to satisfy your needs for autonomy, competence, and relatedness. Maybe it's finally starting that side business, learning a new language, or getting involved in community projects.

So, what are you waiting for? The science is clear: when you align your life with your passions, not only do you feel more alive, but you're also setting yourself up for sustained happiness and motivation. Your brain and your heart will thank you.

What Are You Meant to Do?

The search for a life's purpose is as old as humanity itself, but it's more pressing than ever in a world that offers endless opportunities. We'll explore what it means to find your calling and how this pursuit can transform your everyday life from mundane to extraordinary.

Let's face it - grasping the psychology of fulfillment is crucial. By identifying and pursuing your true passion, your well-being, motivation, and resilience soar. Studies confirm individuals engaged in meaningful activities are not only happier but also healthier and more productive.

You're here because you're itching to figure out what you're meant to do with your life, right? Well, strap in. We're tackling the eternal question: What is my purpose?

First things first, it's important to understand that there is no one-size-fits-all answer. Your purpose may differ from your friend's or even your family member's. And you know what? That's perfectly fine. Embrace the uniqueness of your journey and know that it will lead you to where you are meant to be.

Did You Know? According to psychology research, people who have identified and pursued their calling are more likely to be engaged in their jobs.

Now, let's start with the basics. Your purpose is not just a job title or a specific career path. It's not something that can be found in a quick Google search or a quiz result. Your true calling is much deeper and more meaningful than that.

Your purpose is rooted in your values, passions, and strengths. It's the intersection of what you care about, what you love to do, and what you excel at. It's what gets you out of bed in the morning and fuels your day. But here's the thing: your purpose is not a destination. It's an ongoing journey of self-discovery and growth. As you evolve as a person, your purpose may also shift and change. And that's okay too!

So, how do you uncover your purpose? It isn't a one-off revelation. It's a persistent quest for introspection and exploration. The world's your playground, filled with infinite opportunities. But here's the thing: it's not about just picking any old job or hobby. It's about finding your true calling - that thing that sets your soul on fire and makes you feel like you're living life to the fullest.

Start with some soul-searching. What lights up your heart? What activities make you lose track of time? What do you find yourself constantly drawn to? But here's the twist: once you identify your calling, you can't just sit back and expect it to fall into your lap. You've got to pursue it with everything you've got. And trust me, it won't be easy. There will be obstacles and setbacks along the way. But that's where the magic happens.

You see, when you're engaged in something truly meaningful to you; it transforms your entire life. Suddenly, the mundane becomes extraordinary, and every day feels like an adventure. And the best part? Science is on board with this. Studies show that people who pursue their calling are happier, healthier, and more resilient. They have a sense of purpose that drives them forward, even in the face of adversity.

So, what's holding you back? Start exploring what sets your soul on fire. Don't settle for a life of mediocrity when you could be living an extraordinary one. The journey to finding your calling won't be easy, but it will be worth it. Take it from someone who's been there - it's worth every step.

Did You Know? In many Scandinavian countries, there is a cultural concept similar to 'Ikigai' called 'Hygge,' which emphasizes comfort, contentment, and well-being, arising from engaging in joyful activities.

Apps: 'Good&Co Culture Fit Job Finder' to explore career options that match your personality and values.

Personality and Career Assessment Tests: Tools like the Myers-Briggs Type Indicator or the Strong Interest Inventory can offer valuable insights into your personality and career preferences.

Books: "The Element: How Finding Your Passion Changes Everything" by Ken Robinson explores the concept of living a life in alignment with your genuine passions and talents.

Activity: Purpose Discovery Day

Today's mission is to engage in a series of introspective and actionable exercises designed to help you uncover and clarify your life's purpose. Try to deeply explore your passions, skills, and values and how they align with your life and career paths.

1. Values Assessment: Begin your day by identifying your core values through various prompts and questionnaires. Determine which values are most important to you and how they align with your current life and career. What do you truly care about? What principles guide your life?

2. Passions and Interests Brainstorm: Make a list of activities and topics that excite you or that you find deeply engaging. Reflect on how these could translate into potential career paths or life missions. What brings you joy and fulfillment? What do you love to do in your free time? What could you talk about for hours? List out everything that gets your heart racing. Pinpoint these passions— they're clues to your purpose.

3. Skills Inventory: Take stock of what you're awesome at. Include both hard skills (technical abilities) and soft skills (such as communication and empathy). What are you naturally good at? What skills and abilities do you possess?

4. Life's Milestones: Write your key life experiences that have shaped who you are. Reflect on those life-changing moments. What themes keep showing up? Look for patterns or recurring themes that might point to underlying passions or potential paths.

5. Future Self Visualization: Close your eyes and envision your best life. Who are you with? What are you doing? What achievements you are most proud of? Capture this vision—it's your north star.

6. Make It Happen Goals: Time to bridge the gap. From the visualization, identify concrete goals to help you achieve this envisioned future. What goals will catapult you toward that dream scenario? Break them down into bite-sized, achievable steps.

7. Informational Interviews: If possible, conduct informational interviews (either in person or virtually) with individuals currently in fields or roles you find intriguing. Ask about their path, daily responsibilities, and what they find most fulfilling about their work.

8. Career and Life Path Research: Research different career paths or life trajectories that align with your identified values, skills, and interests. Look at educational requirements, potential job markets, and personal testimonies.

9. Reflective Journaling: Reflect on the day's activities and insights—Journal about how your understanding of your purpose may have changed or deepened.

10. Commitment Plan: Create a plan to pursue further exploration or education in areas of interest. Set specific, time-bound objectives to move you closer to your true calling.

Benefits: This power-packed day is your launchpad to discovering what truly drives you. It's about aligning your life with your passions, skills, and values, setting the stage for fulfillment in every area of your life. Let's ignite that spark and get you moving toward a life that's not just lived, but loved.

Reflective Questions

1. What truly captivates you and makes time fly by?
2. Can you think of someone you know who is truly following their passion, and what insights can you gain from their journey?

3. Which activities or insights from today resonated most with you, and why? What next steps will you take to explore further or pursue your true calling?

Concluding Thoughts

Now that you have some tips for finding your purpose, it's important to remember that everyone's journey is unique. Just because someone else has found their purpose doesn't mean it will be the same for you. Don't compare yourself to others or feel pressured to have it all figured out right away. Trust that the pieces will fall into place as you continue on your path.

Take some time to reflect on these questions in this chapter, seek guidance from those who know you well, and trust your own journey. And finally, don't forget that your purpose is not just about you —it's also about how you can make a positive impact on others and the world around you.

So embrace the journey and remember that it's never too late to discover your purpose. It is an ongoing process that requires self-reflection, exploration, and openness to new experiences. Trust in yourself and follow your heart—your purpose will reveal itself as you continue to grow and evolve.

Remember, your purpose isn't something to be found or achieved—it's already within you. You just have to uncover it and let it guide you toward a life of fulfillment and happiness. Stay curious, keep evolving, and let your purpose unfold in its own time. Embrace the process and enjoy the ride!

CHAPTER 19

DISCOVERING YOUR TALENTS: UNCOVERING AND CULTIVATING HIDDEN POTENTIAL

"Everyone has talent. What's rare is the courage to follow it to the dark places where it leads." — Erica Jong

Do you truly know all your talents? Think again. It's a common tale that most of us only scratch the surface of what we're capable of. Whether you're in a rut or simply curious, uncovering your hidden talents can revolutionize your personal and professional life.

It is time to rebrand yourself. Brand 'You'! Let's create a personal brand that highlights your journey, skills, and where you're headed—not just where you've been. It's storytelling with you as the hero on a quest. Are you ready to craft a compelling narrative that showcases your adaptability, resilience, and the unique value only you bring?

This chapter goes beyond just recognizing your strengths; it's about challenging what you believe you're capable of achieving. Don't limit yourself based on past experiences or preconceived notions. Embrace the unknown and see where it takes you.

Wisdom from the Wise

History shows us that many successful people didn't start out knowing their greatest skills. It is full of stories where people discover their true talents later in life, shifting the course of their journeys.

Take Walt Disney, for example, who started as a cartoonist but built one of the world's most beloved entertainment companies. J. K. Rowling, once a struggling writer, created the Harry Potter series, becoming a best-selling author. Jeff Bezos transformed a small online bookstore into Amazon. He launched Amazon from his garage, transforming it into a global e-commerce and cloud computing giant.

Sir Ken Robinson, an advocate for developing personal talents, emphasized the importance of creating an environment that nurtures rather than undermines creativity and innovation. His work encourages educational systems and workplaces to adapt to their members' individual learning styles and strengths.

Each of these individuals started with modest beginnings, but through innovation and persistence, they created empires that have left indelible marks on the world.

Did You Know? According to research, individuals who incorporate their strengths into their daily routine are six times more likely to feel engaged at work, experience higher levels of happiness, and have reduced stress and anxiety.

The Psychology Behind Talent Discovery: What Are You Really Good At?

Talent isn't just about what you're good at—it's about what makes you feel alive. It's the intersection of ability, creativity, and passion. But how do you tap into these hidden reserves? We'll explore how self-awareness and curiosity are key to unlocking your true potential.

Research in cognitive psychology and neurology suggests that talents are a combination of genetic predispositions and environmental influences. Brain plasticity also plays a significant role, as engaging in new activities can strengthen neural pathways associated with various skills and competencies.

Delving into the science, we find talents are a blend of innate abilities and developed skills. Psychological studies suggest that while some talents are genetic, many are cultivated through exposure, experience, and practice. This means that everyone has the potential to discover and develop new abilities.

Author and psychologist Dr. Angela Duckworth champions the idea of "grit"—the power of passion and perseverance. She suggests that feeling lost can sometimes be part of a more extensive journey towards achieving something truly meaningful, encouraging persistence and continuous effort.

The Increasing Importance of Soft Skills

A 2025 forecast by the World Economic Forum ranks emotional intelligence, creativity, and complex problem-solving as top skills needed in the future job market, reflecting a shift towards uniquely human skills that are less likely to be automated.

Focus on developing these soft skills through workshops, coaching, mentorship, and real-world practice. Additionally, showcase these skills in your professional profiles and interviews to demonstrate your readiness for future challenges and leadership roles. Document these experiences in your professional portfolio to illustrate a well-rounded skill set that blends human insight with technical proficiency.

Technological Displacement and Skills Gap

The World Economic Forum estimates that 85 million jobs may be displaced by a shift in the division of labor between humans and machines by 2025, while 97 million new roles may emerge that are more adapted to the new division of labor.

The job landscape is shifting—don't get left behind. Proactively identify emerging roles and the skills they require. Dedicate time each week to developing these skills. Think of this as future-proofing your career—by staying ahead of trends, you're not just adapting; you're setting the trends.

Personality Tests and Skill Assessments: Tools like the Myers-Briggs Type Indicator or the StrengthsFinder can provide insights into your personality traits and potential talents.

Books: "Now, Discover Your Strengths" by Marcus Buckingham and Donald O. Clifton discusses identifying and playing to your strengths using the StrengthsFinder assessment. "Pathways to Possibility" by Rosamund Stone Zander is a transformative book that helps redefine personal narratives and unlock new possibilities.

Activity: Unleashing Your Inner Talent

Today is all about unlocking the powerhouse of talents lying dormant within you. You're going on a transformative journey to not just discover, but also nurture and expand your unique abilities. This isn't just a challenge; it's an opportunity to dive deep into what makes you tick, using a blend of self-reflection, daring experiments, and valuable feedback. We're on a quest to reveal your hidden gems - talents you might not even realize you have.

1. Skills Deep Dive: Kick off your day with a deep dive into your skills and passions. Grab an online survey or worksheet (think Myers Briggs or Clifton Strengths) to map out both your known and yet-to-be-discovered skills.

2. Tales of Inspiration: Immerse yourself in stories of people who've walked off the beaten path to harness their unique talents. Look for echoes of your own undiscovered skills in their journeys.

3. Experimentation Labs: Jump into a variety of hands-on workshops or tutorials that push you out of your comfort zone. Ever thought about painting, coding, gardening, or poetry? Now's your chance.

4. Joy and Flow Reflections: After each new experience, take a moment to reflect. Did you love it? Did it feel like second nature? Your reactions could point towards your innate talents.

5. Deep Dive Practice: Choose the activity that sparked the most joy and dive deeper. Create something real - a painting, a piece of code, or a poem.

6. Feedback Loop: Share your creations with others and listen to their feedback, focusing especially on insights into your natural abilities.

7. Talent Portfolio: Compile a portfolio of your talents and skills based on today's explorations and the feedback you've received.

8. Growth Blueprint: Sketch out a plan for nurturing and integrating these talents into your life, whether personally or professionally.

9. Journal Journey: End your day with reflective journaling. Reflect on your talents with gratitude and excitement for the journey ahead. How did these activities make you feel? What did you discover about yourself?

Benefits: Embrace this challenge to deepen your self-awareness, boost your self-esteem, and ignite a passion for personal growth. Discovering and refining your talents can open the door to a more rewarding life, both personally and professionally.

Reflective Questions:

1. What's something new you've been itching to try but haven't yet?
2. How can you make talent discovery a regular part of your life?
3. Which activities make you lose track of time, indicating potential hidden talents?

4. How can you weave your talents into your everyday life or career for a more enriching experience?

Concluding Thoughts

As you flip through this chapter, stepping boldly into what's next, keep this in mind: uncovering and growing your talents is a vibrant, never-ending journey.

It demands your curiosity, bravery, and dedication. Discovering and nurturing your talents involves introspection, experimentation, and seeking feedback.

"There is a vitality, a life force, an energy, a quickening that is translated through you into action, and because there is only one of you in all of time, this expression is unique." — Martha Graham

---

When you tap into and leverage your talents, not only do they transform your life, but they also have the power to make a significant difference in the world.

Unleash your unique strengths and let them guide you to a life full of fulfillment and impact. Are you ready to embark on a journey of self-discovery and begin uncovering the talents that make you *uniquely you*? Let's explore the amazing potential you hold!

CHAPTER 20
BUILDING YOUR TRIBE: THE KEY TO NETWORKING SUCCESS

"We are born alone, we live alone, we die alone. Only through our love and friendship can we create the illusion for the moment that we're not alone." — Orson Welles

Let's smash a common myth: Networking isn't about collecting business cards like they're going out of style or racking up LinkedIn connections faster than likes on a viral meme. No, real networking is the art of forging connections that are as profound as they are profitable.

It's about transforming the "What can you do for me?" into "How can we create magic together?" It's not who you know; it's who knows you well enough to vouch for your skills and character.

Ready to transform superficial interactions into deep connections that could open doors for a lifetime?

Wisdom from the Wise

Cultural anthropologist Margaret Mead emphasized the impact of community and shared learning in her research. Her studies suggest that the cohesion of a tribe or community group significantly impacts its members' psychological well-being and cultural development.

Seth Godin, in his book "Tribes," argues that anyone can be a leader, not by managing people but by connecting and leading a group of like-minded individuals. His concept of "tribes" is a powerful testament to building supportive networks in the modern age.

Benjamin Franklin, one of America's founding fathers, was also a master networker. He established the Junto Club—a group of like-minded individuals from diverse professions who met regularly to discuss moral, political, and scientific topics, helping each other succeed.

His Junto Club wasn't just a gathering; it was a masterclass in networking. Franklin knew that a network of well-connected, mutually supportive individuals could change the world—and it did. His club was about pooling collective intelligence to lift every member up. That's networking with style and substance.

Did You Know? The concept of "Ubuntu" in Southern Africa translates to "I am because we are," highlighting the belief in a universal bond that connects all humanity.

Beyond the Business Cards

Here's a slice of truth pie: in today's hyper-connected world, relationships are the real currency in the professional world. This isn't just fluffy talk—it's backed by psychology.

Effective networking is about strategic relationship-building, not just glad-handing. Real networking isn't a transaction; it's an investment in a mutual give-and-take that extends far beyond the initial handshake.

Psychological research confirms that relationships built on trust and mutual respect are more likely to yield long-lasting and significant advantages.

Dive deep into the human psyche, and you'll find we're wired for connection. The dynamics of human behavior and social exchange theory aren't just about feeling good; it's about survival.

Our brains light up when we forge connections, releasing a cocktail of neurotransmitters that scream, "Yes! This feels great!" Leveraging this for networking means turning every handshake into a meaningful exchange.

> Apps: Use 'Meetup' to find and join groups or events that match your professional interests and personal passions.

> Books: "Never Eat Alone" by Keith Ferrazzi explores the intricacies of building and maintaining powerful relationships that transcend professional transactions.

Activity: Community Connection Challenge

Today's mission is to strengthen existing relationships and forge new ones, building a supportive community that enhances personal and collective growth.

1. Reach Out: Reach out to a friend or family member you haven't spoken to in a while. Have a meaningful conversation, or better yet, arrange a meet-up if possible. Focus on listening and reconnecting.

2. Join a Group: Find a local or online group that aligns with your passions and long-term goals. This could be a book club, a fitness class, or a professional networking group.

3. Offer Support: Identify how you can offer support or help to someone in your community. It could be professional advice, emotional support, or hands-on help with a project.

4. Community Event: Attend a community event, even if it's virtual. Engage with participants, exchange ideas, and make at least one new connection.

5. Reflective Journaling: Reflect on your experiences in building your tribe. How did engaging with different people make you feel? What role do you see yourself playing within your community?

Benefits: This exercise enhances feelings of belonging and purpose, reduces feelings of loneliness, and can lead to personal and professional development opportunities.

Reflective Questions:

1. Do you remember the last time you helped someone in your network, expecting nothing in return?
2. How did it feel to reconnect or deepen your social connection?
3. What can you change in your current networking approach to foster stronger, more genuine connections?
4. What can you do regularly to maintain or strengthen your social ties?

Concluding Thoughts

In our interconnected world, mastering the art of networking is crucial for personal and professional development. By forging meaningful connections, we don't just enrich our lives; we uplift society. Let's commit to creating powerful, supportive networks, both online and offline, and elevate each other to new heights.

This week, reach out to three people in your network and offer them something valuable—no strings attached. That's right, no hidden agenda, no expectation of getting something in return. Just pure, unadulterated generosity.

Instead of seeing it as a chore, let's approach it as an opportunity to forge meaningful connections that could lead to unexpected and extraordinary paths. This isn't just networking; it's net-weaving. We're creating a rich tapestry of meaningful and mutually beneficial relationships.

Maybe you've got some knowledge to share that could help someone tackle a problem they're facing. Maybe you know someone who would be the perfect fit for an opportunity they've been searching for. Or maybe you just want to let someone know that you appreciate them and the work they do. Whatever it is, make that connection and see what unfolds. Because here's the thing: the best networks aren't built on transactions; they're built on generosity.

Building your tribe is the key to networking success. When you focus on giving value and creating genuine connections, amazing things happen. Your network becomes a powerful force that propels you forward, opening doors and presenting opportunities you never even knew existed.

Are you ready to build a network that builds you back? Then let's do this. Reach out, make those connections, and watch as your tribe grows stronger, one generous act at a time. And remember, the power of networking lies not in what you can get, but in what you can give. The possibilities are endless.

Let's make them happen together. Together, we rise!

CHAPTER 21
LASER FOCUS: MASTERING THE ART OF CONCENTRATION IN A DISTRACTED WORLD

"Concentrate all your thoughts upon the work in hand. The sun's rays do not burn until brought to a focus." — Alexander Graham Bell

---

Remember the days when the mailman brought just a couple of letters, and that was the day's information intake? Now, our inboxes are bottomless pits, and social media feeds refresh faster than you can blink. We're like kids in a candy store, but the candy is information, and too much of it is making us mentally bloated.

In today's attention economy, your attention isn't just yours to direct, our attention is the currency that everyone is competing for. While the world competes for your focus, making you feel like you're living in a mental pinball machine, the ability to concentrate has become more than just a valuable skill—it's a critical survival tool.

This chapter isn't about tweaking your habits; it's about overhauling how you manage your mind and environment to master the art of focus. Are you ready to turn down the noise and turn up your productivity?

Wisdom from the Wise

Information overload is not a new phenomenon. Even in ancient libraries of Alexandria, scholars faced the daunting task of cataloging and understanding vast accumulations of knowledge. However, the digital age has accelerated this issue exponentially.

Historically, each technological advance, from the printing press to the internet, has exponentially increased the availability and consumption of information, presenting new challenges to human attention and cognition.

The greats—whether they're artists, athletes, or entrepreneurs—know that focus is their secret weapon. Steve Jobs wore the same outfit daily to avoid wasting focus on trivial choices. Elon Musk says that he breaks his entire day into five-minute slots, each fiercely focused.

Cal Newport advocates for embracing boredom. Learning to be okay with being bored can strengthen your mental focus muscle in a world that constantly entertains us. Even when your instincts scream to check that notification, you'll learn to stay the course, transforming potential distractions into moments of concentrated effort.

Nikola Tesla, the pioneering inventor, credited his groundbreaking discoveries to his intense ability to focus and visualize complex engineering solutions in his mind. Tesla's almost supernatural ability to visualize mechanisms in his mind, down to the last detail, showcases the power of intense focus. His practice of mental imaging was more than a just genius at work—it was focus turned to maximum. Nikola Tesla's story is a compelling case for why nurturing our ability to focus can lead to innovations that change the course of history.

Consider the legendary writer Mark Twain, who created some of his most celebrated works in a secluded garden shed. He would retreat there to isolate himself entirely from distractions, enabling him to şelve deeply into the worlds he created. Twain's ability to shut out the external world was pivotal to his creative process, illustrating the profound impact of dedicated workspaces and focused time on creative output.

Carl Jung, a profound thinker and psychiatrist, maintained voluminous collections of books and texts. Despite the vast amount of information at his disposal, Jung was selective in his focus, diving deep into specific topics to develop theories that are still influential today. His approach underscores the importance of depth over breadth in managing information.

Lessons from Jung's Routine:

Selective Learning: Focus on mastering a few areas rather than skimming the surface of many.

Scheduled Reflection: Jung dedicated time to reflection and meditation, crucial for assimilating complex information.

"My mind is like my internet browser. 14 tabs open, 3 of them are frozen, and I have no idea where this music is coming from." - Anonymous

---

Wake Up: Your Focus Needs You

Focus is not just a mental skill; it's a critical determinant of success. Like a laser, focus can cut through the clutter and complexity of any task. Whether you're writing a novel, coding software, or crafting a business strategy, your ability to focus on the task at hand significantly impacts the quality and speed of your work. Understanding how focus works—the neuroscience behind it—isn't just helpful, it's transformative. It can transform how you work, learn, and live. Focus isn't just about finishing tasks; it's about fulfilling your potential.

Deep work isn't just beneficial for creatives; it's crucial across all fields. Neurological studies show that when we focus intensely, our brain's frontal cortex lights up, activating networks associated with complex problem-solving and innovative thinking. Psychology tells us that minimizing multi-tasking and interruptions enhances cognitive efficiency, leading to higher-quality work output in shorter periods.

Your Brain on Focus: It's Science, Not Magic

Cognitive neuroscience shows us that focus isn't just about gritting your teeth and getting through a to-do list—it's about training your brain to select important information while ignoring the irrelevant. We'll explore techniques that bolster this ability, turning you into a mental agility master.

Focus is not just staring at a task until it's done. It's about intentionally directing your cognitive abilities to cut through what's bull and cling to what's golden. It's the difference between knowing a little about everything and knowing everything about something. Focus is about diving deep, not just skimming the surface. And right now, it's under siege from every ping, ding, and ring.

Your frontal cortex, where focus does its magic, is battling against distractions akin to mind candy—tasty but terrible for your productivity and mental health. Whenever you switch tasks without completing them or let a notification pull you away, you're training your brain to be a jack of all trades, master of none. Neuroplasticity means you can rewire your brain, but it also means you need to take charge of what wires you're strengthening.

Did You Know? Multitasking reduces productivity by up to 40%. Focusing on one task at a time is not just efficient: it's crucial.

Understanding the Zeigarnik Effect

The Zeigarnik effect shows that people remember uncompleted or interrupted tasks better than completed tasks. Breaking tasks into smaller, manageable segments that are easier to start and stop can harness this psychological phenomenon and enhance productivity. This method keeps tasks at the forefront of our memory and maintains motivation.

Frequent task switching, as noted in studies from the University of California, Irvine, shows that the average person changes tasks every three minutes, often resulting from digital interruptions. Use apps like 'Forest,' which gamifies focus by growing a virtual tree that will die if you exit the app prematurely. This helps maintain focus on single tasks by minimizing digital interruptions.

Role of Dopamine in Task Completion

Dopamine, a key neurotransmitter linked to pleasure and motivation, is crucial in task initiation and persistence. Neuroscientific research has found that breaking down tasks into smaller parts and rewarding oneself after completing each part can significantly enhance dopamine levels, boosting motivation and focus.

Minimize distractions in your workspace to optimize dopamine release related to task completion. This might include setting up a dedicated, clutter-free work area, using noise-canceling headphones to block external noise, and turning off non-essential notifications on your devices.

The Enemies of Focus

Digital Distractions: Your gadgets are designed to addict you. Every notification is a dopamine hit that steals your focus. Let's talk about how to cut this off.

Multitasking Myth: Doing multiple things at once doesn't make you a multi-tasking hero; it makes you a half-assing zero. It's time to do one thing brilliantly instead of ten things poorly.

Stress and Fatigue: If your mind is a mess, your focus will be too. Stress clouds thinking; fatigue kills creativity. We'll tackle how to manage these focus-killers.

Tech That Helps, Not Hinders: Use apps and tools that block out distractions, not introduce new ones. Freedom, Focus@Will, and Forest can help keep your digital environment clean.

> Apps: 'Freedom' or 'Forest' help limit distractions by blocking disruptive apps and websites. They're like personal trainers for your brain. 'Focus@Will' for music that increases concentration and focus.

> Books: Cal Newport's "Deep Work" is your handbook for success in a distracted world —essential reading for anyone serious about improving their focus.

Activity: Laser Focus Bootcamp

Today's mission is to master the art of deep concentration by engaging in a structured "Laser Focus Bootcamp" that enhances your ability to fully immerse in tasks, boosting creativity and productivity.

1. Preparation Phase: Choose a quiet, comfortable space where you are least likely to be disturbed. This could be a home office, a library, or even a quiet corner of a café.

2. Eliminate Distractions: Just turn off your phone notifications, clear unnecessary items from your desk, and prepare all the materials you might need in advance (notes, books, software tools, etc.).

3. Focus Session Planning: Choose a task that requires your full attention and creativity. Tasks such as writing a report, developing a software module, and creating a piece of art. If you find it easier to concentrate, consider using headphones and playing instrumental music.

4. Time Blocking: Schedule a solid two-hour block where you will work uninterrupted. Use a timer to enforce this period strictly.

5. Execution: Begin your work session by briefly reminding yourself of the goal. Then, dive into the task with full intensity. Refocus by visualizing your task as the focal point of a beam of light, gathering all your mental resources towards it.

6. Review and Reflect: At the end of the session, assess the quality and quantity of the work you have achieved. Write about your experience, noting what worked well and what didn't. Reflect on how the absence of distractions affected your work output and creativity.

Benefits: This exercise not only improves your work quality but also decreases stress by eliminating the fragmentation of constant task-switching.

Reflective Questions:

1. What distractions do you find most disruptive, and what strategies could you implement to mitigate them?
2. What differences did you notice in your work output or quality during the deep work session compared to your everyday work routine?
3. What strategies helped you maintain your focus during this time, and how can you apply these strategies daily?

Concluding Thoughts

Alright, here's the deal. To be unstoppable in a noisy world, you must get laser-focused on what truly matters. It's not simply about producing more work—it's about setting yourself up for those life-changing wins that'll leave you feeling like a total rockstar.

But let's be real here: mastering focus isn't some overnight magic trick. It's a skill you have to work on, one moment at a time. So, here's your challenge for this week: pick one distraction that's been bothering you and get rid of it. Whether it's those constant phone notifications or that clutter on your desk, it's time to take control. You might be surprised at how these little changes can totally transform your every day.

So, are you ready to unleash the true power of focus and take your life to the next level? It's time to cut through the noise, ditch the distractions, and become the unstoppable force you were meant to be. Own your attention, own your future!

CHAPTER 22

NAVIGATING CHANGE: EMBRACING ADAPTABILITY AND RESILIENCE

"It is not the strongest of the species that survives, nor the most intelligent that survives. It is the one that is most adaptable to change."— Charles Darwin

Change isn't just a part of life; it's the pulse of life itself, beating a rhythm of endless possibilities into every moment and decision. Think of it as the world's most influential personal trainer, constantly pushing you out of your comfort zone into new experiences that stretch and strengthen you.

Imagine one morning you wake up and decide to take an alternative route to work. It's just a tiny change, but suddenly, you're seeing new landscapes, original faces, and unfamiliar coffee shops with the steamy allure of fresh pastries. It's exciting, isn't it?

Whether it's the unexpected phone call that shifts your day's direction, the sudden downpour that alters your path, or the new job opportunity that turns your career on its head, embracing change is like saying yes to the universe's invitation to grow, explore, and truly live.

Change doesn't tiptoe gently into our lives—it crashes in, unannounced and often unwelcome, upending our routines and expectations. Change is the one constant we can all count on, whether in our personal lives or careers.

This chapter isn't about merely surviving the onslaught of change, but learning to thrive within it. How do we turn disruption into opportunity? How do we adapt to change and become agents of change ourselves? It's time to stop bracing against the winds of change and start becoming the wind.

Let's dive in and transform our approach to change from reactive to proactive, from surviving to thriving.

Wisdom from the Wise

Think of Charles Darwin. When he talked about the 'survival of the fittest,' he wasn't championing the strongest or the smartest, but the most adaptable. Darwin didn't just theorize evolution; he handed us the playbook for thriving in a changing world: adapt or die.

His theory of natural selection is not just about species—it's a profound metaphor for businesses, careers, and personal growth. The fittest? They're the adapters, the innovators, the resilient.

J. K. Rowling, who faced many rejections before publishing the Harry Potter series, once said, "It is impossible to live without failing at something unless you live so cautiously that you might as well not have lived at all." Embrace failure as a necessary precursor to success. It's not just about bouncing back; it's about bouncing forward.

Your Brain and Change: It's a Love-Hate Relationship

Stability is a myth. The reality? Our world—and your life in it—is in perpetual motion. Neuroscience doesn't just back this up; it celebrates it! Neuroscience reveals that a phenomenon called neuroplasticity allows our brains to adapt. It's about leveraging this built-in agility of the brain to survive, change, and thrive in it.

Think of neuroplasticity as your brain's natural workout regimen—it flexes and grows with use, especially when faced with new challenges. You do push-ups for your brain when you learn to embrace rather than brace against change. This isn't just coping with change; it's harnessing it to build mental muscle and resilience.

Change triggers the amygdala, the part of the brain responsible for emotional responses, which can activate our primal fear reactions. This is part of our brain's inherent mechanism to protect us from perceived threats, historically including unfamiliar and potentially dangerous situations.

Did You Know? People who regularly embrace new experiences show increased levels of brain plasticity. Yes, trying new things makes you brainier.

Your brain might be hard-wired to resist change, but guess what? You can rewire it! To mitigate these instinctual responses, integrate brain training activities that enhance neural flexibility and resilience, such as mindfulness practices or cognitive-behavioral techniques.

Start every day with a five-minute meditation session. Picture yourself embracing change and navigating challenges successfully. It's like a mental workout for building your change muscle. The more you practice, the stronger you push past the fear.

Psychologically, people often perceive change as a threat to stability, which triggers anxiety and resistance. This resistance can manifest because of uncertainty about the future and losing control over familiar situations.

Change is scary because it's uncertain, right? But what if you could flip that feeling on its head? Instead of dreading change, start small and make it a game. Switch up your coffee order, take a different route to work, or try a new workout class. Small wins in embracing uncertainty can lead to big confidence and resilience gains in handling more significant life changes.

Adaptability is a crucial skill in managing the fear of change effectively. Research shows that individuals with higher adaptability can better manage and reduce the stress associated with significant life changes. Change is not just necessary; it's growth!

Remind yourself that every challenge is an opportunity to learn and expand. Keep a journal of what each new experience teaches you and how it contributes to your growth. This mindset shift isn't just positive thinking—it's making you a powerhouse of adaptability.

Apps: Try 'Insight Timer' for a mindfulness boost or 'FutureMe' to send advice or reminders to your future self.

Books: "Adapt" by Tim Harford discusses thriving in a complex and constantly changing world. It's a manual for mastering adaptability.

Activity: Flexibility Fitness

This challenge is all about stepping out of your comfort zone to spark creativity, adaptability, and embrace the unpredictable aspects of life. It turns the anxiety of uncertainty into a powerful engine for growth and innovation. Here's how you're going to do it:

1. Meditation Practice: Kick off your day with 10 minutes of meditation focused on acceptance. Choose a guided session that preps you to welcome the unknown with open arms, setting a proactive and positive vibe for what lies ahead.

2. Small Changes, Big Impacts: Mix up something you do out of habit. Brush your teeth with your opposite hand, find a new way to your job, or reorganize your desk. Pay attention to how it makes you feel and what it brings up for you.

3. Learn Something New: Spend an hour on an activity that's out of your wheelhouse. Dive into a pottery class, hit a yoga mat for beginners, or crack the code with an intro to programming. Immerse yourself and enjoy the process of being a newbie.

4. Adventure Without a Map: Explore a new area in your city without using GPS. Let your curiosity be your guide and take in everything around you with fresh eyes. You'll be amazed at what you discover.

5. Forget What Your Mom Told You, Talk to Strangers: Strike up a conversation with someone new. It could be at a coffee shop, in a park, or on your adventure. Ask open questions and really listen to what they share.

6. Journal Your Journey: End your day by writing down what happened. Reflect on what stepping outside your comfort zone taught you about yourself. How does embracing new experiences prepare you to deal with change and challenges elsewhere in your life?

Benefits: Embarking on this challenge boosts your mental agility and creative potential while dialing down the fear of the unknown. By actively seeking new experiences, you're teaching your brain to be more adaptable and less intimidated by change, unlocking endless opportunities for growth in all areas of your life.

Reflective Questions:

1. How did changing your routine or environment affect your day?
2. What did you learn about your ability to adapt to new situations?
3. Reflect on a past change that initially seemed daunting but was beneficial. What did it teach you?
4. What changes are you currently resisting that might reshape your future for the better?

Concluding Thoughts

In summary, navigating change is all about embracing adaptability and resilience. It's not about avoiding the tough stuff; it's about facing it with courage and determination. So, go out there and make change your ally, not your enemy. Your future self will thank you for it.

So, here's your challenge for this week: pick one change you've been avoiding like the plague. Maybe it's having that difficult conversation, starting that new project, or finally signing up for that class you've been eyeing. Whatever it is, it's time to face it head-on.

Being adaptable in the face of changing circumstances can greatly reduce stress. This means being open to adjusting plans and expectations as situations evolve. Cultivate a mindset that views challenges as opportunities for growth. And always have a contingency plan. This readiness can alleviate anxiety about potential problems.

Now, I'm not saying it's going to be easy. Change can be messy, uncomfortable, and downright painful at times. But you know what? It's also beautiful. It's a chance to grow, learn, and discover unknown parts of yourself you never knew existed.

As Lana Lang wisely said, "Life is about change; sometimes it's painful, sometimes it's beautiful, but most of the time it's both." Embrace the beauty and the pain, for both are integral to the tapestry of life's richest experiences.

Remember, you are stronger than you think. You have the power to adapt, overcome, and thrive in the face of change. So, take a deep breath, put on your game face, and dive in. You've got this!

CHAPTER 23
FINANCIAL FITNESS: TURNING MONEY MANAGEMENT FROM STRESS TO SUCCESS

"Do not save what is left after spending but spend what is left after saving." — Warren Buffett

In a world where 'financial stability' sounds like an oxymoron, dealing with financial stress is as enjoyable as a root canal, but equally important. It's time to take control of your finances and stop making excuses. You know that managing your money is crucial to living the life you want, but for some reason, you keep putting it off. Well, not anymore!

Are you letting your financial life run on autopilot, crossing your fingers that it all works out? That ends now. Managing your money doesn't have to be a constant struggle or a day-to-day grind. It's time to take control, shape your financial future, and turn it into a strategic success. It's not just about earning more money, but about managing and planning your finances to achieve your life goals without stress. This chapter isn't just about managing money, but mastering it. Let's transform anxiety into empowerment, confusion into clarity, and turn your financial path into a runway for success.

Wisdom from the Wise

Our relationship with money is complex. It's also tied up with our sense of self-worth and freedom. Financial stress isn't just about numbers; it's about the stories we tell ourselves about what those numbers mean.

Think of Warren Buffett, the Oracle of Omaha, who advocates for simple and effective financial principles such as living below one's means and investing wisely. His approach to personal finance and investing has made him one of the wealthiest individuals in the world. Warren Buffett doesn't just understand money; he understands human nature. His strategy—focusing on long-term value over short-term gain and not letting fear or greed guide his decisions—can be your strategy, too.

Hetty Green, as known as the "Witch of Wall Street," was an intelligent and highly successful investor between the late 19th and early 20th centuries. Despite her wealth, she lived frugally, highlighting her practical approach to managing and accumulating wealth.

George S. Clason advises in "The Richest Man in Babylon," "Pay yourself first." This timeless principle is about treating your savings and investments as non-negotiable expenses. Austin Kleon might add, "Money is fuel for your creative life. Manage it well, and you buy yourself the freedom to be creative."

Did You Know? In ancient Rome, citizens used salt as currency, from where the word "salary" originated. They literally got paid in salt!

Why Financial Fitness Matters

Money isn't just currency, it's psychology in action. Every spending decision reflects your habits, fears, and desires. Our feelings about money are often rooted deeper than in the wallet. They tap into our need for security, our fear of scarcity, and our dreams of abundance. Financial stress isn't just about balancing numbers; it's about balancing emotions and expectations. Understanding why you spend the way you do—recognizing those emotional triggers and cognitive biases—can help you break bad habits and make smarter choices. It's about aligning your financial behaviors with your deepest values, not your fleeting whims.

Think about financial fitness as you think about your physical health: everything else is more complicated without it. It's not about getting rich quickly; it's about building a life where money is a tool, not a trap. Financial stability gives you choices, freedom, and, most importantly, peace of mind.

Financial stress can significantly affect mental health, relationships, and overall life satisfaction. Studies have shown that people who manage their finances well experience lower levels of anxiety and depression. Critical components of financial wellness include budgeting, saving, investing, and managing debt.

Apps: 'Mint' or 'You Need a Budget (YNAB)' for efficiently managing budgets and tracking expenses.

Books: "The Total Money Makeover" by Dave Ramsey offers a straightforward plan for achieving financial health

Activity: Financial Health Day

Today aims to understand personal finances better and develop a plan for financial security and growth.

1. Start Simple: If you haven't got a budget, today's the day to make one. Keep tabs on your spending over the next week. It's eye-opening to see where your cash flows and how you can tweak habits to stash more cash.

2. Spend Smart: Just for today, track every dime you spend. Jot it down in a notebook or your favorite budget app.

3. Money Check-Up: Take a good look at your monthly bank statements. Spot any money leaks? Now's the time to plug them.

4. Dream Big, Start Small: Nail down one short-term and

one long-term financial dream. Whether it's saving for a chill vacation or gearing up for retirement, writing it down makes it real.

5. Finance 101: Dedicate an hour to up your personal finance game. Discover the essentials of budgeting, saving, investing, and avoiding debt.

6. Action Plan: Armed with today's insights, sketch out steps to hit those financial targets.

Benefits: Taking part in this exercise is an effective way to cultivate financial awareness and discipline, both of which are essential for promoting long-term financial well-being and minimizing stress.

Reflective Questions:

1. What insights did you gain from tracking your spending?
2. What are your main financial goals for the next year, and what steps are you taking to achieve them?
3. How does your current spending align with your values and long-term aspirations?
4. How can better financial management improve your quality of life?

Concluding Thoughts

Money—it makes the world go round, but sometimes it feels like it's spinning us out of control. From bills that multiply like rabbits to the elusive quest for savings, financial stress can feel like a shadow lurking in every purchase, every bill, and every peek at the bank account.

It is like a bad roommate; it's always there, eating your food and leaving dirty dishes in the sink of your mind. Whether it's bills, savings, or the daunting task of budgeting, managing money often feels daunting.

Managing your finances wisely is vital to living a balanced and stress-free life. You have the power to change your financial situation right now. All it takes is one small step in the right direction.

Budgeting, saving for emergencies, and investing in your future is foundational to financial fitness. So, pick one area of your finances that you've been neglecting and tackle it head-on. Set up that emergency fund, start investing for your future, or cut out those unnecessary expenses that are holding you back.

Remember, this isn't about perfection; it's about progress. You don't have to have it all figured out today, but you do need to start somewhere. Every little bit counts and every smart financial decision you make brings you closer to the life you deserve.

So, are you ready to take charge of your money and start living life on your own terms? It's time to stop surviving and start thriving.

This is your wake-up call to take action and transform your relationship with money. Don't wait another day. Start your journey to financial fitness right now and watch as your life begins to change in ways you never thought possible. Let's do this!

CHAPTER 24

THE ART OF DISAPPEARING: FINDING PRIVACY IN A SHARE-EVERYTHING WORLD

"Talking to myself is the only way I can be sure of intelligent conversation." — Edmund Blackadder

---

In today's digital fishbowl, seeking privacy and solitude is like being a magician trying to perform a disappearing act while the audience is live-streaming your every move.

Living in the age of information, where our lives are often open books (or open social media feeds), carving out privacy and solitude is a modern-day odyssey. It's about navigating a sea of tweets, pings, and notifications, in search of the elusive island of 'Personal Space.'

In an age where social media demands constant sharing and surveillance technology grows ever more pervasive, the art of disappearing—maintaining privacy and carving out personal space—has become both a challenge and a vital necessity.

This chapter explores strategies for safeguarding your personal information and reclaiming the often-overlooked right to privacy. Are you ready to navigate the complexities of a share-everything world and master the art of disappearing?

Wisdom from the Wise

The revelations made by Edward Snowden concerning government surveillance programs emphasize the level at which our personal information has been and can be collected. Snowden's actions serve as a powerful reminder of the fundamental right to privacy and spark critical debates about the delicate balance between security and personal privacy.

Sherry Turkle, an MIT professor and psychologist, argues that real solitude is where self-reflection and personal growth happen. Her research emphasizes the need for moments of non-sharing to maintain our psychological well-being and develop a stable sense of self.

Neurobiology of Privacy and Stress

Neuroscientific research reveals that lack of privacy increases psychological stress. The amygdala, a brain region involved in processing stress and emotion, shows heightened activity when individuals feel their privacy is invaded, mirroring the body's fight-or-flight response.

Feel like you're always on? That's because your brain's alarm system (hello, amygdala!) is in overdrive without privacy. Cut the noise! Schedule 'no screen' times and treat them as sacred. Your mind needs these moments to unwind and reset. It's not just relaxing; it's a requirement for mental health.

Psychologically, solitude is crucial for self-reflection and cognitive autonomy. Studies indicate that uninterrupted alone time is essential for allowing the brain to process and reflect without external influence, fostering a healthier mental state.

Alone time isn't lonely—it's powerful. It's the golden ticket to clarity and creativity. Declare parts of your day as non-negotiable periods of solitude. Turn off your devices, and let your mind meander. This isn't just downtime; it's where you meet your real self, minus the filters and likes.

Reclaiming Your Private Sphere

Today's information age is a double-edged sword—connected yet congested, informative yet invasive. Seeking solitude and privacy becomes an act of defiance, a way to reclaim pieces of our identity from the ever-expanding web of social networks, data trails, and virtual personas.

The human need for privacy is more than a preference; it's a psychological necessity. It's where we retreat to process, reflect, and be unobserved and uninfluenced—a mental sanctuary becoming increasingly rare in our always-on, share-everything culture. Our need for privacy is wired into our psyche—it's a sanctuary for self-reflection, independence, and individuality. Yet, in our interconnected world, the lines between public and private blur, challenging our ability to safeguard this psychological haven.

Educate yourself on digital privacy. Knowledge is power—understand how your data is used, stored, and shared. Empower yourself to make informed choices. Be a role model for digital balance. In demonstrating your commitment to privacy and solitude, you inspire others to consider their digital habits and spaces. Choose what to share. In a share-everything culture, be selective. Your life isn't a reality show unless you sign the contract. Cultivate real-world connections. Balance your online interactions with face-to-face connections. Sometimes, the best way to reclaim privacy is to enter the physical world.

Apps: Signal for encrypted communications that keep your messages secure; DuckDuckGo for private browsing that doesn't track your online activities; and Offtime to help you unplug from your devices and enjoy undisturbed time.

Books: Kevin Mitnick's "The Art of Invisibility" provides insights into protecting yourself online from hackers and snoops.

Activity: Privacy Reclamation Day

Today's mission is to spend a day focused on enhancing your personal privacy and understanding the implications of the digital footprint in a highly connected world. Are you ready to refine the art of disappearing and reclaim your privacy in this interconnected world? Let's take the steps together to ensure our personal spaces remain just that—personal.

1. Digital Footprint Review: Start your day by auditing your current digital footprint. Check your social media privacy settings, search for your name online to see what information is publicly accessible, and review the permissions granted to mobile apps and websites. It's your digital wardrobe—ensure it only reveals what you're comfortable sharing.

2. Account Clean-Up: Begin deactivating accounts you no longer use, unsubscribe from unnecessary newsletters, and delete apps you do not use or that request too much personal information.

3. Encryption Implementation: Implement encryption tools for your emails and messages. Install and set up secure communication apps like Signal or Telegram to protect your personal communications.

4. VPN Usage: Subscribe to a reputable VPN service and learn how to use it to safeguard your online browsing and protect your internet privacy from potential eavesdropping.

5. Personal Data Management Workshop: Educate yourself on the best practices for personal data management and learn how to store your sensitive documents and photos, both online and offline securely.

6. Digital Detox: Implement 'digital detoxes.' Regularly set aside time to unplug and disconnect. Think of it as taking your psyche on a spa retreat, away from the noise of the online world. Set boundaries for technology use. It's like establishing a no-fly zone over your personal time. Designate tech-free hours or zones in your home where the digital world is politely but firmly asked to wait outside.

7. Reflect on Sharing Habits: Reflect on your current social media and online sharing habits. Determine which practices might risk your privacy and consider ways to share more innovatively and less frequently.

8. Privacy Goals Setting: Customize your privacy settings. It's like setting up a security system for your digital home. Know what's public, what's private, and who has the keys to your information kingdom. Set specific, achievable goals for maintaining your digital privacy, such as regular privacy settings reviews and digital detox periods.

9. Create a Physical Sanctuary: Designate a space in your home as a tech-free zone—a haven for reading, meditation, or simply being. It's your personal fortress of solitude. It's about creating your own pocket of silence amidst the digital hustle, a personal Zen Garden amid a cybernetic jungle.

10. Relaxation and Disconnection: Indulge in 'analog activities.' Read a physical book, write with pen and paper, and cook from a recipe book. These activities don't just provide a break from screens; they reconnect you with the tactile world. Journal the old-fashioned way. In a world where thoughts are often typed, try putting pen to paper. It's a private dialog with yourself, with no 'send' button involved.

11. Privacy Protection Plan: Draft a privacy protection plan that outlines steps to maintain your privacy. Include routine checks of privacy settings, digital detoxes, and continuous education on privacy practices.

Benefits: Practice good digital hygiene and be mindful of how you share information to safeguard your privacy and reduce the risk of identity theft and exposure to personal data.

Reflective Questions:

1. What were the most surprising discoveries about your digital footprint during today's audit?
2. How do you plan to maintain and enhance your digital privacy based on today's activities?
3. How might your life change if you shared less online?

4. What are the benefits and challenges of stepping back from constant connectivity?

Concluding Thoughts

In a world where we're constantly bombarded with notifications, emails, and endless digital chatter, the art of disappearing has never been more crucial. It's not just about having a little "me time"—it's about protecting your identity, your autonomy, and your mental well-being.

Look, I get it. It's easy to get caught up in the never-ending cycle of likes, comments, and shares. But here's the thing: if you don't take control of your digital life, it will control you. You need to find harmony in the chaos, a melody of tranquility amidst the relentless online orchestra.

So how do you do it? Remember that privacy and solitude aren't just settings on your phone—they're states of mind. You have to decide when to connect and when to retreat consciously. Reclaiming privacy involves choosing when, how, and to what extent we share our lives with the world. You have to set boundaries and make sure that your inner life remains fulfilling and free from intrusion.

And don't be afraid of silence. In a world where we're constantly connected, silence isn't just a luxury—it's a necessity. It's in these moments of disconnection that we often find our deepest connections with ourselves. Privacy is crucial for psychological well-being, autonomy, and security.

So here's your wake-up call: take control of your digital life. Find your moments of solitude. Protect your personal space. And remember, the art of disappearing isn't about vanishing completely—it's about finding the courage to be present in your own life, on your own terms.

CHAPTER 25

OVERCOMING STAGE FRIGHT: STRATEGIES FOR CONQUERING PUBLIC SPEAKING ANXIETY

"Pursue something so important that even if you fail, the world is better off with you having tried." — Tim O'Reilly

When it's your moment to shine on that stage, does your mouth suddenly feel like the Sahara desert? Are your hands shaking like a leaf in a thunderstorm? Does your mind suddenly decide to take a vacation to nowhere? Yeah, I've been there too.

Dealing with stage freight is like being stuck in a room with a distorted mirror that magnifies every perceived flaw. It's a relentless critic that follows you around, commenting on every move, every reflection, every piece of your words.

Stage fright is no joke, and it doesn't discriminate between newbies and veteran speakers. But here's the deal: you don't have to live with this fear forever.

This chapter is your roadmap to transforming anxiety into confidence, turning dread into readiness. Get ready to transform, because by the end of this, you'll be owning that spotlight like it's your birthright!

Wisdom from the Wise

Great speakers throughout history weren't born that way—they practiced. Their stories will help us see that overcoming public speaking anxiety is possible and a path many of the greats have trodden.

For instance, Winston Churchill, despite being one of the greatest orators of the 20th century, spent countless hours preparing his speeches due to a fear of public speaking. Similarly, contemporary singer Adele has openly shared her battles with severe stage fright, yet she continues to deliver powerful performances.

Barbra Streisand, a legend in music and film, experienced debilitating stage fright that kept her from performing live for many years. However, she overcame her fears and returned to the stage, captivating audiences with her voice.

Thomas Jefferson, the third President of the United States, was known for his exceptional writing abilities but was not comfortable with public speaking. He often expressed a preference for writing reports and documents over delivering speeches. Similarly, Mahatma Gandhi, one of the most iconic figures in the struggle for India's independence, initially faced significant fear of public speaking. He overcame this challenge over time, becoming an inspirational speaker.

Even Sir Laurence Olivier, one of the greatest actors of the 20th century, struggled with severe stage fright throughout his illustrious career. His openness about his anxiety helped to destigmatize the issue among performers, showing that even the most skilled can experience these fears.

Dr. Amy Cuddy, a social psychologist, recommends using power poses before going on stage to increase feelings of confidence and reduce stress. Her research suggests that body language profoundly impacts our hormones and feelings of assertiveness.

Why Public Speaking Scares Us?

Understanding the roots of public speaking anxiety is crucial.

It's often not just about the fear of forgetting words or failing—it's about how we perceive those risks and our ability to handle them. We'll dive into why the spotlight feels so intimidating and how changing our perspective can dramatically reduce our fears.

The fear of being judged or failing in front of others is the underlying cause of stage fright, which activates the body's fight-or-flight response. Understanding this fear's psychological and physiological aspects is crucial to managing it. Cognitive-behavioral therapy (CBT) techniques are effective in addressing these fears.

Studies on performance psychology show that stage fright can be reduced through different mental and physical preparation techniques. These include visualization, controlled breathing, and desensitization processes, which help you reduce your anxiety and improve your performance outcomes.

Apps: Use apps like Speeko or Orai, which provide feedback on your pacing, tone, and clarity.

Books: "The Confident Speaker" by Harrison Monarth and Larina Kase offers a comprehensive guide to overcoming public speaking anxiety with practical tips and strategies.

Activity: Stage Confidence Day

Today's mission is to engage in practical exercises designed to reduce public speaking anxiety and build confidence. This challenge aims to equip you with effective techniques for managing nerves and improving your performance in public speaking situations.

1. Understanding Anxiety: First things first, it's important to acknowledge that feeling nervous is completely normal. In fact, studies have shown that a certain level of anxiety can actually improve performance. So instead of trying to suppress or ignore your nerves, try embracing them as a sign that you care about your presentation. Start your day by learning about the physiological and psychological aspects of public speaking anxiety. Use resources like articles, videos, or books to understand why public speaking can induce fear and how common it is.

2. Breathing Exercises: Practice deep breathing exercises designed explicitly for anxiety-reduction. Focus on diaphragmatic breathing techniques that help you calm your nervous system and reduce the physical symptoms of stress. If you start feeling overwhelmed or anxious during your presentation, take a moment to pause and take deep breaths. This will help calm your nerves and slow down your heart rate. It can also give you a few seconds to collect your thoughts and refocus on delivering your presentation.

3. Mirror Practice: Stand before a mirror and practice a quick speech or presentation. Observe your body language and try to relax your posture. Make eye contact with your reflection to simulate making eye contact with an audience.

4. Record and Review: Record your practice session on your phone or camera. Watch the playback, noting areas of strength and aspects where you can improve, such as vocal tone, pacing, and gestures.

5. Practice Makes Perfect: One of the best ways to combat stage fright is to be prepared. Take the time to research your topic, organize your thoughts, and create a well-structured presentation. Then, practice delivering it multiple times until you feel comfortable with the content and flow. This will not only help you become more confident in your delivery, but it will also make you more familiar with the material and less likely to stumble on stage.

6. Small Group Presentation: Organize a small group of friends, family, or colleagues and present a brief talk. Choose a topic you are passionate about to help reduce some anxiety.

7. Connect with the Audience: Remember, your audience is made up of real people just like you. Instead of viewing them as intimidating judges, try to connect with them on a personal level. Make eye contact, smile, and use relatable examples to make your presentation more engaging. This will not only help ease your nerves, but it will also make the experience more enjoyable for both you and your audience.

8. Constructive Feedback: Ask for specific feedback on both content and delivery. Encourage your audience to highlight what you did well and areas for improvement.

9. Visualization Techniques: Visualization is a powerful tool for overcoming anxiety. Take some time to close your eyes and imagine yourself delivering a successful presentation with ease. Visualize the audience engaging with your content and giving positive feedback. This can help boost your confidence and reduce any negative thoughts or fears.

10. Public Speaking Tips and Tricks: Review tips and tricks from professional speakers to help you manage stage fright. These might include strategies for engaging the audience, using humor, or handling unexpected issues during a speech. (I love Simon Sinek's videos about this topic, it helped me a lot before my first keynote speaking performance.)

11. Reflective Journaling: Spend some time in the evening reflecting on your experiences throughout the day. Write about how your feelings towards public speaking have changed and what strategies you found most helpful.

12. Relaxation Techniques: End your day with relaxation techniques that you enjoy, such as yoga, a warm bath, or listening to calming music.

Benefits: This intensive day of practice and learning aims to reduce your public speaking anxiety, building up your confidence and capability to address an audience effectively. By actively confronting your fears and practicing in a supportive environment, you develop skills that enhance your communication ability in all areas of life.

Reflective Questions

1. What specific aspect of public performance most triggers your anxiety?
2. Which anxiety-reduction technique helped you the most during your presentation?
3. How can applying these strategies change your approach to public speaking or performance?

Did You Know? A study found that performers who focused on the joy of sharing their music rather than on their anxieties experienced significantly less performance anxiety.

Concluding Thoughts

Overcoming stage fright isn't just about easing nerves—it's about unlocking your potential to influence, inspire, and connect with others. Each step you take builds your skills and confidence. It involves a combination of mental preparation, physical relaxation techniques, and practical performance experience.

Choose one technique from this chapter—whether it's a breathing exercise, visualization, or practicing in front of friends—and incorporate it into your preparation for your next public speaking event or performance. Observe the impact on your anxiety levels and performance quality.

Maya Angelou once said: "There is no greater agony than bearing an untold story inside you."

Are you ready to unlock your inner superstar and amaze the world? Don't let stage fright hold you back from showcasing your incredible talents in the spotlight! With some guidance and practice, you can conquer your fears and shine like never before. So, are you up for the challenge?

Let's take these strategies and turn your anxiety into an engine for spectacular performances!

CHAPTER 26
DANCING WITH DOUBT: OVERCOMING THE FEAR OF FAILURE

"I have missed more than 9,000 shots in my career. I have lost almost 300 games. 26 times, I've been trusted to take the game-winning shot and missed. I've failed over and over and over again in my life. And that is why I succeed." — Michael Jordan

The fear of failure often feels like the monster under the bed. It's always lurking, waiting for the lights to go off. Remember when you were a kid convinced that if your foot dangled off the bed, something would grab it? That's how we treat failure—as if it's something waiting to snatch us the moment we step out of line.

In life's journey, few emotions are as universally experienced and as deeply paralyzing as the fear of failure. It lurks in the minds of students stepping into an examination hall, entrepreneurs launching new ventures, artists facing a blank canvas, and individuals facing daily challenges.

This chapter turns on the light. No more monsters, just a new game plan. Ready to stop fearing failure and start steering it?

Wisdom from the Wise

Great thinkers and achievers throughout history have often spoken about the role of failure in success—such as J. K. Rowling, Steve Jobs, and Michael Jordan—and we see that failure is often a precursor to monumental success.

Thomas Edison's work exemplifies the productive embrace of failure. His attempts to invent a commercially viable electric light bulb resulted in over a thousand unsuccessful tries before he succeeded. Edison famously reframed these attempts by saying, "I have not failed. I've just found 10,000 ways that won't work."

Sir James Dyson, the inventor of the Dyson vacuum cleaner, faced 5,126 failed prototypes over 15 years before successfully creating his famed bagless vacuum cleaner. He asserts that each failure taught him something new and was invaluable. Dyson's perseverance highlights the essential role of persistence and a positive attitude toward failure.

Sir Edmund Hillary and Tenzing Norgay became among the first two men, confirmed to have reached the summit of Mount Everest. Hillary's venture required overcoming immense fears of the unknown and physical limits, showcasing the power of confronting and overcoming one's deepest fears to achieve incredible feats.

Did You Know? The Five Why's Technique: Originally developed by Sakichi Toyoda for Toyota's manufacturing process, this technique involves asking "why" five times to understand the root cause of a failure, turning it into a learning opportunity rather than a defeat.

Understanding the Dynamics of Failure

Fear of failure is a tricky beast. We often fear not the failure itself but the fallout—judgment, embarrassment, or the dent in our self-esteem. We see failure as a stop sign rather than a detour. But here's the catch: avoiding failure is like avoiding exercise. You might be safe, but you won't be strong.

The fear of failure, technically known as 'atychiphobia,' is rooted in our evolutionary biology. Historically, failure in hunting, battle, or community standing could mean the difference between life and death. In its most primal form, fear served as a safeguard, a mechanism to avoid threats. Though the saber-toothed tigers have vanished in modern times, the instinctual response to perceived threats to our ego or self-image persists.

Did You Know? A NASA study found that engineers and scientists who made more mistakes were ultimately more successful than their peers, suggesting that early failures lead to more prosperous learning opportunities.

Psychologically, fear of failure is linked to self-worth. We equate our success with our value as people. This is like measuring the ocean's worth by the number of boats it can hold. We need to separate our endeavors from our ego. Your projects may fail, but you are not a failure.

Psychologists link fear of failure to lowered self-esteem, anxiety, and a tendency to avoid risk, which can inhibit growth and innovation. The ability to learn from failure is a crucial aspect of the growth mindset, a concept developed by psychologist Carol Dweck, emphasizing the potential to create and improve through dedication and hard work. In this mindset, we perceive failure not as evidence of lack of intelligence, but as a chance for intellectual growth and the exploration of our capabilities.

Studies in behavioral psychology suggest that how individuals perceive and react to failure affects their likelihood of future success. People who see failure as a chance to grow are stronger and keep going, but those who see it as a weakness tend to avoid challenges, holding themselves back.

Neuroscientists find that exposure to manageable amounts of

stress (like experiencing and overcoming small failures) can make our brains more resilient to future stress. This phenomenon, known as *stress inoculation*, suggests that small, controlled exposures to failure can build our resilience day to day.

Carol Dweck's research on growth mindsets highlights the importance of believing that skills and intelligence can be improved through dedication and hard work. To foster a growth mindset, it is crucial to embrace challenges and see failure as an opportunity for growth, rather than a setback.

Effort Over Outcome: Cultivate an appreciation for effort and learning, regardless of the outcome. This shifts the focus from fearing failure to valuing the growth that comes from the attempt.

Praise the Process: When evaluating your actions, emphasize the strategies, choices, and efforts you made rather than the result.

Apps: Tools like Reflectly or Daylio offer journaling features that help users record and reflect on both successes and failures, fostering a habit of learning from every experience.

Books: "Failing Forward: Turning Mistakes into Stepping Stones for Success" by John Maxwell offers actionable advice on converting mistakes into growth pathways.

Activity: Fearless Day Challenge

Today, we're going to tackle the fear of failure head-on. I'm here to guide you through a series of empowering activities designed to transform your relationship with failure—all in one action-packed day.

1. Face Your Fears: Kick off the day by getting real with yourself. Grab a journal and spill the beans about what aspect of failure freaks you out the most. Is it the fear of being judged, a hit to your self-esteem, or missing out on opportunities? Pinpointing your fears is your first step to conquering them.

2. Flip the Script on Failure: It's time to redefine what failure means to you. Write a new definition that focuses on growth and learning, not loss and disappointment. This mental shift is crucial for changing how you perceive failure.

3. Try Something New: Step out of your comfort zone and try an activity you've been avoiding because of fear of failing. Whether it's experimenting with a new recipe, joining a fitness class, or tackling a DIY project, it's all about broadening your horizons.

4. Reflect and Learn: After completing the activity, take a moment to reflect. What did you learn, regardless of the outcome? Concentrate on the journey and any new skills you've developed, not just the end result.

5. Visualize and Embrace Failure: Dedicate some time to visualizing a scenario where you face an enormous challenge and fail. See yourself handling the situation gracefully and learning from it.

6. Expose Yourself to Failure: This week, I want you to step out of your comfort zone and into the "Growth Zone." Pick a challenge that scares you, something you've been avoiding because you're afraid to fail. It could be anything—pitching an idea at work, trying a new hobby, or even asking someone out. Just go for it!

7. Share and Learn from Failures: Have an open conversation with a friend or colleague about past failures. This is a great way to understand that failure is a common part of growth and learning.

8. Lean on Your Support Network: Ask for advice on overcoming fear and collect strategies that might work for you. It's all about strengthening your support system.

8. Reflect on Your Day: Wind down by journaling about your day. What did you learn about yourself and your approach to failure? How can you apply these insights moving forward?

Benefits: This challenge is your golden ticket to boosting your courage, strengthening your resilience, and reshaping how you view failure: not as a setback, but as a springboard for growth.

Reflective Questions:

1. How did facing your fear of failure in a controlled manner change your feelings about it?
2. What can you do differently in the future when faced with the possibility of failure?

Concluding Thoughts: Fear as a Catalyst for Growth

Let's end this chapter with a powerful message that you need to hear: Nobody wants to fail. But guess what? Failure isn't the enemy. It's your secret weapon for growth. Every time you stumble, you're learning what doesn't work. And that's valuable knowledge, my friend.

Plan your approach, take action, and then reflect on what happens. What did you learn? How did it feel? Write it down in your Resilience Diary. Because growth isn't just about succeeding; it's about learning from every experience, good or bad. Remember, every small step counts.

The journey towards overcoming the fear of failure is not about achieving perfection but about embracing imperfection with grace and courage. Embracing failure means making peace with imperfection and understanding that setbacks are part of the journey to greatness. With the right mindset and tools, you can turn negatives into positives.

So, are you ready to turn your next setback into your biggest comeback? Let's learn to bounce back stronger, smarter, and more resilient than ever before. It's time to face your fears head-on and unlock your full potential. Let's do this!

CHAPTER 27

SUSTAINING PASSION FOR WORK: KEEPING THE FLAME ALIVE IN LONG-TERM CAREERS

"Your work is going to fill a large part of your life, and the only way to be truly satisfied is to do what you believe is great work. And the only way to do great work is to love what you do." — Steve Jobs

Let's talk about the moment you realize that the job you once jumped out of bed for now barely gets you out of it. Sustaining passion for work is like a muscle; it needs regular exercise to grow stronger. But instead of lifting weights, you're lifting beliefs, ideas, and attitudes.

It's like looking in the mirror and instead of asking, "Mirror, mirror on the wall, who's the fairest of them all?" you ask, "How can I be the best version of myself today?"

It's a typical scene: after years in your dream job, the excitement dwindles, and what was once thrilling now feels like a drag. But here's the kicker—it doesn't have to be this way. You can totally bring that spark back to life and keep it blazing!

This chapter isn't just about stoking the fire; it's about turning it into a lasting blaze.

Wisdom from the Wise

Julia Child didn't start cooking until she was 36, but there was no looking back once she found her passion. Her journey is a testament to the power of discovering and nurturing what excites you, no matter your stage in life. Her continued passion and curiosity about cooking transformed not just her career but also how America cooks. From a government worker to a beloved TV chef, it shows that with curiosity and persistence, you can keep your passion alive and kicking, regardless of age or career stage.

In ancient Greece, the concept of 'thymos' was used to describe a spirit of spiritedness and assertiveness that was considered essential for a fulfilling life. Understanding that confidence has been valued as a virtue for millennia can empower you to embrace your inner strength as a part of your personal and professional development.

The Psychology Behind Work Passion

But why does the spark fade?

Passion at work isn't just about having fun; it's a key driver of high performance, innovation, and personal fulfillment. Without active efforts to reignite that initial enthusiasm, we risk sliding into monotony, leading to burnout, a drop in performance, and dissatisfaction. Your work should light you up, not drag you down. Passion at work leads to better performance, more innovation, and deeper satisfaction—it's the secret sauce that can make the huge difference between just surviving and absolutely thriving in your career.

Psychologists often distinguish between harmonious passion, which enriches your life, and obsessive passion, which might drive success but at the cost of personal happiness and health. Understanding and fostering the right kind of passion is vital for sustainable success without burning out.

Occupational psychology research reveals that being passionate about work is strongly connected to intrinsic motivation, which is the urge to do something because it's interesting or enjoyable. This type of motivation is more sustainable than extrinsic motivation, driven by external rewards or pressures.

Benefits of Cultural Diversity in the Workplace

A diverse workplace is not just a moral imperative but a strategic advantage. Studies have shown that culturally diverse teams are more creative and innovative. These teams bring a range of perspectives that enhance problem-solving capabilities and can boost overall happiness and productivity. This diversity also makes a company more attractive to potential employees from varied backgrounds, enhancing recruitment and retention.

Get excited about diversity! Here's the thing—different perspectives are like pieces of a jigsaw puzzle. When you put them together, they create a masterpiece. Encourage brainstorming sessions that invite diverse perspectives, and watch as the magic happens. Diversity isn't just nice to have; it's a rocket fuel for creativity and innovation. Be the catalyst in your workplace that celebrates and stimulates this diversity.

Did You Know? Studies have found that professionals who engage in hobbies or creative activities outside of work are more likely to be innovative in their jobs.

Workspace Design in Home Environments

The design and organization of a home workspace can greatly influence productivity and mental well-being. A study found that individuals with a dedicated, well-organized workspace reported higher productivity and reduced stress levels compared to those without.

Command your space, don't let it command you. Set up a workspace that signals to your brain, "This is where I succeed." Whether it's a corner of your living room or a separate office, make it a place where chaos can't find you. This space is your stage—own it!

The Psychology of Remote Work and Employee Engagement

Remote work can lead to feelings of detachment from the organization's goals, affecting employee engagement and productivity. Surveys indicate that employees who feel disconnected often exhibit lower job satisfaction and higher turnover intentions.

Engage like your team's energy depends on it—because it does. Be proactive in reaching out, be generous with praise, and be consistent with feedback. Turn routine check-ins into moments of motivation. Remember, engagement isn't a checkbox; it's the heartbeat of your team.

Apps: Tools like 'Coursera' or 'Udemy' make learning new skills accessible and fun.

Get Inspired by Books: Read "Drive: The Surprising Truth About What Motivates Us" by Daniel H. Pink to understand what fuels your drive and how to harness it for lasting passion in your work.

Activity: Career Passion Revival Day

Today's mission is to reignite and sustain your passion for your career, especially if you've been in the same field for a long time.

1. Career Highlights Revisit: Start your day by recalling why you chose your career path. Reflect on your initial passions and career highlights. Journal of these reflections to capture your early motivations and memorable achievements.

2. Inspirational Stories: Read or watch stories about people who have successfully rejuvenated their careers. Focus on stories within your industry or related fields to find relevant inspiration and actionable ideas.

3. Industry Trends Review: Update yourself on your field's latest trends and innovations. Explore how these changes might impact your role and how you can engage with them to bring fresh energy into your daily work.

4. Skill Expansion: Identify new skills that are becoming important in your industry. Select an online course or tutorial and begin a learning session to integrate these new skills into your repertoire.

5. Creative Project Initiation: Start a small project related to an aspect of your work that excites you. This could be something as simple as redesigning a process, drafting an article related to your field, or brainstorming a new product idea.

6. Professional Networking: Reach out to colleagues, mentors, or new contacts within your industry. Discuss your projects and ask for feedback. Networking can reignite your enthusiasm and provide new perspectives.

7. Future Visioning: Envision your career future, considering the insights and trends you explored earlier. What new roles or achievements would you like to aim for? How can you align your current passions with long-term goals?

8. Goal Setting: Based on your vision, set concrete, achievable goals that reignite your passion. These should include short-term goals to build momentum and long-term goals to strive for.

Benefits: This challenge helps you rediscover what made you passionate about your work and introduces ways to integrate new, exciting elements into your career. By focusing on personal growth and industry trends, you can sustain your enthusiasm and remain engaged and satisfied with your professional life.

Reflective Questions

1. What aspects of your work are you most passionate about, and how can you focus more on these areas?
2. What did you rediscover about your passion for your career today?
3. Which new skills or projects are you most excited to explore further?

Concluding Thoughts

Remember, sustaining passion for your work isn't a one-time fix —it's a continuous commitment. By staying curious, embracing new challenges, and balancing your life, you can enjoy a fulfilling career that keeps you excited for decades.

This week, take one step towards reigniting your work passion. Maybe it's enrolling in a course, pitching a new project idea, or planning a team outing. Whatever it is, make it something that reminds you why you loved your job in the first place.

Think of your career like a long-running TV show that needs a new twist every season to keep the audience hooked. What new twist can you introduce in your professional life to keep your story interesting and engaging?

"Do not listen to those who weep and complain, for their disease is contagious," said Og Mandino. Let this be a reminder to stay positive, proactive, and find the silver linings in your work challenges.

CHAPTER 28

HARNESSING THE POWER OF STORYTELLING: WHY YOUR STORY MATTERS

"We are, as a species, addicted to story. Even when the body goes to sleep, the mind stays up all night, telling itself stories."
—Jonathan Gottschall

You have a story inside of you - it could be about your product, your passion, or your journey. And guess what? The way you tell that story could completely change the game. It has the power to captivate your audience and make you stand out.

Even in brief interactions, a good story can engage, entertain, and inform, creating a memorable connection with your audience. It's time to say goodbye to boring, uninspired presentations.

Today, we're diving into the art of storytelling. We're going to learn how to weave compelling narratives that not only entertain but also enlighten and inspire.

Whether you're a leader, an educator, a marketer, or an entrepreneur, storytelling is not just a nice-to-have, it's absolutely essential.

Wisdom from the Wise

We all know that storytelling is one of the oldest yet the most powerful forms of communication. It's how civilizations pass down knowledge, cultures express their values, and individuals share their experiences. Homer, the ancient Greek poet credited with composing The Iliad and The Odyssey, used storytelling not just to entertain but to preserve history and instill moral values. His epic poems have influenced Western narrative traditions and highlight the enduring power of storytelling to shape cultures.

Martin Luther King Jr.'s iconic "I Have a Dream" speech is a masterclass in storytelling. He painted a vivid picture of a divided nation and a unified future, using narrative techniques that stirred emotions and called to action. The "I Have a Dream" segment of King's speech was improvised, showcasing his skill as a speaker and deep connection to his message and audience.

His speech went beyond mere words; it was a call to action, galvanizing listeners to drive forward social change. Through his narrative, King showed us how powerful stories can not only inspire but also mobilize people to come together and make history.

"The universe is made of stories, not of atoms." — Muriel Rukeyser

---

Imagine if Steven Spielberg had decided not to tell the stories that came to him. The world would never have known "E.T.," "Schindler's List," or "Jurassic Park." Spielberg's journey from a young boy making amateur films to one of the most influential film-makers in Hollywood exemplifies the power of storytelling not just as a form of entertainment but as a medium that can inspire, challenge, and transform society.

Annette Simmons once said, "People don't want more information. They are up to their eyeballs in information. They want faith —faith in you, your goals, your success, in the story you tell." This underscores the importance of storytelling, not just for conveying information, but for building relationships.

Science of Storytelling

Storytelling isn't just an art; it's a strategic tool rooted in psychology. Stories stimulate emotions and can influence our thoughts and decisions in profound ways. They also enhance memory retention by engaging more parts of the brain-the motor cortex, sensory cortex, and frontal cortex-which are involved in processing experiences, emotions, and actions.

Stories are more than entertainment—they're the fundamental way humans communicate, understand, and perceive the world. They shape our thoughts, influence our decisions, and define our beliefs. Harnessing the power of storytelling means tapping into a core feature of human psychology to convey messages, foster connections, and drive change more effectively.

Neuroscientific research shows that when we hear stories, our brain releases dopamine into the system, making the experience more memorable and impactful. And guess what, stories have the power to activate neural coupling, a process that allows the listener's brain to mirror the storyteller's brain, establishing a strong empathetic link.

You're lighting up your listener's brain when you tell a story, engaging them on multiple levels. The brain doesn't just hear a story; it experiences it. The regions involved in processing senses, emotions, and implications all activate, making storytelling one of the most effective ways to convey messages and drive engagement.

Did You Know? Studies have shown that stories can increase fundraising by up to 77% when used in charity campaigns, highlighting their power to persuade and motivate action.

Creative Insights

Embrace multimedia communication. Sometimes a well-placed GIF speaks louder than a paragraph. Use visuals, videos, and audio to enhance your message and keep your audience engaged.

Master the art of the metaphor. A well-placed metaphor can illuminate complex ideas better than any lengthy explanation. It's like turning on a light in a dark room.

Inject storytelling into your communication. People may forget facts, but they remember stories. Craft your message like a mini-narrative, with a clear beginning, middle, and end.

Explore the potential of visual storytelling. A compelling image, infographic, or video can convey your message more effectively than paragraphs of text.

Use humor wisely. A touch of humor can make your communication more relatable and engaging, but be mindful of your audience and the context.

Practice active listening. Communication isn't just about talking; it's about listening. In a world full of noise, being a good listener can make your words even more powerful. In a world full of broadcasters, being a listener makes you a rare and valued presence. It's not just about waiting for your turn to speak, but about truly understanding and engaging.

Apps: 'StoryChief' for effectively organizing and crafting your stories and narratives.

Books: "The Storyteller's Secret" by Carmine Gallo explores how some of the world's most inspiring leaders use storytelling to ignite change, influence others, and create success.

Activity: Storyteller's Day

Today's mission is to deepen your storytelling skills through creative, reflective, and interactive exercises. It's your turn now to use your ability to craft and convey compelling stories that engage, inform, and inspire your audience. So why not try it out and see where your imagination takes you?

1. Inspirational Stories: Begin the day by reading or listening to powerful stories from renowned storytellers across various mediums—literature, film, podcasts, or speeches. Note what makes each story impactful, such as emotional depth, character development, or a surprising plot twist.

2. Reflective Writing: Take a moment to think about what stories have resonated with you in the past. What made them stand out? Was it the characters, the plot twists, or the underlying message? This exercise will help you identify what elements make a story impactful and memorable.

3. Personal Narrative: Share a personal experience that has shaped who you are today. This activity will not only allow you to practice storytelling but also help you connect with your audience on a deeper level by sharing a vulnerable and relatable story.

4. Story Circle: Host a storytelling session where you tell your story aloud, either in person or virtually. Gather a group of friends or colleagues and have each person share a personal story based on a specific theme. Pay attention to your pacing, tone, and audience engagement. This activity will not only help you practice storytelling but also foster connection and empathy among the group

5. Elevator Pitch: Imagine you have 60 seconds in an elevator with someone who could potentially change your life. How would you use that time to tell your story and make a lasting impression? This activity will help you practice crafting a concise and impactful pitch for your ideas or projects.

6. Visual Storytelling: Take a photo or use an image as inspiration for a story. This exercise will challenge you to think creatively and find new ways to convey your message through visuals.

7. Plot Development: Construct a compelling plot. Start with a basic outline and expand each section, focusing on creating tension and intrigue that leads to a climax. Ensure your story has a clear beginning, middle, and end.

8. Rewrite the Ending: Take a story or movie with an unsatisfying ending and rewrite it to your liking. This exercise will challenge you to think critically about storytelling and how different choices can impact the overall message of a story.

9. Perspective Shift: Write a story from the perspective of a character or person who is different from you. This exercise will challenge your empathy and allow you to explore different perspectives and experiences.

10. Reflective Journaling: After your presentation, journal about the experience. How did the audience react, and what can you learn from their reactions?

Benefits: Sharing stories is an amazing way to improve your communication skills, ignite your creativity, and make deeper emotional connections with others.

Reflective Questions

1. Think of a time when a story significantly influenced your decision. What elements of the story were most impactful?
2. How can you incorporate storytelling into daily communications to enhance your leadership and influence?

Concluding Thoughts

Storytelling isn't just about spinning tales; it's the key to making genuine connections. When you get storytelling right, you don't just boost your ability to communicate—you transform your relationships and your impact on others. Remember, stories aren't just narratives; they're the lens through which we view ourselves and the world. Taking charge of your story is taking charge of how the world sees you.

This week, I challenge you to find just one moment where storytelling can elevate your personal or professional life. Create a narrative with the power to persuade, captivate, or inspire. Pay close attention to the reactions you get. It's a chance to see how incorporating stories more often could revolutionize your way of connecting.

Your stories are more than just words; they're your imprint on the world, a way to influence, motivate, and make a difference. Never underestimate the impact of a compelling story—it has the potential to alter not just your path, but also the paths of those around you.

To embrace storytelling is to embrace a form of power—the power to affect change, to motivate, and to lead. It doesn't matter if you're in a boardroom, at a conference, or in front of your team; your storytelling ability shapes how others perceive and react to you. Are you ready to tap into the power of storytelling and revolutionize your communication and leadership style?

CHAPTER 29

SHOULD I STAY OR SHOULD I GO?: MAKING THE BIG DECISION ABOUT YOUR JOB

"Your work is going to fill a large part of your life, and the only way to be truly satisfied is to do what you believe is great work. And the only way to do great work is to love what you do. If you haven't found it yet, keep looking. Don't settle. As with all matters of the heart, you'll know when you find it." — Steve Jobs

---

Quitting can be one of the most challenging career decisions. You need to consider your job satisfaction, career goals, and the risks of leaping into the unknown.

Feeling unsure whether to stay in your current job or move on can be both unsettling and overwhelming. You're not alone.

This chapter aims to guide you through this complex decision-making process clearly and confidently.

As Nietzsche said: "He who has a why to live for can bear almost any how." Let's try to find ours!

Wisdom from the Wise

Steve Jobs stepping down from Apple in 1985, the company he helped start, is a well-known case of pursuing fresh opportunities (although he eventually came back). He left because of internal conflicts and differences in his vision for the company, showing how disagreements in values and objectives can lead to someone leaving.

Herminia Ibarra, an organizational behavior professor at London Business School, suggests that sometimes you need to act your way into a new way of thinking rather than think your way into a new way of acting. Small steps toward exploring new opportunities can provide more clarity than extensive deliberation if you're indecisive.

Consider the existentialists' view, like that of Jean-Paul Sartre, who argued that humans are "condemned to be free," tasked with continually defining ourselves and our life's direction. This philosophical perspective can transform our approach to feeling lost from despair to empowerment and opportunity.

Did You Know? Studies show that employees who feel stagnant in their careers are twice as likely to think about quitting compared to those who believe they have promising career prospects.

Understanding Job Dissatisfaction & The Psychology of Change

Before you decide anything, it's important to pinpoint why you're considering leaving. Is it the job itself, the company culture, a lack of growth opportunities, or perhaps something external affecting your satisfaction? We'll explore common factors that lead to job dissatisfaction and how to address them.

The decision to leave a job often hinges on many factors, including personal fulfillment, career growth opportunities, work-life balance, and financial security. Understanding your core motivations and the potential impact of leaving your current position is crucial to making an informed decision.

Psychological theories related to job satisfaction, such as Herzberg's Motivation-Hygiene Theory, provide insight into why people may choose to stay or leave a job. This theory suggests that recognition, achievement, and growth lead to job satisfaction, while poor working conditions and salary can cause job dissatisfaction.

The sensation of being without direction often arises when there is a misalignment between an individual's day-to-day activities and their fundamental values or a disruption in what psychologists call as the "life narrative"—the ongoing story we tell ourselves about our identity and future direction. This disconnection might lead to a lack of engagement and a feeling of floating without an anchor.

Humans crave certainty and lacking it can cause significant stress and anxiety. Existential psychology offers valuable perspectives on why we sometimes feel lost. It suggests that such feelings can be an opportunity for growth, prompting us to reevaluate our paths and make meaningful adjustments. It emphasizes that crisis points can lead to profound personal development and a renewed sense of purpose.

> Apps: 'LinkedIn' to research job opportunities and network with industry peers. 'Daylio' for mood tracking and activity correlation, helping you identify what brings satisfaction and what feels lacking.

> Books: "Quit: The Power of Knowing When to Walk Away" by Annie Duke explores the science and strategy behind quitting as a tactical decision.

Activity: Job Decision Day

Today's mission is to spend a single day engaging in comprehensive, structured activities to help you decide whether to stay in your current job or pursue a new opportunity. This challenge will equip you with practical tools to analyze your current job satisfaction, future career goals, and the benefits and drawbacks of making a change.

1. Current Job Analysis: Begin your day by assessing your current job—your job satisfaction, career growth opportunities, company culture, and work-life balance. Use a scoring system to rate each aspect.

2. Personal Fulfillment Review: Reflect on how well your job aligns with your values and long-term career goals. Journal about times when you have felt most satisfied and frustrated at work.

3. Future Career Aspirations: Outline your career aspirations and what you need from a job to feel fulfilled. Consider what changes or advancements you expect in your industry and how they align with your career path.

4. Pros and Cons of Staying vs. Leaving: Create a list of the pros and cons of staying where you are versus looking for a new opportunity. Be truly honest with yourself about the potential risks and rewards of each option.

5. Market Research: Research the current job market in your field. Look at available positions, required skills, and potential employers. Evaluate how competitive the market is and what opportunities exist for someone with your qualifications.

6. Mentor or Peer Consultation: Discuss your situation with a mentor or trusted peer. Get their insights on your career plans, the pros and cons list, and any advice they might have based on their experiences.

7. Role Play Scenarios: Engage in role-playing exercises where you envision yourself accepting a new job offer or deciding to stay. Reflect on the emotional and practical implications of each scenario.

8. Decision-Making Strategy: To further clarify your choice, use decision-making tools such as the Decision Balance

Sheet or SWOT Analysis (Strengths, Weaknesses, Opportunities, Threats).

9. Reflective Review: Spend the evening reviewing the day's findings. Assess the clarity you've gained and whether your initial feelings about your job have shifted.

Benefits: This focused challenge helps clarify your thoughts regarding your current job and future career aspirations, providing a structured approach to a significant life decision.

Reflective Questions:

1. What are the main reasons making you consider leaving your job?
2. How does staying in your current position versus leaving align with your long-term career and personal goals?
3. What next steps will you take following your decision, whether you choose to stay or go?

Concluding Thoughts

If you're thinking about quitting your job, don't just up and leave on a whim. That's a recipe for disaster. Instead, I want you to take one week - just seven days - and commit to doing the exercises in this chapter. No excuses, no backing out. This is your chance to get real with yourself and figure out what you really want.

The decision to quit a job should be based on a thorough evaluation of job satisfaction, financial security, personal goals, and market conditions. During this week, you're going to be a detective. Gather all the information you can about your job, your satisfaction, and what you really want out of life.

Talk to people you trust, get their advice, and most importantly, listen to your gut. Pay attention to what makes you light up inside and what makes you want to hit the snooze button on life.

At the end of the week, it's decision time. Pick a date, circle it on your calendar, and make a pact with yourself to make a choice. You're either all in or all out.

Now, I know this can be scary. Change is never easy, and the unknown can be downright terrifying. But here's the thing: the best choice is the one that moves you closer to the life you want to live. Not the life your parents want for you, not the life society tells you to want, but the life that makes you feel alive and fulfilled.

So, take a deep breath, trust yourself, and make the decision that aligns with your personal and professional growth goals. Whether you decide to stay or go, the most important thing is that you're being true to yourself and what you really want.

CHAPTER 30

REKINDLING THE FLAME: A CREATIVE APPROACH TO BEATING BURNOUT

"The only people for me are the mad ones, the ones who are mad to live, mad to talk, mad to be saved, desirous of everything at the same time, the ones who never yawn or say a commonplace thing, but burn, burn, burn like fabulous yellow roman candles exploding like spiders across the stars." — Jack Kerouac, On the Road

---

Imagine burnout as the world's worst stage manager in the theater of your life, insisting on endless rehearsals, full-throttle performances, and no days off. The result? A star performer (that's you) who's forgotten the joy of the spotlight and yearns for the quiet of the wings.

Unfortunately, burnout gradually dims the spotlight on your passions and enthusiasm until you're left wondering why you stepped on stage in the first place. It sneaks up like a thief in the night, stealing away enthusiasm and energy and leaving behind a shell of fatigue and disinterest.

Burnout is more than just being tired; it's a deep, mental, and emotional exhaustion where even passions become chores, and motivation feels like a myth.

You may find yourself questioning: "What is the point?"

Burnout is a state of emotional, physical, and mental exhaustion caused by excessive and prolonged stress. It occurs when you feel overwhelmed, emotionally drained, and unable to meet constant demands. As the stress continues, you begin to lose the interest and motivation that led you to take on a specific role in the first place. It's the feeling that you've got nothing left to give, even though demands keep coming.

If this sounds familiar, you're not alone, and this chapter is here to help you turn things around.

Wisdom from the Wise

Did you know that the term "burnout" was first used by a psychologist named Herbert Freudenberger in the 1970s? He came up with the term to describe the negative effects of having high ideals and enduring severe stress in professions aimed at helping others. Burnout isn't a recent phenomenon, but our always-on, hyper-connected world has sped up its prevalence. Today, it's recognized across a range of stressful occupations and lifestyles.

Christina Maslach, a social psychologist and one of the leading researchers on burnout, emphasizes the role of the workplace environment in contributing to or mitigating burnout. She advocates for organizational change, focusing on workload management, community building, and ensuring consistency of values.

Did You Know? Studies show that employees with high control over their work activities are less likely to experience burnout.

Understanding the Dynamics of Burnout

What exactly is burnout? It's more than just feeling blue; that has been recognized by the World Health Organization, and it has the potential to negatively impact your health, happiness, and job performance. We'll break down the signs of burnout, why it happens, and why recognizing it early can save your career—and your well-being.

Burnout specifically affects individuals in intense and demanding roles but can impact anyone who feels overworked and undervalued. It's not just being overwhelmed by overwork; it's a chronic state that leads to diminished performance, cynicism, and a sense of ineffectiveness.

Burnout doesn't happen overnight. Gradually, it grows unnoticed because of ongoing stress and excessive work. Research in organizational and health psychology identifies three key dimensions of burnout: *emotional exhaustion, depersonalization (or cynicism),* and *reduced personal accomplishment.* Understanding these components can help individuals and organizations create more effective strategies to combat burnout.

Chronic stress associated with burnout leads to functional changes in the prefrontal cortex, often resulting in decreased cognitive flexibility and increased emotional reactivity. Neuroscientists have observed that sustained high cortisol levels, a hallmark of chronic stress, can alter the structure and function of the brain, reducing the brain's gray matter.

Psychologically, burnout is often seen because of prolonged emotional strain coupled with decreased accomplishment and a loss of personal identity. From the lens of Maslow's Hierarchy of Needs, burnout could stem from unmet needs at different levels, particularly esteem and self-actualization.

Apps: Lumosity or Peak to train your brain
with cognitive and critical thinking games.

Books: "Burnout: The Secret to Unlocking
the Stress Cycle" by Emily Nagoski and
Amelia Nagoski provides a scientific and
personal approach to understanding and
dealing with burnout.

Activity: Burnout Breakthrough Day

Today's mission is to address and ease symptoms of burnout through a series of creative and therapeutic activities. This challenge aims to renew your energy, enhance your well-being, and stimulate your creativity, providing you with tools to manage and prevent burnout.

1. Burnout Self-Assessment: Begin your day with a self-assessment to identify signs of burnout you may be experiencing, such as exhaustion, cynicism, or feelings of inefficacy. Establishing clear boundaries between work and personal life is essential to prevent burnout, with structured work hours and designated downtime being crucial for long-term well-being.

2. Mindfulness Meditation: Engage in a mindfulness meditation focused on acknowledging these feelings without judgment. Use breathing techniques to foster calmness and presence.

3. Art Therapy Session: Take part in an art therapy activity, such as painting, drawing, or sculpting. Focus on expressing your current emotions through your creations, which can provide relief and new perspectives on underlying stressors.

4. Journaling for Insight: Write in your journal about the thoughts and feelings that surfaced during your art session. Reflect on how engaging in creative activities impacts your mood and stress levels.

5. Nature Walk: Walk in a nearby park or natural setting. Engage all your senses to notice the surrounding environment, to help you reduce stress and improve your mental health.

6. Ecotherapy Exercises: In nature, perform ecotherapy exercises such as grounding (barefoot walking), hugging a tree, or simply sitting and observing the landscape. These activities help reduce burnout symptoms by reconnecting you with the earth and its healing properties.

7. Social Connection: Connect with a friend, family member, or colleague who uplifts your spirits. Choose a light, enjoyable activity together, such as having coffee or watching a comedy show.

8. Community Art Project: If possible, take part in a community-driven art project or a group creative workshop. Engaging with a community can reignite a sense of purpose and belonging, which is crucial for combating feelings of burnout.

9. Wind Down: End your day with relaxation techniques you find most effective, such as yoga, a warm bath, listening to white noise or calming music. These activities can help reset your stress response system.

10. Burnout Prevention Plan: Reflect on the day's activities and how they affected your feelings of burnout. Draft a burnout prevention plan incorporating daily or weekly activities that have proven beneficial for your mental and emotional health.

Benefits: This comprehensive day-long challenge helps you actively combat burnout by engaging in stimulating and creative activities. It offers strategies to restore energy, reduce stress, and reconnect with your creative and joyful self, ultimately helping you develop resilience against future burnout.

Reflective Questions:

1. What are the major sources of stress in your life, and how can you address them?
2. Which activities helped you feel more rejuvenated and less burnt out?
3. How can you integrate these strategies into your routine to maintain energy and prevent burnout?

Concluding Thoughts

In confronting burnout, we're not just seeking rest; we're looking to rediscover our zest. It's about finding balance, rekindling passion, and remembering that the show of life is as much about the backstage rest as it is about the onstage performance.

Burnout is a significant psychological state resulting from prolonged stress, characterized by exhaustion, cynicism, and feelings of reduced effectiveness. Strategies to manage burnout include setting boundaries, developing stress-relief routines, and maintaining strong social support networks.

This week, take charge of your life by identifying one thing you can change in your daily routine to reduce stress. Whether it's delegating a task, pursuing a new hobby, or simply taking your time for relaxation, just try to prioritize your well-being. By taking action and monitoring how this change affects your feelings of burnout, you can discover new ways to lead a more fulfilling and balanced life. Remember, every small change can make a big difference.

In Anne Lamott's wise words, "Almost everything will work again if you unplug it for a few minutes, including you." Consider this chapter your guide to unplugging and rebooting to return to life's stage refreshed. Your future self will thank you for it.

CHAPTER 31
BALANCING POWER AND EMPATHY: MASTERING THE DUAL ROLES OF AUTHORITY AND CARETAKER

"My own heroes are the dreamers, those men and women who tried to make the world a better place than when they found it, whether in small ways or great ones. Some succeeded, some failed, and most had mixed results... but it is the effort that's heroic, as I see it. Win or lose, I admire those who fight the good fight." — George R.R. Martin

---

Ever feel caught between being the boss everyone respects and the leader everyone loves? Finding that sweet spot between exerting authority and showing empathy is a common challenge.

Why not both? The truth is, effective leadership isn't just about calling the shots—it's about connecting with your team in a way that drives results and fosters a positive environment.

Too harsh, and you risk alienating your team; too lenient, and you may lose their respect. If you struggle to find that sweet spot between being authoritative and accessible, this chapter is your game plan. It's time to transform your leadership by mastering the balance between power and empathy.

Wisdom from the Wise

Eleanor Roosevelt reshaped the role of a First Lady, using her position to advocate fiercely for human rights while maintaining profound connections with the public through her empathetic approach. Her leadership style shows how power and deep empathy can lead to meaningful change and lasting influence.

Simon Sinek, the author of "Leaders Eat Last," believes that influential leaders prioritize the well-being of their team over their own comfort. This perspective underscores the importance of empathy in leadership, suggesting that true power lies in putting others first.

Did You Know? Research shows that companies that prioritize empathy have higher levels of employee satisfaction and lower rates of employee turnover.

The Science Behind Effective Leadership

Influential leaders understand that their actual power lies not in directives and demands, but in their ability to inspire and engage their team. Leadership isn't just about setting directions or driving performance. It's about people—motivating, understanding, and guiding them towards shared goals.

When you balance firm leadership with genuine empathy, you create a dynamic workplace where people are motivated, productive, and loyal. Let's break down why this balance isn't just nice to have—it's a must-have for any leader looking to make an impact.

Here's a quick neuroscience lesson: when people feel understood and valued, their trust in leadership increases. Psychological research highlights the importance of emotional intelligence in leadership.

Emotional intelligence—the skill of understanding, managing, and expressing your emotions, along with navigating interpersonal relationships with empathy and wisdom—is fundamental to successful leadership. Leaders who excel in emotional intelligence are adept at navigating team dynamics and achieving stellar outcomes without burning out their teams.

Apps: 'Mood Meter' for developing emotional intelligence through mood tracking and analysis.

Books: "Primal Leadership" by Daniel Goleman, Richard Boyatzis, and Annie McKee discuss the role of emotional intelligence in effective leadership. Dive into emotional intelligence's role in leadership— trust me, it's a game-changer.

Activity: Power-Empathy Equilibrium Challenge

Today's mission is to focus meaningfully on achieving a balance between exercising authority and showing empathy, which is essential for effective leadership and harmonious relationships. This challenge involves a series of reflective, interactive, and developmental exercises designed to enhance your ability to lead with strength while maintaining a deep connection to the needs and feelings of others.

1. Empathy and Authority Overview: Begin by exploring the concepts of empathy and authority. Read articles or watch videos discussing the psychological impacts of traits in leadership and personal relationships.

2. Self-Assessment: Reflect on your own leadership style or relationship management. Identify instances where you may lean more towards authority or empathy and consider the outcomes of these tendencies.

3. Empathy Practice: Engage in role-playing exercises focusing on highly empathetic scenarios. Practice responding to complex emotional situations, such as handling a team member's personal crisis or mediating a conflict.

4. Authority Scenarios: Switch to role-playing scenarios that require authoritative decision-making. Practice making and communicating tough decisions, such as delegating tasks or enforcing rules.

5. Balanced Response Development: Using insights gained from the morning's role-plays, develop new strategies for situations where you will need both authority and empathy. Create responses that blend firm decision-making with understanding and care.

6. Feedback Gathering: If possible, involve peers or mentors in your exercises and ask for feedback on your approach. Use this feedback to refine your ability to balance empathy with authority effectively.

7. Implementing Techniques: Apply your new strategies in real-world interactions throughout the afternoon. This could be in professional settings, like leading a meeting, or personal settings, like interacting with family.

8. Reflective Observation: After each interaction, take a moment to reflect on how well you balanced authority and empathy. Note what worked, what didn't, and how people responded to your approach.

Benefits: This challenge enhances your leadership skills and improves interpersonal relationships by fostering a balanced approach that values both assertiveness and understanding. It can lead to more effective team management, healthier personal relationships, and a greater sense of personal fulfillment.

Reflective Questions:

1. How can you improve your emotional intelligence to become a more empathetic leader?
2. What steps can you take to make sure your authority is both respected and fair?
3. How can you further develop your skills to maintain this balance in the future?

Concluding Thoughts

Listen up, leaders! It's time for a wake-up call. If you think being a good leader is just about wielding power, think again. The secret sauce to effective leadership is balancing power with empathy. This isn't about being everyone's best friend. It's about creating a workplace where people actually want to be. Where they feel heard, valued, and motivated to give their best. The most influential leaders are the ones who truly care. They understand that empathy isn't a weakness, it's a strength. It's what sets them apart from the rest.

So, here's your challenge for the week: Choose one leadership skill from this chapter and put it into action. Maybe it's starting an open feedback policy or taking an emotional intelligence course. Whatever it is, make it count. And watch what happens. Watch how it transforms your team dynamics. How it drives everyone, including you, to step up and do better.

By adopting this balanced approach, you're not just improving your leadership skills. You're setting a new standard. You're showing your team what real leadership looks like. It's time to step up to the plate. It's time to lead with both power and empathy. And watch as your team soars to new heights under your guidance.

So, are you ready? Are you ready to be the leader your team deserves? Because the world needs more leaders like you!

CHAPTER 32
NAVIGATING COGNITIVE DISSONANCE: UNDERSTANDING AND RESOLVING INTERNAL CONFLICTS

"And will I tell you that these three lived happily ever after? I will not, for no one ever does. But there was happiness. And they did live." — Stephen King

Ever notice yourself justifying a bad habit even though you know it's harmful? Or are you wrestling with the guilt of not living up to your own standards?

That's cognitive dissonance—your brain's struggle to hold two conflicting beliefs or values at the same time. It's uncomfortable, it's confusing, and it's totally human!

Cognitive dissonance is the mental discomfort we experience when holding two or more conflicting beliefs. It's not just a modern phenomenon, it's a timeless aspect of the human condition that has intrigued some of the greatest thinkers in history.

This chapter will not only help you understand this psychological phenomenon, but also provide practical strategies that you can implement in your everyday to harmonize your beliefs and actions.

Wisdom from the Wise

From Aristotle's ancient philosophies to Freud's psychoanalytical theories, exploring these historical perspectives, can connect us to the internal struggles that continue to challenge us today.

Aristotle, the father of Western philosophy, delved deep into the nature of ethics and psychology. He introduced the concept of 'virtue ethics,' suggesting that moral virtue comes from habit—our actions must align with our values to achieve eudaimonia or true happiness. For Aristotle, the conflict between what we believe to be right and our actions leads to moral inconsistencies that disrupt our quest for a virtuous life. Understanding this helps us see cognitive dissonance not just as discomfort but as a pivotal force pushing us toward greater personal integrity.

René Descartes, a pivotal figure in the Scientific Revolution, is best known for his assertion, "I think, therefore I am." Descartes wrestled with the reliability of human perception and the truth of existence. His approach began by questioning everything that could be questioned, leading to undeniable truths in the end. This approach highlights a form of cognitive dissonance where questioning our perceptions and beliefs can lead to a clearer, more confident understanding of the world and ourselves.

Through his groundbreaking theories of the ego, superego, and id, **Sigmund Freud**, often referred to as the father of psychoanalysis, added a new perspective to our understanding of human psychology. Freud suggested that cognitive dissonance often arises from the conflict between the id (instinctual desires), the superego (moral control), and the ego (reality). His exploration of these conflicting forces reveals why we often feel torn inside, as our base desires clash with societal expectations and our own moral standards.

Carl Jung, a student of Freud who developed his own theories, introduced the idea of the Shadow—the darker, often unacknowledged part of our personality. Jung believed that true psychological harmony comes from integrating the Shadow with the conscious self, acknowledging all parts of our being. This integration process directly addresses cognitive dissonance by encouraging us to accept conflicting parts of ourselves, leading to a more unified and authentic existence.

These historical giants didn't just live in their heads; they used their insights to teach us how to live better on our own. They showed that cognitive dissonance isn't just a modern dilemma but a catalyst for growth, pushing us toward a more authentic and integrated self. So, let's take a cue from these masters—embrace the dissonance, lean into the discomfort, and watch as it reshapes us into stronger, wiser beings.

Why Do Our Minds Play Tricks on Us?

Psychologist Leon Festinger introduced the theory of cognitive dissonance in the 1950s, and it has since become one of the most influential theories in psychology. It suggests that people have an inherent desire to achieve internal consistency. When inconsistency (dissonance) is experienced, individuals strive to reduce the dissonance and achieve consonance.

Why is cognitive dissonance so powerful? It taps into our fundamental need for self-consistency. Psychologists have studied this phenomenon extensively and found that dissonance can lead to irrational decisions, stress, and even low self-esteem. It can affect everything from simple decision-making to key behaviors, such as smoking or recycling.

The discomfort it causes can lead to irrational and sometimes destructive behavior as individuals try to reduce or eliminate the dissonance without considering the best course of action. Strategies for managing cognitive dissonance include increasing self-awareness, adjusting behaviors or beliefs, and accepting the complexity of human psychology. Dealing with dissonance effectively can lead to greater personal integrity and consistency in actions and beliefs.

Apps: Mindfulness apps like Simple Habit can help you stay aware and reflective, which are critical skills in managing dissonance.

Books: "Mistakes Were Made (But Not by Me)" by Carol Tavris and Elliot Aronson explores how self-justification and cognitive dissonance affect our actions and beliefs.

Activity: Cognitive Harmony Day

Today's mission is to spend mindful time dedicated to understanding and addressing cognitive dissonance—the discomfort one experiences when holding conflicting beliefs or attitudes. This challenge involves a series of reflective, analytical, and therapeutic activities designed to identify areas of dissonance, understand their impact, and develop strategies to resolve these internal conflicts, promoting mental clarity and emotional well-being.

1. Journaling for Dissonance: Begin your day with a journaling exercise focused on areas where you've felt conflict between your actions and beliefs. This could involve decisions in your personal life, career, or social behaviors.

2. Education on Cognitive Dissonance: Spend some time learning about cognitive dissonance theory. Understand the psychological research behind why we experience dissonance and its effects on our well-being.

3. Beliefs and Behaviors Mapping: Create a map or chart that lists your fundamental beliefs and corresponding behaviors. Identify where mismatches occur and note the emotions and thoughts that arise from these mismatches.

4. Role-Playing Scenarios: Engage in role-playing exercises to explore these conflicts more deeply. Act out situations where cognitive dissonance arises and experiment with different responses to see how they feel.

5. Reconciliation Techniques: Learn and apply techniques to reconcile conflicting beliefs and behaviors. This might involve behavioral modification techniques, re-framing strategies, seeking new information, and aligning your beliefs with your actions.

6. Mindfulness and Meditation: Use mindfulness exercises to sit with the discomfort of dissonance without immediately trying to resolve it. This can provide deeper insights into why you hold certain beliefs and how they impact your actions.

7. Discussion with Peers or Mentors: Discuss your findings and feelings with a trusted peer or mentor. An outside perspective can provide new insights and help reassess your beliefs or behaviors.

8. Feedback Incorporation: Take any feedback received and consider how it can help you adjust your approach to resolving cognitive dissonance.

9. Action Plan Development: Develop an ongoing plan to monitor and address future instances of cognitive dissonance. Set up regular check-ins with yourself through journaling or meditation to maintain cognitive harmony.

Benefits: This focused challenge helps you better understand the psychological mechanisms behind cognitive dissonance and provides practical tools for managing and resolving internal conflicts. This promotes excellent mental health, consistent behavior aligned with your beliefs, and improved decision-making processes.

Reflective Questions:

1. What were the most significant areas of cognitive dissonance you identified today, and why do they affect you?
2. How do you plan to apply the strategies you learned today to reduce dissonance in your daily life?

Concluding Thoughts

You know that uncomfortable feeling when your beliefs and your actions don't quite line up? That's cognitive dissonance, and it can be an actual source of stress and anxiety in our lives. But here's the thing: navigating cognitive dissonance isn't about choosing one belief over another. It's about understanding your values deeply and aligning your life with them.

When you take the time to really dig into what matters most to you, you can start making choices that feel authentic and true to who you are. And that, my friend, is how you reduce that psychological discomfort and start living a more fulfilling life.

So here's my challenge to you this week: pick one area of dissonance in your life and take a small step toward resolving it. It doesn't have to be a massive overhaul - just one minor change that helps decrease the gap between your actions and your values.

Maybe it's finally having that tough conversation with a friend or family member. Maybe it's setting boundaries at work so you can prioritize your well-being. Or maybe it's making a commitment to yourself to start that hobby or project you've been putting off.

Whatever it is, remember that small steps can lead to big changes in how you feel about yourself and the decisions you make. So don't be afraid to take that first step towards a more authentic, aligned life. And if you need a little extra motivation, just remember: you're capable of incredible things when you stay true to yourself and your values.

So let's get out there and start making those changes, one small step at a time. You've got this!

CHAPTER 33
BOOSTING PRODUCTIVITY: CUTTING-EDGE METHODS TO INCREASE OUTPUT WITHOUT BURNOUT

"Instead of wondering when your next vacation is, maybe you should set up a life you don't need to escape from." — Seth Godin

Let's be real; the traditional idea of "working longer" isn't cutting it anymore. Working leads to burnout, not success in a world where we're constantly pulled in directions. What if I told you that achieving more could actually involve doing less?

Today's pace is relentless. Our devices ping, screens flicker, and notifications pop—each demanding a slice of our ever-thinning attention span. How did we get here, and more importantly, how can we navigate this new reality without capsizing our personal and professional lives?

This chapter isn't about squeezing hours into your day—it's all about making each hour count smarter for you. Ready to up your productivity game without hitting a wall? Let's get started!

Wisdom from the Wise

Henry Ford didn't just innovate cars; he revolutionized workplace productivity. Henry Ford famously reduced his workers' hours from 10 to 8 per day and doubled their pay, finding that shorter shifts increased overall productivity and worker satisfaction. His approach revolutionized industrial productivity and showed that less can indeed be more when it comes to efficient work.

Einstein's Timeless Strategy - Compartmentalization: Albert Einstein, though living in a less distracted era, structured his days around deep, uninterrupted blocks of work, interspersed with periods dedicated to his other passions, like playing the violin or corresponding with friends. He intuitively knew what science now confirms: multitasking is a myth that hinders, not helps, our productivity. By compartmentalizing his day, Einstein achieved an astonishing level of productivity without succumbing to burnout.

Drawing on the simplicity of Einstein's wardrobe—a uniform of similar outfits—we can reduce our daily decisions to save cognitive energy for more important tasks. Einstein wore similar outfits daily to eliminate trivial choices. We can apply this principle by simplifying decisions, automating mundane tasks, and setting themes for days of the week—like 'Meeting-Free Mondays' or 'Creative Fridays'.

Time Blocking - A Lesson from Tesla: Nikola Tesla, a pioneer in both invention and thought, segmented his work into strict blocks of time, dedicating undistracted periods to his experiments and studies. Like Tesla, use time blocking to make your schedule tangible, allotting specific hours to specific tasks, thereby reducing the urge to multitask.

The 'Two Pizza Rule' - Keeping Meetings Efficient: Borrowed from Jeff Bezos, if two pizzas cannot feed everyone in the meeting, then the meeting is considered too crowded. Keeping gatherings small ensures they remain focused and efficient, saving precious time.

Our culture often equates busyness with productivity, but this is a fallacy that needs debunking. True productivity isn't measured by how full your schedule is but by the impact of what you achieve.

Emphasizing Quality Over Quantity: Taking a cue from Einstein's miracle year, where he published four groundbreaking papers, we learn that significant achievements come from depth, not breadth, of focus. Prioritize tasks that have the most substantial impact, and give them the attention they deserve.

The Role of Downtime - Recharging the Mind: Einstein's leisure time was as integral to his routine as his work. Scheduled breaks—true breaks, free from digital intrusion—can recharge the mind and spur creativity. Recognizing the value of rest, both as recuperation and as a subconscious problem-solving tool, is crucial in our relentless world.

Exploring the Science; Be More Efficient, Not Busier

People often get it wrong by thinking productivity is about working longer, but actual productivity is about working smarter. This means using technology to manage time better and optimizing our energy levels throughout the day.

Productivity isn't some term; it's a crucial skill set for those aiming to excel without burning out. It's all about using your time, focus, and energy. Here, we redefine productivity. It's not about doing more but achieving through focused effort and strategic breaks. By grasping and applying the principles of productivity science, you can not only boost your output but also enhance your creativity and satisfaction.

It's all about your mindset—literally. Recent studies on the brain show that our effective work occurs in periods of effort, followed by breaks. According to psychology, we're most productive when we work in sync with our body rhythms and match our tasks to our energy levels. The concept of ultradian rhythms—natural cycles of concentration that ebb and flow throughout the day—teaches us that respecting these biological patterns can enhance productivity while preventing fatigue. Ignoring these natural rhythms can sabotage your efficiency.

Did You Know? Modern research supports taking regular breaks to improve concentration and prevent decision fatigue. Studies recommend a quick break every 90 minutes to optimize cognitive performance.

Overwhelmed by Options: The Paradox of Choice

In the digital age, we face many choices, from the videos we watch to the tools we use to manage our tasks. This plethora can lead to decision fatigue, draining our energy before we even tackle our actual work. Decision fatigue has become the silent productivity killer in a world brimming with options and opportunities. Every choice we make—from the brand of coffee we drink to the projects we prioritize—drains a bit of our mental energy.

According to the Law of Accelerating Returns proposed by futurist Ray Kurzweil, technology evolves exponentially rather than linearly. This means that each new generation of technology arrives faster than its predecessor, doubling the rate of progress in increasingly shorter time frames.

Feeling overwhelmed by tech updates? Flip the script: instead of seeing constant change as a hurdle, view it as an exhilarating challenge. Set a goal to learn one new tech skill each month—whether it's a new app, a software program, or a tech gadget. Make it fun, make it a game, and suddenly, you're not just keeping up; you're leading the charge.

Studies show that after about 50 hours of work per week, productivity decreases, and the quality of work suffers. Continuously working without adequate breaks can lead to reduced effectiveness and burnout.

More hours don't mean better work. Recognize when you're just spinning your wheels and take a strategic pause. Challenge yourself to redefine productivity: quality over quantity. Set precise cutoff times for work and stick to them. Use the extra time to recharge and watch your work quality soar. Remember, a well-rested mind is a more productive mind.

Studies have shown that long-term stress can cause notable health problems, such as heart disease, diabetes, depression, and anxiety. The American Psychological Association states that the majority of Americans (more than 75%) experience at least one symptom of stress every month.

Think of stress management as an essential part of your health regimen, just like eating right or exercising. Don't wait until you feel overwhelmed to start. Integrate small stress-reduction techniques into every day. Set a timer for three minutes of deep breathing each morning or a five-minute meditation during your lunch break. Start small but start today—your body and mind will thank you.

Adaptation Fatigue in the Digital Age

A study by the International Journal of Information Management found that continuous adaptation to new technologies can lead to 'adaptation fatigue', where individuals become tired and less productive because of the constant need to learn new systems and interfaces.

If you're feeling burnt out by the constant need to adapt, it's time to sharpen your core competencies. Focus on building robust problem-solving, critical thinking, and creative skills. These don't require updates or new downloads—they enhance your ability to use any technology effectively. Remember, it's not about the tool but how you use it. Apply the 'just-in-time' learning approach. Instead of trying to learn everything, focus on the technologies relevant to your life or work as they emerge.

Apps: 'RescueTime' tracks how you spend your time and identifies areas for improvement. 'Trello' for task management and project organization. 'Zapier' is used to automate workflows between apps and services.

Books: Timothy Ferriss's "The 4-Hour Workweek" explores working less and achieving more by eliminating waste and focusing on efficiency.

Activity: Productivity Power-Up Day

Today's mission is to enhance productivity through innovative methods that prevent burnout. This challenge uses time management techniques, mental exercises, and strategic breaks to optimize your productivity while safeguarding your mental and physical well-being.

1. Energizing Start: Begin with a physical activity that increases energy levels, like a quick workout, yoga, or a brisk walk. Follow this with a healthy, energizing breakfast to set a positive tone for the day.

2. Task Prioritization: Use the Eisenhower Box technique to prioritize tasks by their level of urgency and importance. Focus your energy on tasks that are both urgent and important, planning your day around these priorities.

3. Pomodoro Technique: Use the Pomodoro Technique, which involves working in concentrated intervals of 25 minutes and taking 5-minute breaks in between. This technique allows for sustained focus without causing tiredness.

4. Task Batching: Group similar tasks together to decrease task-switching time and increase flow. This could involve batching all emails, calls, or creative tasks in specific blocks.

5. Technology Leverage: Try using productivity tools and apps to streamline your work. Tools like task managers, timers, and distraction blockers can significantly enhance your efficiency.

6. Mind Mapping: For complex projects, create mind maps to visualize tasks and their relationships. This can help clarify your next steps and simplify the execution process.

7. Nature Break: Take a more extended break to connect with nature, whether walking in the park or simply stepping outside for fresh air. Nature restores mental energy and fosters creativity.

8. Progress Review: Evaluate your productivity for the day so far. Adjust your plan based on what's been effective and what hasn't, setting yourself up for a productive end to the day.

9. Relaxation Techniques: To wind down from the day and prevent burnout, engage in relaxation techniques such as deep breathing, progressive muscle relaxation, or meditation.

10. Plan for Tomorrow: Briefly plan your next day, applying insights from today's productivity efforts. Anticipate potential challenges and think about how to overcome them.

Benefits: This focused productivity day not only boosts your output for the day but also teaches you sustainable practices to maintain high productivity without risking burnout.

Reflective Questions:

1. Which productivity techniques were most effective for you, and why? How can you better adjust these techniques to suit your daily work routine and prevent burnout?
2. What part of your day do you feel most productive, and how can you use this to schedule your tasks? What are your top three productivity killers?
3. What tasks can you automate or delegate to focus more on high-impact activities?

Concluding Thoughts

Do you want to be more productive? I am sure you do. It's not really about the hacks or the tricks. It's about creating a lifestyle that works for you. Enhancing productivity involves more than increasing work hours; it requires strategic planning, understanding personal energy cycles, and using modern tools and methods.

Here's the deal: your productivity is personal. What works for your coworker might not work for you, and that's okay. The key is to find strategies that respect your mental and physical health because that's what's going to drive sustained performance. Respecting your natural productivity rhythms and regular breaks can significantly boost output and prevent burnout.

So, here's what I want you to do. This week, I want you to choose one productivity technique from this chapter. Maybe it's the Pomodoro Technique, maybe it's time blocking whatever speaks to you. And I want you to integrate it into your routine. Really commit to it. But here's the important part: I want you to observe the changes. Not just in your output, but in your well-being. Because actual productivity, the kind that lasts, means working not just harder, but smarter and healthier.

You have the power to transform your workday. You can achieve new heights of productivity without sacrificing your well-being. But it starts with you. It starts with applying these creative strategies to work smarter, not harder.

So, are you ready? Are you ready to boost your productivity, to increase your output without burnout? Then let's do this. Let's apply these methods and create a productive lifestyle that works for you.

CHAPTER 34
THE FITNESS QUEST: UNLOCKING YOUR INNER WORKOUT WARRIOR

"Take care of your body. It's the only place you have to live." - Jim Rohn

Finding motivation for physical fitness can sometimes feel like trying to start a car on a frosty morning. You know it's good for you, but the comfort of the couch, much like a warm blanket, is oh-so-enticing. It's the battle of the gym versus the gravitational pull of the sofa.

Regular exercise, often viewed as a chore or a distant dream whispered to oneself on New Year's Eve, is a common struggle. In an era where our fingers get more exercise scrolling through feeds than our bodies do in a week, motivating ourselves to exercise can be a Herculean task.

We all want the health benefits of fitness, but the journey from couch to crunches is fraught with mental hurdles and temptations. Breaking the inertia requires more than just willpower; it involves rewiring our perception of fitness.

Wisdom from the Wise

Bruce Lee was more than just a martial artist; he was also a fitness pioneer who combined different disciplines to enhance his physical abilities. His philosophy, "Be water, my friend," underscores the importance of adaptability in fitness—a reminder that our training should be fluid and responsive to our body's needs.

Consider the discipline of Olympic athletes like Usain Bolt, whose rigorous training and strict dietary regimes highlight the profound commitment to physical health. Their routines show that maintaining peak physical condition requires consistent effort and dedication.

Did You Know? Ancient Greeks valued physical fitness highly, integrating it into their daily lives as a civil duty to ensure that the body was as fit as the mind.

Psychology of Exercise

Why do we often find ourselves crafting elaborate excuses to skip the gym (or living room floor)? It's a blend of psychological factors: fear of judgment, the discomfort of change, and the daunting expectation of instant results. Recognizing these mental barriers is the first step in dismantling them.

Our internal tug-of-war over exercise is deeply rooted in human psychology. Our struggle with fitness often stems from a 'pleasure-pain' principle. It's a clash between the primitive part of our brain, craving ease and comfort, and the higher self, seeking growth and vitality. We're wired to seek immediate gratification and avoid discomfort, even knowing the long-term benefits.

Psychological studies often cite lack of time, perceived difficulty, and low enjoyment as the primary barriers to regular exercise. Research in the Journal of Behavioral Medicine indicates that setting manageable goals and focusing on immediate positive feelings post-exercise, like increased energy and mood, can significantly counteract these barriers.

Here's the truth—you've got time. You just need to see it. Instead of waiting for that elusive 'perfect time' to exercise, grab it wherever you can. Got 15 minutes before dinner? Do a quick workout. Waiting for laundry? Get some steps in. Change how you view exercise; it's not a marathon session at the gym but any moment you decide to move. Focus on how fantastic and energized you feel afterward, and let that feeling pull you back day after day.

Start small. Setting monumental fitness goals can be overwhelming. Begin with achievable targets—a 10-minute walk, a few yoga poses, a quick bike ride, and a home workout session. Small wins pave the way to more significant triumphs. Find your fitness 'why.' Connect exercise to something meaningful. Is it about health, feeling good, or being strong for your loved ones? Anchor your fitness journey for this purpose.

Neuroscientific research reveals that regular physical activity stimulates the production of neurotransmitters like dopamine and serotonin, which play key roles in mood regulation and reward mechanisms. A study from the University of California showed that just 20 minutes of moderate exercise can boost dopamine levels, enhancing mood and motivation.

Your brain loves rewards, and exercise is like a jackpot of happy chemicals—dopamine, serotonin, you name it. So, how about tricking your brain into loving exercise? Start with something so fun it doesn't feel like a workout. Dance around your living room, play tag with your kids, or take a brisk walk in your favorite part of town. Keep it short and sweet; even 10 minutes can shift your mood and kick those brain chemicals into high gear.

Beyond the immediate mood boost, regular physical activity has profound long-term health benefits. According to the World Health Organization, consistent exercise reduces the risk of heart disease, diabetes, depression, and several types of cancer by up to 50%.

Don't just exercise; envision your future self—healthier, stronger, and bursting with energy. Create a vision board or jot down your health goals. Every workout is a step closer to that vision. When you connect exercise to your dreams for your future self, every sweat session becomes a building block to a vibrant, healthier life.

Creative Insights

Turn your workout into a **game**. Use apps that gamify fitness or create personal challenges. Imagine you're a character leveling up with each workout.

Invent **workout rituals**. Create pre- and post-workout rituals that you enjoy. It could be a special smoothie, a favorite playlist, or a relaxing shower ritual after exercise.

Craft a motivational fitness **playlist**. Let music be your personal trainer. The right tunes can turn a sluggish jog into a heroic sprint.

Experiment with **different** activities. Fitness isn't one-size-fits-all. Try dancing, hiking, swimming, or martial arts. Find what makes you feel alive and excited.

Join a class or a fitness **community**. The camaraderie can be a powerful motivator, turning exercise into a social and enjoyable activity.

Celebrate **progress**, not just **perfection**. Every day your exercise is a win. Keep a workout log and celebrate your consistency and improvements. Focus on how exercise makes you feel rather than how it makes you look. Celebrate the energy boost, the mood elevation, and the sense of achievement.

Be kind to yourself on off days. Fitness is a journey, not a destination. There will be days off the wagon. What matters is getting back on without self-judgment. Embrace rest as part of the journey. Fitness isn't just about movement; it's about recovery, too. Understand and respect your body's need for rest. Reframe setbacks as setups. Did you miss a workout? Have you struggled through a routine? Each is an opportunity to learn and adjust, not a reason to criticize yourself.

Apps: 'MyFitnessPal' for tracking diet and exercise, helping you stay accountable, and informing you about your nutritional intake. 'Strava' for tracking cycling and running activities, connecting you with a community of athletes for motivation and friendly competition.

Books: "Becoming a Supple Leopard" by Dr. Kelly Starrett offers invaluable advice on resolving pain, preventing injury, and optimizing athletic performance.

Activity: Total Health Turnaround

Today's mission is to engage in a day-long series of activities designed to kick-start improvements in your physical health. This fun and practical exercise is crafted to enhance your understanding of personal health needs, boost your physical activity levels, and promote healthier eating habits, all within a single day.

1. Hydration Boost: Give your body a hydration boost and jump-start your metabolism by starting your day with a glass of water infused with lemon. Commit to staying hydrated throughout the day, aiming for 8-10 glasses of water.

2. Energizing Breakfast: Prepare yourself an energizing breakfast that combines protein, healthy fats, and fiber. Consider options like a smoothie bowl, oatmeal topped with nuts and fruits, or scrambled eggs mixed with vegetables.

3. Quick Cardio Session: Engage in a 20-minute cardio exercise of your choice. This could be a brisk walk, a run, a cycling, or a high-intensity interval training (HIIT) session.

4. Fitness Goal Setting: Post-workout, take a moment to set a fitness goal for the next month. Whether it's increasing the distance you run, improving your flexibility, or building strength, write it down and outline the steps you'll take to achieve it.

5. Healthy Lunch Cooking: Cook a healthy lunch focusing on whole foods. Use plenty of vegetables, lean proteins, and whole grains. Just try to avoid processed foods and those high in unhealthy fats and sugar.

6. Learn About Nutrition: Spend 30 minutes reading about nutrition—specifically, learn about the benefits of whole foods versus processed foods and how different nutrients contribute to physical health.

7. Yoga or Stretching: Take part in a yoga class or do a stretching routine at home. Focus on poses and stretches that enhance flexibility and muscle relaxation.

8. Mindfulness and Breathing: Integrate mindfulness by concentrating on your breathing during each pose, which helps enhance the connection between body and mind.

9. Digital Detox: Spend your evening free from screens. Instead, engage in relaxing activities that promote your health, like reading, meditating, or taking a warm bath.

10. Healthy Dinner and Preparation for Tomorrow: Prepare a light, nutritious dinner, and plan your meals for the next day to maintain momentum.

Benefits: This activity is designed to jump-start your physical health improvements by combining exercise, proper hydration, nutritious eating, and mental wellness practices. It sets the foundation for ongoing healthy habits and gives you practical experience in managing a healthier lifestyle.

Reflective Questions:

1. What was the most challenging part of today's health-focused activities, and how did you overcome it?
2. How did you feel physically and mentally after today's exercise? How can you incorporate today's lessons and practices into your everyday routine?

Concluding Thoughts

Exercise isn't just about physical fitness; it's a celebration of what your body can do, a testament to your willpower, and a journey towards self-care. It isn't just about sculpting a body; it's about forging a spirit of resilience, strength, and unstoppable determination. It's about finding joy in movement and strength in perseverance!

Changing the way we think about exercise - seeing it as a powerful catalyst for personal growth rather than a mundane task - is key to overcoming this. Embracing a holistic approach to fitness includes strength, stamina, flexibility, nutrition, and mental resilience. It's a commitment to your best self.

As you embark on this quest, remember that the strongest muscle is your heart. Exercise it with joy, determination, and a touch of playfulness. It's about discovering what makes you feel strong, vibrant, and alive.

In the wise words of Muhammad Ali, "I hated every minute of training, but I said, 'Don't quit. Suffer now and live the rest of your life as a champion.'" Let this spirit guide you. Embrace the sweat, the effort, the discipline, and become the champion of your own fitness story.

CHAPTER 35
MASTERING MINDFULNESS: THE FOMO FIASCO, EMBRACING THE HERE AND NOW

"Mindfulness isn't difficult; we just need to remember to do it." — Sharon Salzberg

Ever feel like you're everywhere but here? Our minds are often pulled in a million directions in today's hyper-connected world. It feels like we're always one scroll away from discovering someone living our dream life on a beach we've never visited with a dog we've always wanted.

FOMO—the sneaky suspicion that everyone is having more fun than you, possibly at a party you weren't invited to, where they're probably riding unicorns.

This disconnect can drain our energy, diminish our focus, and escalate our stress levels. Mindfulness offers a powerful antidote, teaching us to anchor ourselves in the here and now.

Forget the autopilot. It's time to take the controls and truly experience the ride.

Wisdom from the Wise

Thich Nhat Hanh, a Vietnamese Zen master, brought mindfulness to the West with his teachings on meditation, mindfulness, and peace. He taught that the most profound joys are found not in extraordinary events but in understanding the extraordinary nature of ordinary moments. His approach transforms everyday tasks into profound opportunities for mindfulness. His work has shown how mindfulness can bring about peaceful transformations in individuals and societies.

Jon Kabat-Zinn, the visionary who founded the Mindfulness-Based Stress Reduction (MBSR) program, revolutionized the accessibility of mindfulness for Western audiences. His programs and books show how mindfulness meditation can reduce stress and enhance life quality.

Paul Arden might quip, "Don't just think, observe. The world is what YOU think of it, so think of it DIFFERENTLY, and your life will change." George Lois would likely add, "If your head isn't in it, where are you?" These insights remind us that mindfulness is about diving deeply into the experience of living, not just skimming the surface.

Psychological Roots and Consequences of FOMO

At its core, FOMO (The Fear of Missing Out) is about social anxiety and our innate desire to belong. It taps into our deep-seated fear that we're missing out on critical experiences, leading to a perpetual state of dissatisfaction and comparison.

A 2021 study published in the Journal of Social and Clinical Psychology found that individuals experiencing high levels of FOMO exhibit signs of general dysphoria, anxiety, and lower overall life satisfaction. This emotional strain often stems from a perceived deficit in one's personal life compared to others perceived through social media.

Neuroimaging studies have shown that social comparison, mainly mediated by social media, activates the brain's reward centers while simultaneously engaging areas linked to pain and discomfort. This dual activation suggests that social media can provide immediate gratification but also contributes to long-term psychological stress.

Instead, embrace JOMO—the Joy of Missing Out. It's the satisfying feeling when you're content doing your own thing, not worried about what others are doing. Celebrate your moments of JOMO!

Did You Know? Mindfulness can significantly reduce the cortisol levels associated with stress, leading to better health outcomes and enhanced well-being.

Since your brain processes social media interactions with both reward and discomfort, retrain your brain to seek rewards from healthier sources. Incorporate daily practices that promote positive brain chemistry, like exercise, which boosts endorphins, or engage in hobbies that increase dopamine levels, such as painting or playing music. This shift will help reduce the reliance on social media for your emotional highs.

A comparative study across cultures found that FOMO levels are notably higher in societies that prioritize individual success and external validation through social media, such as the United States and parts of Europe, compared to more collectivist cultures like Japan or South Korea, where community and group cohesion provide a buffer against such pressures.

Actively seek and create environments that reflect the values of collective enjoyment and community involvement. This could mean joining local clubs, volunteer groups, or sports teams. Immersing yourself in these settings can diminish the personal pressure to "keep up" with superficial social media standards, fostering a healthier, community-focused lifestyle that combats FOMO at its roots.

How to be Here & Now?

Mindfulness isn't just trendy—it's transformative. It's about tuning in to the now, not tuning out the world. This practice isn't an escape; it's an engagement. It strengthens your ability to attend to the present moment without judgment, enhancing both mental clarity and emotional calm.

Think of mindfulness as the ultimate life hack—it doesn't change the game's rules but changes how you play it, making every moment more intense, more vivid, and more meaningful.

Mindfulness is all about intentionally focusing on the present moment without judgment. It's about observing our thoughts, feelings, and sensations as they are, not as we want them to be - noticing the colors, sounds, and sensations of now rather than getting lost in 'what was' or 'what might be.'

This practice isn't just about inner peace—it's about accessing a level of clarity and engagement most people don't even know they're missing. This practice roots us, providing a clearer perspective and helping us navigate life with greater clarity and intention.

Mindfulness does more than calm the mind; it rewires it. Research shows that mindfulness can literally change our brains, making us more focused and better decision-makers. It also effectively reduces symptoms of anxiety, depression, and stress by taming the amygdala.

Regular mindfulness practice can improve your brain's gray matter, boosting areas responsible for attention, emotion regulation, and mental flexibility.

You might think that mindfulness is about emptying your mind. Well, it is not- it is about filling it with the moment you're living. It's not just about feeling better; it's about literally changing your brain for the better.

Apps: 'Insight Timer' offers a plethora of guided meditations that cater to various focus areas—from reducing anxiety to enhancing creativity.

Books: "Wherever You Go, There You Are" by Jon Kabat-Zinn breaks down mindfulness into digestible, actionable pieces for everyday life.

Activity: Mindful Moments

Today's activity focuses on integrating mindfulness practices into everyday life, enhancing present-moment awareness, and promoting a sense of peace and centeredness.

1. Morning Meditation: Start your day with a 10-minute guided meditation focusing on breath awareness. Pay attention to moments when your thoughts drift and gently guide them back to focusing on your breath each time. Use an app or a guided video to help facilitate the process.

2. Mindful Eating: During breakfast, focus solely on the experience of eating. Notice your food's textures, flavors, and sensations, eating slowly without distractions like TV or smartphones.

3. Mindful Walking: Take a 15-minute mindful walk, whether during a break at work or in your neighborhood. Concentrate on the sensations of walking, feeling each step and the rhythm of your breath.

4. Limit Notifications: Every ping pulls you back into the world of comparison. Be selective about what gets your attention.

5. Mindful Social Media Use: It's not about quitting Instagram, TikTok, or Facebook; it's about using them intentionally. Remember, social media is a curated gallery, not a documentary of someone's life.

6. Create a FOMO Jar: Whenever you feel FOMO, write something you're grateful for or a fun memory and put it in the jar. When you're feeling down, read them as reminders of your own rich life.

7. Mindfulness Reminders: Set three reminders on your

phone randomly during the day. When each alarm goes off, pause whatever you're doing and take a minute to engage fully with your current activity or sensation.

8. Evening Reflection: Reflect on your day through a mindfulness journal. Note moments when you felt most present and any challenges you experienced staying mindful.

Benefits: This exercise helps reduce stress, improve concentration, enhance emotional reactivity, and increase overall well-being through heightened awareness of the present moment. The benefits of mindfulness extend beyond personal well-being to improve interpersonal relationships and professional performance.

Reflective Questions:

1. What moments were you fully present for today, and what did you notice?
2. What ordinary moment today brought you unexpected joy, and why?
3. How might incorporating mindfulness into your daily routine improve your life?

Concluding Thoughts

FOMO thrives in the gap between reality and perception. We close that gap by embracing the present and appreciating our own experiences. It's time to get real with ourselves. Life isn't about doing it all; it's about finding joy and fulfillment in the things we choose to invest our time and energy in. And let's be honest, when we start comparing our lives to everyone else's highlight reel, it's a surefire way to kill our own happiness.

So, here's what we're going to do. We're flipping the script on FOMO. Instead of focusing on what everyone else is doing, we're going to focus on our own journey, our own wins, and our own happiness. All that noise about what's happening elsewhere? It's just background static compared to the incredible story of your life.

This week, I challenge you to embrace Micro-Mindfulness Practices. Pay attention to the small, easily overlooked moments and sensations in your day. Dare yourself to find the extraordinary in the ordinary. Every single moment is an opportunity to practice mindfulness, and I want you to seize those opportunities and see what you discover.

Are you ready to upgrade your mental software and experience life in high definition? Then let's embark on this journey of presence together and uncover just how amazing your life can be when you're fully engaged in the here and now.

Remember, mastering mindfulness is the key to overcoming the FOMO Fiasco. Embrace the present, appreciate your own experiences, and watch your life transform before your eyes. You've got this!

CHAPTER 36

THE JOY QUEST: NAVIGATING HAPPINESS IN A 'BUY NOW' WORLD

"Very little is needed to make a happy life; it is all within your-self, in your way of thinking." — Marcus Aurelius

---

In the supermarket of life, we often mistake happiness for the latest shiny thing on the shelf. Society's aisles are filled with glittering promises of joy, just a credit card swipe away. Can true happiness really be found in your shopping cart?

We're drenched in a culture that equates cool stuff with happiness, especially if it makes for an awesome Instagram post. Success seems to be measured in square footage and happiness in megapixels.

In this consumer-driven world, happiness often comes wrapped in shiny packaging with a price tag. But beneath that glossy surface, there's a deeper craving for something real, something money can't buy.

Living happily in a materialistic society is like being on a diet at an all-you-can-eat buffet. Yet, the real challenge is finding nourishment that truly feeds the soul, not just the shopping cart.

Wisdom from the Wise

Epicurus, a philosopher from ancient Greece, established a highly influential philosophy school. According to his teachings, the ultimate goal in life is to attain happiness by actively seeking pleasure and evading pain. This pursuit of pleasure is considered the highest good. His ideas emphasize the importance of friendship, freedom, and self-analysis as key components of happiness.

Did You Know? A landmark study by Brickman et al. (1978) on lottery winners and accident victims found that despite initial increases or decreases in happiness, individuals returned to a baseline level of happiness over time. This phenomenon, known as hedonic adaptation, suggests that new acquisitions bring only temporary joy.

The Science of Happiness in the Modern World

Living happily in a materialistic society is like being on a diet at an all-you-can-eat buffet. Everywhere you look, something is tempting you to indulge, promising satisfaction. Yet, the real challenge is finding nourishment that truly feeds the soul, not just the shopping cart.

Our brains crave instant gratification, and in a society full of material temptations, it's easy to confuse acquiring things with actually accomplishing things. But true happiness often lies off the beaten path of consumerism in the quieter spaces of meaningful experiences and connections.

The human mind is a curious beast, easily seduced by the allure of the new and shiny. Yet, this lure of materialism is like fast food for the soul—momentarily satisfying but ultimately unfulfilling. Unraveling this requires a bold reevaluation of what truly nourishes us.

Take a moment to assess your joy. Think about when you feel the most alive. Spoiler: It rarely happens while standing in a checkout line. It's about those special moments when we connect, create, and sometimes just sit back and reflect.

Cultivate an anti-consumerism hobby. Gardening, hiking, painting—these activities root you in experiences and personal growth, not accumulating stuff.

Focus on experiences, not possessions. The joy of doing typically outlasts the joy of owning. Plan adventures, learn new skills, and create memories—these treasures don't lose their luster.

Practice mindfulness in consumption. Before buying, ask, "Do I need this, or do I just want it?" It's about being a conscious consumer, not a passive shopper.

Creative Insights

Organize an anti-materialism challenge. Go a month without buying anything non-essential. Document the journey—the struggles, the revelations, and the triumphs.

Experiment with minimalist living. It's like stripping the layers of excess to reveal the art of living simply yet richly. Engage in 'decluttering' exercises. Simplify your space and life. Sometimes, less really is more, especially when it creates room for growth and clarity.

Cultivate gratitude. It shifts the focus from what you don't have to what you do have. An attitude of gratitude can be the richest form of wealth.

Dive into the world of barter and trade. It's an adventure in value exchange that can be more rewarding and socially engaging than traditional shopping.

Embrace the DIY culture. Making, repairing, and upcycling can be deeply satisfying—a rebellion against the disposable culture.

Navigating the Materialistic Maze

Question the narrative. Every ad, every shiny new trend, is a story being sold. Set personal values as your compass. Let these guide your decisions, purchases, and lifestyle. Write your own story, one where happiness isn't barcode-scannable.

Find richness in frugality. There's a unique joy in finding value in the underrated, in stretching resources, in the triumph of ingenuity over impulse.

Discover joy in giving. There's immense happiness in generosity —sharing time, resources, and skills. It's a happiness that comes back tenfold.

Apps: 'Eventbrite' to discover local events and experiences that can enrich your life beyond material possessions

Books: "The Art of Happiness" by the Dalai Lama and Howard Cutler explores the concept of happiness and how to achieve it in everyday life.

Activity: Happiness Without Purchase Day

Today's mission is to spend a day exploring and cultivating personal happiness without relying on consumerism. This challenge aims to disconnect from the instant gratification of 'buy now' impulses and focus on activities and practices that foster genuine, sustainable joy.

1. Digital Detox Initiation: Begin the day by disconnecting from digital shopping platforms, social media, and any other online consumer activities. Turn off notifications to minimize distractions.

2. Gratitude Meditation: Start with a gratitude meditation focusing on the non-material aspects of your life that bring you joy, such as relationships, achievements, or personal growth.

3. Nature Connection: Engage in an activity that allows you to connect with nature, such as a walk in a local park, gardening, or simply sitting outside in a natural setting. Focus on the beauty and calm of the environment.

4. Creative Expression: Dedicate time to a creative endeavor that doesn't involve consumption. You can choose from various creative outlets, such as drawing, writing, playing music, or any other form that uplifts your spirit.

5. Volunteering: Take part in a local community service or volunteering opportunity. Giving back can enhance feelings of happiness and fulfillment.

6. Connection with Loved Ones: Arrange to spend quality time with family or friends. Focus on activities that strengthen bonds, such as playing games, cooking together, or sharing stories.

7. Journaling Session: Reflect on your experiences through journaling. Focus on how the day's activities made you feel and what you discovered about your sources of happiness.

8. Learn Something New: Spend some time learning a new skill or topic that interests you, not related to consumerism. This could be a language lesson, a craft tutorial, or a scientific documentary.

9. Happiness Planning: Outline a plan to incorporate today's successful activities into your routine—set goals to engage in these happiness-boosting activities at least once a week.

Benefits: This activity hopefully helps you highlight and enhance the elements of life that contribute to true happiness beyond material goods. By focusing on experiences, relationships, creativity, and giving, you can build a more fulfilling and joyful life.

Reflective Questions:

1. What non-material aspects of today brought you the most joy, and why?
2. How can you reduce the impulse to seek happiness through purchases based on today's experiences?

Concluding Thoughts

We're living in a world that's constantly trying to sell us the idea that happiness comes with a price tag. It's like we're all on this never-ending quest for joy, but we're looking for it in all the wrong places. In a society consumed by the "buy now, be happy now" ideology, the most profound act of rebellion is to reject this materialistic narrative and discover happiness outside of consumerism. Sure, money can buy comfort - and don't get me wrong, comfort is great - but it's not the end game. It's not what's going to fill that void inside or make you feel truly fulfilled.

Happiness is a journey, not a destination. It's a path paved with meaningful experiences, deep connections with the people surrounding you, and a healthy dose of defiance against the idea that you need to buy more to be more.

So here's my challenge to you: start your own Joy Quest. Navigate this crazy, commercialized world we live in, but do it on your own terms. Find the things that light you up inside, that make you feel alive and connected and whole - and spoiler alert: those things probably aren't going to have a brand name attached.

It's time to rebel against the status quo and create your own definition of happiness. Because at the end of the day, the best things in life aren't things at all. They're the moments, the people, and the experiences that make you feel like the most authentic version of yourself.

So go out there and find your joy, rebel. The Quest is waiting for you to seize it!

CHAPTER 37

UNPLUGGING THE MATRIX: ESCAPING SOCIAL MEDIA'S SIREN SONG

"Technology doesn't just do things for us. It does things to us, changing not just what we do but who we are." — Sherry Turkle

Picture the scene: you open an app to check the weather, only to find yourself, an hour later, deep in the profile of someone you barely know, analyzing their vacation photos. Or consider the near-universal experience of crafting a post, deleting it, rewriting it, and then pondering over whether to post it at all. These moments are the modern-day comedies of our digital lives—equal parts amusing and perplexing.

In today's digitally dominated world, social media is like a sprawling, vibrant city that never sleeps. It's bustling, chaotic, and brimming with endless information. However, just like a bustling city, it can also be overwhelming, leaving us lost in its digital alleys.

In the dazzling world of social media, everyone else's life looks like a highlight reel. It's easy to get hooked, scrolling through a never-ending feed of vacation snaps, gourmet meals, and picture-perfect moments.

But when does staying connected start disconnecting us from the real world?

Did You Know? Research in the Journal of Social and Clinical Psychology highlights that individuals who spend more time on social media daily feel more socially isolated than those who spend less time. The study suggests that over-engagement in virtual spaces can lead to detrimental comparisons that erode self-esteem and increase loneliness. According to a survey by the Pew Research Center, about 60% of social media users feel inadequate about their own life achievements when comparing themselves to others online.

The Psychology of Social Media Addiction

Social media, the modern-day Pandora's box, opens a world of connection yet often leads us down a vicious circle of comparison, distraction, and relentless pursuit of digital acknowledgment. It's a world where 'the currency is likes' and 'the language is emojis,' but the conversation is often one-sided.

Caught in the social media vortex, it's like being at a masquerade ball where everyone competes for the shiniest mask. Swipe after swipe, like after like, we find ourselves drifting further from shore, entangled in the nets of curated realities and virtual validations.

Social media taps into our basic human needs for connection and validation. However, it can morph into an addictive loop, where the quest for likes and followers hijacks our brain's reward system.

Social media taps into several fundamental aspects of human psychology. It offers us social connection, a platform for self-expression, and a window into the lives of others. However, it can also feed into our anxieties, insecurities, and the innate tendency to compare ourselves with others.

Our brains get a dopamine hit every time we receive a like or a comment, turning social media into a digital slot machine. We're wired to seek connection and validation, but when they come from a screen, they can leave us feeling empty and craving more.

Neuroimaging studies, including those published in the journal Psychiatry Research, have shown that social media interaction strongly activates dopamine pathways like other rewarding behaviors, such as gambling. Additionally, the National Institute of Health found that getting likes on social media can boost dopamine levels in the brain by 14%, similar to the pleasure derived from eating chocolate. This becomes especially clear when users receive positive feedback, such as likes and comments on their posts.

To counteract this 'reward addiction', consciously diversify your sources of dopamine. Engage in offline activities that also release dopamine but in a more controlled and less addictive manner, such as completing a workout, mastering a new skill, or volunteering. These activities provide a healthier balance to the instant gratification of social media. For example, regular exercise has been shown to boost dopamine by up to 25%, providing a more stable and healthy uplift in mood.

Practical Advice

Social media addiction is like being stuck in a loop of a soap opera. You know it's the same plot over and over, but you just can't stop watching. Every scroll, like, and share is a step deeper into the digital rabbit hole, where time warps and reality blurs.

Picture the scene: you open an app to check the weather, only to find yourself, an hour later, deep in the profile of someone you barely know, analyzing their vacation photos. Or consider the near-universal experience of crafting a post, deleting it, rewriting it, and then pondering over whether to post it at all. These moments are the modern-day comedies of our digital lives—equal parts amusing and perplexing.

Create a 'no-phone zone' in your home—a sanctuary where the

digital world is not invited. Let this be a space for undistracted presence, whether it's at the dinner table or right before bed. Disconnect to reconnect with yourself and those around you.

Audit your social media consumption. Set time limits. Allocate specific times for social media, perhaps 20 minutes thrice a day. This helps prevent constant, mindless scrolling and keeps usage in check. Use app features or external tools to monitor and limit your social media usage. Just as you might track calories for a diet, track your social media intake. Awareness is the first step to change.

Be mindful of your usage. Ask yourself, "Why am I scrolling?" Is it habit, boredom, or genuine interest? Being conscious of your motives can help break the autopilot cycle.

Focus on meaningful interactions. Comment on friends' posts, engage in discussions, or share content that genuinely interests you rather than passively scrolling.

Creative Insights

Transform your feed. Curate your social media to include accounts that inspire, educate, and uplift you rather than those that fuel comparison and inadequacy. Actively manage your feed. Instead of engaging with accounts that provoke negative feelings, choose to follow accounts that inspire and motivate you.

Start a 'lifelog' journal. For every half-hour spent on social media, jot down something productive or enjoyable you could do instead. The solution can be as uncomplicated as reading a book, taking a walk, or giving a friend a call.

Engage in digital detox challenges. Commit to a day or even a week without social media. Notice the changes in your mood, productivity, and interactions.

Replace the habit with a new one. If you reach for your phone out of habit, try replacing it with a new habit, like solving a quick puzzle, sketching, or practicing deep breathing. Explore new hobbies that require your full attention. Immersive activities like painting, cooking, or hiking can provide a fulfilling escape from the digital world.

Reconnect with nature. Nature has its own rhythm, far removed from the frenetic pace of online life. Regular doses of the great outdoors can be incredibly therapeutic.

> Apps: 'Offtime' helps users unplug by blocking distracting apps and filtering communications. 'Moment' tracks overall phone usage and provides coaching to help decrease screen time.

> Books: "Digital Minimalism" by Cal Newport offers a philosophy for technology use that prioritizes long-term happiness over momentary satisfaction.

Activity: Digital Detox Challenge

Today's mission is to spend a day significantly reducing or completely abstaining from social media use, aiming to understand and mitigate its impact on your mental health and well-being. This challenge helps you break the habit of mindlessly scrolling, increases your awareness, and promotes meaningful connections and activities in the real world.

1. Intention Setting: Begin the day by setting clear intentions. Write down your goals for this digital detox, such as increasing focus, reducing anxiety, or improving sleep.

2. Notification Management: Turn off all non-essential notifications or set your devices to "Do Not Disturb" mode to minimize digital interruptions.

3. Media Consumption Reflection: Spend some time reflecting on your typical social media habits. Journal about what triggers your social media use, how long you spend on different platforms, and how these habits affect your mood and productivity.

4. Mindfulness Meditation: Engage in a mindfulness meditation focused on present-moment awareness. Use guided audio if helpful, focusing on breathing and the senses to ground yourself in the here and now.

5. Engage in Real-World Activities: Replace the time you typically spend on social media with real-world activities that can enhance your well-being. This can involve taking a stroll, enjoying a good book, or pursuing a hobby that brings you joy.

6. Social Interaction: Plan a face-to-face interaction with a friend, family member, or neighbor. Focus on making meaningful connections without the interference of digital devices.

7. Learn About Social Media Psychology: Educate yourself about the psychological effects of social media. Watch documentaries or read articles or books that explore how social media is designed to be addictive and its impact on mental health.

8. Cognitive-Behavioral Techniques: Learn and apply cognitive-behavioral techniques to manage urges to check social media. Practice recognizing distorted thoughts and replacing them with more rational responses.

9. Evening Reflection: Reflect on your experience throughout the day. Note any difficulties you faced, how you felt during and after the detox, and any insights you gained about your relationship with social media.

10. Future Use Plan: Develop a plan for more mindful social media use moving forward. Set specific guidelines for when and how you'll engage with social media, focusing on intentional rather than habitual use.

Benefits: This challenge helps you recognize and modify your social media habits, leading to improved mental health, enhanced real-life relationships, and increased personal productivity.

Reflective Questions:

1. How does your current social media use align with your personal values and life goals?
2. What might you gain in your personal and professional life by reducing your digital footprint?

Concluding Thoughts

We're all plugged into this digital matrix, constantly scrolling, liking, and sharing. But here's the thing - it's time to wake up and take control of our lives again!

Listen up, because this is important. Navigating social media isn't about quitting cold turkey. It's about being smart, intentional, and finding a balance that works for you. It's like walking through a busy city - you gotta enjoy the sights and sounds without getting lost in the chaos.

So, how do we escape the siren song of social media? It starts with being mindful. When you're online, make sure it's enhancing your life, not taking away from it. And when you unplug, really unplug. Reconnect with yourself, with the people around you, and with the world beyond your screen.

Dare to press pause. Step back. Savor those unplugged moments. Because in a world that's always on, the best connection is a genuine conversation.

Remember, your life is made up of real experiences, not just digital echoes. So, take control, find your balance, and don't let social media run your life. You've got this!

CHAPTER 38

THE FRIENDSHIP GARDEN: CULTIVATING CONNECTIONS THAT COUNT

"Friendship is born at that moment when one person says to another, 'What! You too? I thought I was the only one.'" — C.S. Lewis

Nurturing meaningful friendships in today's world is like tending a garden in the middle of a concrete jungle. Amidst the hustle and bustle, finding and maintaining these oases of connection requires intention, care, and a bit of green thumb magic.

In a time where our social circles often exist more on screens than, the art of cultivating deep, meaningful friendships seems to belong to a bygone era.

In an age where 'friends' can be added with a click and 'likes' are mistaken for meaningful interactions, genuine friendships can seem like an endangered species. Yet, these relationships are crucial to our happiness and well-being, offering a much-needed antidote to the isolation of modern life.

Did You Know? According to the American Sociological Review, the number of Americans with no close friends has tripled in recent decades. Busy schedules and frequent relocations are cited as common barriers.

Practical Advice

Human beings are social creatures. Friendship, at its core, is about connection and belonging. Our friendships provide emotional support, boost our happiness, and even affect our physical health.

These bonds contribute to our sense of identity and purpose. They're the antidotes to loneliness, the safety nets of our emotional well-being. The challenge is not just in making friends, but in keeping them close in a world that often pulls us apart.

Consistency is key. Regular check-ins, whether through a text, a call, or a coffee date, keep the roots of friendship strong. It's the steady drip of water that keeps the soil of friendship fertile.

Make the first move. Reach out, make plans, and show interest in each other's lives. Friendships are a two-way street, but sometimes, you need to be the one to start the engine. Embrace vulnerability. Sharing your thoughts, fears, and dreams is the soil where deep connections grow. Vulnerability breeds intimacy, turning acquaintances into confidants.

Quality over quantity. It's better to have a few close friends than many acquaintances. Prioritize building stronger relationships with a select few.

Creative Insights

Create friendship rituals. Whether it's a monthly brunch, a yearly trip, or a weekly phone call, establish traditions that keep you connected.

Start a shared hobby or interest. It could be a book club, a music group, or a sports team. Shared activities create shared memories and strengthen bonds. Organize a themed gathering or a unique shared experience. It could be a costume dinner party, a group hike to an unusual destination, or a night of stargazing. Shared experiences create shared memories, the bedrock of friendship.

Be open to friendships in unexpected places across generations, cultures, and backgrounds. Sometimes, meaningful connections are found where we least expect them. These diverse perspectives can enrich your life in ways you never expected.

Learn the art of listening. Sometimes, being a good friend means simply being there, offering a listening ear without judgment or interruption. In conversations, focus entirely on the other person. Listening is one of the most powerful tools in building solid and empathetic connections.

Apps: 'Meetup' is for finding and joining local groups with similar interests and is ideal for cultivating new friendships. 'Bumble BFF' for making new friends who share your hobbies and lifestyle online.

Books: "How to Win Friends and Influence People" by Dale Carnegie, a timeless guide for building and maintaining strong personal connections.

Activity: Cultivating Connections Day

Today's mission is to deepen existing relationships and forge new, meaningful connections. This challenge combines social psychology principles with actionable networking exercises to enhance your social well-being and expand your support network.

1. Relationship Inventory: Start by reflecting on your current social circle. Identify the most meaningful relationships to you and consider how you might strengthen these connections.

2. Intention Setting: Set clear intentions for the day, focusing on what qualities you want to cultivate in your relationships, such as empathy, trust, or supportiveness.

3. Reach Out: Actively reach out to friends or family members you haven't spoken to in a while. Send a thoughtful message, make a phone call, or arrange a meet-up if possible.

4. Memory Sharing: Share a fond memory or express gratitude for their presence in your life, which can strengthen bonds and increase feelings of connectedness.

5. Interest Group Participation: Join a club or group that aligns with your interests. Whether it's a book club, sports team, or art class, engaging in shared activities can foster new friendships.

6. Active Listening Exercises: Practice active listening during your interactions today. Focus entirely on what others are saying without planning your response. Reflect on how this affects the conversation and connection.

7. Empathy Challenge: Try to see things from the perspective of others during your conversations. This practice can deepen your understanding of their experiences and strengthen your emotional connections.

8. Journaling: Spend some time in the evening journaling about your experiences throughout the day. Reflect on how the activities made you feel and what you learned about your relationships.

9. Future Connection Planning: Based on today's experiences, plan for how you will continue to cultivate meaningful relationships—set goals for regular check-ins with friends, ongoing community involvement, or continued participation in group activities.

Benefits: This day-long challenge enhances your interpersonal skills, expands your social network, and deepens your existing relationships.

Reflective Questions:

1. What are the most important qualities you look for in a friend, and how can you develop these qualities within yourself?
2. How can you better nurture your existing friendships to strengthen those bonds?

3. What did you learn about your current relationships, and how can you enhance these connections?
4. Which new connections did you find most promising, and how will you develop these further?

Concluding Thoughts

In this crazy, fast-paced world, it's easy to let those connections slip. But let me tell you something: friendships are the secret sauce that makes life worth living.

Think of it like a garden. You can't just plant some seeds and expect a lush, beautiful space to magically appear. No, you've got to put in the work. You've got to water it, weed it, and give it some TLC (Tender Loving Care). And guess what? Friendships are exactly the same.

It's not always easy, I get it. We're all busy, we've all got a million things on our plates. But if you want those deep, meaningful connections that light up your life, you've got to make them a priority.

So here's what I want you to do. Start small. Reach out to that friend you haven't talked to in a while. Set up a coffee date, a phone call, whatever works. And when you're together, really be present. Listen, laugh, share.

Those are the moments that matter. Because at the end of the day, friendships are what make the journey worthwhile. They're the ones who celebrate your wins, pick you up when you're down, and remind you of who you are when you forget.

So go out there and cultivate those connections. Put in the effort and watch as your friendship garden blooms into something truly beautiful. Trust me, it's worth it.

CHAPTER 39
AGE REIMAGINED: WHY THE 40S ARE THE NEW 30S

"Age is an issue of mind over matter. If you don't mind, it doesn't matter." — Mark Twain

Whoever said, "Life begins at 40!" wasn't kidding. Welcome to the club where 40 is the new 30, only with more style, wisdom, and a much better credit score. It's the age where you finally start to master the art of not sweating the small stuff—mainly because you forgot where you put your glasses.

Embracing aging in today's world is like being part of an exclusive club where experience meets energy. Gone are the days when hitting 40 meant slowing down. Now, it's about shifting gears, rediscovering passions, and living life with a vigor that would make your 30-year-old self a tad envious.

The 40s are a psychological renaissance—a time when self-confidence blooms, the pressure to conform wanes, and life's priorities become clearer. It's a sweet spot where the zest of youth meets the richness of experience.

Wisdom from the Wise

"I didn't become a designer until I was 40, but that gave me over 20 years of experience and perspective that significantly informed my work," — Vera Wang.

Vera Wang's journey into fashion design at 40 exemplifies how midlife is not the beginning of a decline, but potentially the start of the most productive and creative period of one's life.

Adopt the '40s is the new 30s' mantra. It's more than a catch-phrase; it's a mindset. Embrace the energy and curiosity of your 30s with the bonus of 40-something wisdom. Celebrate the milestones, both big and small. Every year is an achievement, a testament to your journey. Throw the party, take the trip, live it up—your 40s are a time to revel in life.

Did You Know? Research in developmental psychology shows that individuals in their 40s often experience enhanced emotional well-being and stability. The 40s are typically marked by increased self-awareness and emotional intelligence, contributing to more fulfilling personal and professional relationships.

Physiological and Cognitive Development in the 40s

Contrary to common misconceptions, middle age can be a period of significant brain development and cognitive resilience. Neuroscientific studies show that brain plasticity continues into middle age, allowing adults to continue learning and improving cognitive functions well into their 40s and beyond.

Don't just settle into the familiar—shake it up! Learning isn't just for the young; it's your secret weapon to keep your mind sharp. Grab that guitar, sign up for a language class, or dive into digital painting. These can stimulate neuroplasticity, helping to maintain cognitive agility and mental acuity.

Challenge your brain daily, and watch your mental agility hit levels that your 30-year-old self could only dream of. It's not just fun; it's brain evolution!

Thanks to medical advancements and improved knowledge about health, people in their 40s are healthier than ever. If you thought your 40s were all about slowing down, think again! It's time to double down on your health.

Get that heart pumping with activities you love—cycling, dancing, swimming. Mix it up with strength training to keep your muscles guessing. Remember, a healthy body is your ticket to a dynamic life. Regular check-ups? Non-negotiable. Make your well-being a top priority, and your body will thank you with energy that lasts!

"Life would be infinitely happier if we could only be born at the age of eighty and gradually approach eighteen." — Mark Twain

---

Individuals in their 40s often hold significant societal and economic roles, leveraging their experience and expertise. They will probably be in leadership positions and influence policy and corporate strategies, contributing substantially to economic productivity and societal development. Now's the time to flex your emotional muscles.

Use your 40s to deepen relationships and enhance your understanding of yourself and others. Have you got a knack for sensing moods and motives? Use it to strengthen your personal and professional relationships. Being emotionally savvy means handling life's ups and downs gracefully—make emotional intelligence a part of your daily routine.

You've got the experience; now share the wisdom! Whether it's at work or in your community, step up and lead. Mentor the next generation, spearhead a project, or volunteer for a cause that lights you up. Your 40s are your leadership years—make them count by leaving a mark that matters. It's about making an impact, one bold step at a time.

Technological advancements have made it easier for people in their 40s to maintain health, connect with others, and manage their personal and professional lives efficiently.

Embrace technology to supercharge your daily life. Not just for keeping up with the kids or managing your calendar—use tech to enhance your health, learn new skills, and connect with friends or networks. From smartwatches that track your fitness to apps that help you meditate or learn, let technology be your partner in crafting a fulfilling, balanced life

Creative Insights

Create a **"Fabulous at 40"** bucket list. Think of all the things you wanted to do in your 30s but didn't. Now's the time to dive into those dreams with the gusto of a 30-year-old and the savvy of a 40-year-old.

Reinvent your style. Experiment with fashion, try a new look. Your 40s are your style playground—sophisticated, playful, or downright rebellious. Explore new hobbies or revisit old ones. Want to learn guitar, write a book, or take up pottery? There's no better time than your 40s to explore these passions.

Nurture intergenerational friendships. These connections keep perspectives fresh and dynamic, combining the vibrancy of youth with the depth of maturity.

Prioritize health and well-being. Your 40s are the perfect time to invest in your health—not just for longevity but for quality of life. Cultivate a positive attitude towards aging. It's not about denying the years; it's about celebrating them. Each year adds to your story, your essence, your you.

Apps: 'Duolingo' for learning new languages and 'Strava' for tracking fitness goals.

Books: "Artist's Way" by Julia Cameron, "Midlife: A Philosophical Guide" by Kieran Setiya, "Designing Your Life: How to Build a Well-Lived, Joyful Life" by Bill Burnett and Dave Evans, and "Younger Next Year: Live Strong, Fit, and Sexy—Until You're 80 and Beyond" by Chris Crowley and Henry S. Lodge, which guides on living vigorously into your later years.

Activity: Ageless Vitality Day

Today's mission is to dedicate a day to embracing and enhancing vitality at any age, focusing especially on redefining what it means to be in your 40s. This challenge involves activities that promote physical health, mental acuity, and emotional well-being, demonstrating that age can indeed be just a number.

1. Energizing Workout: Start with a workout tailored to increase stamina and strength, such as a mix of cardio and resistance training. Emphasize exercises that have proved beneficial for those in their 40s, like Pilates, for core strength and stability.

2. Inspirational Reading: Read stories or articles about people who found new passions and success in their 40s and beyond, illustrating that personal growth does not stop at any age.

3. Brain Games: Engage in activities designed to enhance cognitive function, such as puzzles, strategy games, or learning a new skill or language. These exercises help keep the brain sharp and improve memory and problem-solving skills.

4. Creative Expression: Spend some time on a creative hobby you enjoy or have always wanted to try, such as painting, writing, or playing a musical instrument. Creative activities stimulate mental flexibility and innovation.

5. Healthy Cooking Session: Prepare a meal focusing on anti-aging nutrients like antioxidants and omega-3 fatty acids.

6. Wellness Workshop: Participate in a workshop or online seminar about holistic wellness practices that support aging gracefully, including meditation, yoga, or tai chi.

7. Social Interaction: Organize a meet-up with friends or family virtually or in person. Social connections are vital for emotional health and can significantly impact mental well-being as we age.

8. Gratitude Reflection: Reflect on your life's achievements and experiences so far. Writing a gratitude list can enhance positive feelings and satisfaction with life's journey.

9. Relaxation Techniques: Engage in relaxation practices such as deep breathing exercises, progressive muscle relaxation, or a warm bath. These help soothe the mind and body, promoting better sleep and recovery.

10. Future Goals Setting: Set goals for the next decade. Planning for the future can invigorate your approach to daily life and provide clear milestones to strive toward.

Benefits: This activity promotes an age-positive approach to life, particularly as you enter your 40s. It encourages maintaining physical health, mental sharpness, and emotional resilience, vital to a fulfilling and vibrant life regardless of age.

Reflective Questions:

1. What activities did you find most beneficial for feeling rejuvenated and why?
2. What are the most exciting possibilities that your 40s offer you?
3. How can you use your experience and knowledge to make a positive impact on your personal and professional life?

Concluding Thoughts

The 40s are a new beginning, not just a continuation of the 30s. Forget everything you've heard about the 40s being a time when life slows down. That's old thinking, and it's time for a major reality check!

Here's the truth: your 40s are not just another decade—they're a whole new state of mind. This is the time when you've got the freedom, self-awareness, and a hunger for adventure all coming together in one incredible package. So, what are you waiting for? It's time to open your arms wide and shout, "Bring it on!"

I want you to remember one thing: age is just a number, but attitude is everything. This isn't about trying to be someone you're not; it's about living fully, laughing loudly, and loving every step of the journey. You've got the wisdom of 40 and the heart of 30—that's a powerful combination!

This is your moment to shine, to innovate, and to lead a life that's bursting with purpose and meaning. You're not just living; you're thriving. So, are you ready to make these the best years of your life?

It's time to step into this exciting chapter with passion, purpose, and a hunger for new adventures. Don't let anyone tell you that your best days are behind you. Your best days are happening right now, and the best is yet to come!

Let's embrace this era together and show the world what it means to be in your 40s. It's not about slowing down; it's about rising up and making every moment count. So, let's get out there and make these years the most incredible yet!

CHAPTER 40

TIME FOR A TUNE-UP: THE ART OF SELF-REFLECTION AND PERSONAL GROWTH

"Stop looking at who you are now; start looking at who you could become." — George Lois

---

Picture yourself driving a car without ever inspecting the oil or inflating the tires. It wouldn't run very well, would it? The same goes for our personal and professional lives.

Neglecting self-reflection is like ignoring a blinking check engine light. Without regular self-reflection, we risk running on empty, stuck in old patterns that don't serve us well.

Our brains are like high-performance vehicles; they need regular pit stops or they risk burning out. Neglecting self-care isn't just detrimental to our mental and physical health; it's like trying to sprint a marathon—eventually, you'll hit the wall.

This chapter is about taking the time to do a thorough tune-up of your most important vehicle—yourself.

So, let's roll up our sleeves, grab some tools, and start tuning!

Wisdom from the Wise

Think about Michael Jordan's career. He continually assessed his performances and worked relentlessly on his weaknesses, which helped him become one of the greatest basketball players of all time. His commitment to self-improvement and reflection was key to his success.

Marcus Aurelius, the Roman Emperor, and Stoic philosopher, left behind a series of personal writings known as Meditations. These reflections, initially written for his own guidance and self-improvement, provide insight into his philosophical practices and the importance of self-reflection for personal growth and ethical living.

Cleopatra VII, the final reigning leader of Egypt's Ptolemaic Kingdom, understood the power of legacy and used her influence to try to extend her reign and impact. Her political maneuvers, alliances, and cultural patronage aimed to secure her legacy within the realms of world history.

Mel Robbins might say, "Self-reflection is the school of wisdom." If you're not learning about yourself, you're missing out on your best teacher—you. Paul Arden might say, "It's not how good you are, it's how good you want to be"—and self-reflection is how you get there.

Did You Know? Regular self-reflection is linked to higher emotional intelligence and better decision-making skills, making you more agile in both personal and professional spheres. Additionally, studies show that regular self-reflection can result in significantly lower stress levels and greater life satisfaction.

The Science of Self-Reflection

You know how your phone keeps nagging you about software

updates? Yes, they're annoying as hell, but you do them anyway because you know they keep your device running like a well-oiled machine. Well, guess what? Your brain needs those updates too, and that's where self-reflection comes in.

Self-reflection isn't some fluffy, feel-good exercise; it's an essential practice for anyone serious about personal and professional growth. It lets you understand your motivations, challenges, successes, and failures. Self-reflection helps you navigate your path with greater clarity and purpose, ensuring you're not just going through the motions, but growing through them. It is about building a mindset that values growth over comfort and progress over stagnation.

Let's tap into the mechanics of the mind: self-reflection boosts neuroplasticity, enhancing your brain's ability to adapt and evolve. Every time you reflect, you're essentially wiring your brain to develop new, more effective patterns of thought and behavior. It's about strengthening your mental muscles through regular exercise—only instead of lifting weights, you're lifting thoughts, turning them over, and examining them from every angle.

Self-reflection integrates past events with present concerns, and it's crucial for learning from experiences. It's like updating your internal software to improve decision-making, increase emotional intelligence, and sharpen problem-solving skills. Reflecting isn't just about looking back; it's about connecting the dots in a way that maps out a clearer road ahead.

Apps: 'Day One' for journaling or 'Reflectly' to guide your self-reflection with AI-driven insights.

Books: Marcus Aurelius's Meditations offer timeless wisdom on self-reflection from one of history's greatest philosophers.

Activity: Legacy Builder

Today's mission is to reflect deeply on the impact you want to leave in the world, crafting a personal legacy that aligns with your values and life's work.

1. Legacy Visioning: Spend some quiet time thinking about how you want to be remembered. What values do you want your life to represent? What impact do you want to have on your community or the world?

2. Life Review: Look back over your life and identify the actions and decisions that you feel proud of. Consider how these instances reflect the legacy you wish to build.

3. Gap Analysis: Identify any gaps between your current path and the legacy you wish to leave. What changes or improvements do you need to make to align your actions with your desired legacy?

4. Legacy Actions: Outline specific actions you can take to start building your legacy now. This could involve starting a community project, mentoring others, or changing your professional life to focus more on impactful work.

5. Commitment Letter: Write a letter to yourself outlining your legacy goals and the steps you will take to achieve them. Set a date in the future to review this letter and assess your progress.

Benefits: This exercise helps clarify your long-term goals and ensures that your daily actions contribute to a meaningful, impactful life. It fosters a sense of purpose and commitment to living according to your deepest values.

Reflective Questions:

1. What have you learned about yourself this month?
2. What are the most valuable lessons you've learned from this challenge?
3. What recent success or failure have you not thoroughly examined?
4. How will you apply these lessons moving forward to continue your growth and development?

Concluding Thoughts

Here's the thing: if you want to future-proof your life, you need to understand where you are right now. It's not always pretty, but it's necessary. Self-reflection is like a GPS for your personal growth journey. It helps you navigate the twists and turns, avoid the roadblocks, and ultimately reach your destination.

This week, I'm challenging you to do a little mental maintenance. Grab a pen and paper, open up a fresh document on your laptop, or even use the notes app on your phone—whatever works for you. Just start writing. It doesn't have to be a novel; a few sentences each day will do the trick.

Use this time to reflect on your day, the choices you made, and the direction you're headed. Don't just go through the motions; really think about how you're feeling and what you're learning. Trust me, by the end of the week, you'll be blown away by the clarity and insight you've gained.

So, are you ready for a tune-up? Start your self-reflection practice today and watch as your life shifts into high gear. Remember, you're in the driver's seat, and this is one update you don't want to skip.

CHAPTER 41

THE LAST SLICE DILEMMA: DECIDING WHO GETS THE LAST PIECE OF PIZZA

"You can't have just one slice of pizza. If you do, you are capable of things that scare me." — Jim Gaffigan

---

In every pizza-loving gathering, there comes a critical moment—a moment of truth that is as inevitable as it is fraught with unspoken tension. It's the moment when just one slice of pizza remains in the box, and everyone covertly yearns for it.

This slice, often pepperoni-laden or dripping with cheese, sits there like a culinary Holy Grail, its mere existence posing a silent question to the group: Who deserves the last piece? This isn't merely a choice. It's a social Rubik's Cube, where every move reveals something about us.

This isn't just about hunger; it's a delicate dance of desire, etiquette, and social dynamics. Welcome to the "Last Slice Dilemma!"

Did You Know? Psychological studies have shown that decisions about dividing resources like food can enhance or diminish a sense of community. How we share food can affect our relationships, impacting feelings of trust and connectedness.

The Psychology of Sharing

At its core, this dilemma incorporates the psychology of sharing, a concept that has been ingrained in us since childhood. "Sharing is caring," we're told. But as the last slice sits there, almost mocking us with its deliciousness, we find our primal selves at odds with societal norms. Here lies a perfect opportunity to delve into the psychology of group behavior. Why do some people boldly claim the last piece while others hold back?

Every group, whether friends or family, operates on a set of unspoken rules. Who usually takes the lead? Who is the peacemaker? Observing the dynamics when the last slice is at stake can be revealing. The bold one might leap at it without a second thought, the altruist might push it toward the group's quietest member, or there might be those who pretend they've had enough, but their eyes tell a different story.

The decision of who gets the last slice of pizza can evoke strong emotional responses because of social and psychological dynamics, such as fairness, generosity, and self-control. Research in social psychology highlights that people who offer the last piece to others are often seen as more likable and socially conscious.

Make it a moment of generosity, not a battle. Offer that last slice with a smile and make a joke out of it. It's not just a piece of pizza; it's a chance to be remembered as someone who cares more about the company than the meal. This small act is huge—it says you're thoughtful and generous. That's how you leave a great impression.

Creative Solutions

Situations involving scarcity, like the last slice of pizza, can trigger stress responses, leading to competitive or hoarding behaviors. Studies in behavioral economics have shown that scarcity can cloud judgment, pushing people to act more impulsively.

Challenge the scarcity mindset by stepping back and offering the slice to someone else. Turn this into a moment of mindfulness where you consciously decide not to let a trivial scarcity trigger you. Laugh about it and suggest sharing it. It's just pizza, but your reaction can set the tone for bigger issues.

Social norms and etiquette play a crucial in deciding who should take the last piece of pizza. In many cultures, offering the last piece to others is considered polite, and doing so can be a sign of respect and consideration.

Use this as a teachable moment, especially if kids are watching. Demonstrate what it means to be considerate and kind. Say something like, "It's important to think of others before ourselves." This helps reinforce positive behaviors and shows that manners matter, even over something as simple as the last slice of pizza.

The decision of who takes the last slice often occurs under social pressure, where individuals might feel the need to conform to the actions of others. Studies in psychology show that individuals tend to mimic the actions of their peers in social environments.

Be the leader in decision-making moments. If everyone hesitates, step up with a playful proposal to share the slice or make it a fun contest. Leading the decision can break the tension and turn an awkward moment into a memorable one.

How groups handle minor disputes like the last slice of pizza can reflect their general approach to conflict resolution. Managing such situations with humor and fairness can prevent conflicts and foster a positive group dynamic.

Propose a creative compromise. Say, "Let's split it, or let's see who can earn it with the best joke!" Using humor to diffuse the situation shows you're a problem solver who values harmony over conflict. It's a way to keep things light and remind everyone that it's more about the shared experience than the last piece of the pie.

Apps: Decision-making apps like 'Tiny Decisions' or 'Decision Roulette' to randomize who gets the last slice, adding fun and fairness to the decision.

Books: "Predictably Irrational" by Dan Ariely explores how our decisions are often influenced by hidden forces. "The Joy of Conflict Resolution" by Gary Harper explores the transformative potential of resolving everyday conflicts, applicable even in scenarios as simple as sharing pizza.

Activity: The Last Slice Games

1. The Pizza Lottery: Turn the decision into a game. Write names on slips of paper and draw the winner. It adds an element of chance and fun to the decision.

2. Splitting the Spoils: Why not propose cutting the slice into smaller pieces? It's a diplomatic solution that emphasizes fairness.

3. Merit-Based Allocation: Turn it into a playful debate. Who deserves it the most and why? This can lead to hilarious justifications and light-hearted banter.

4. Deferred Gratification: Introduce a rule where whoever forgoes the slice this time gets first dibs next time. It's a test of willpower and long-term thinking.

5. The Last Slice Challenge: Create a mini-contest. It could be a trivia question or a silly physical challenge. The winner earns the slice.

6. Anonymous Vote: Let democracy decide. Everyone votes for who they think should get the slice. It's fair and can be quite revealing about group dynamics.

Reflective Questions:

1. Recall a time when you faced a similar 'last slice' dilemma. How did it resolve, and how did you feel about the outcome?
2. What does your approach to such dilemmas say about your values and principles?

Concluding Thoughts

Alright, let's talk about something that might seem silly at first glance but actually reveals a ton about human behavior - the last slice of the pizza dilemma. You know what I'm talking about, right? You're at a gathering, there's one slice left in the box, and suddenly everyone's eyeing it like it's the most valuable thing in the room.

But here's the thing: how we handle this moment says a lot about us as individuals and as a society. It's not just about satisfying our hunger; it's about fairness, kindness, and maybe even a little bit of sacrifice. Think about it this way - when you're faced with that last slice, you have a choice. You can grab it for yourself, or you can offer it to someone else. And that decision, as small as it may seem, is actually a reflection of your values and the kind of relationships you want to build.

So next time you find yourself in this situation, I challenge you to pause and consider the bigger picture. Use it as an opportunity to practice empathy, generosity, and maybe even a little bit of self-control. Because at the end of the day, it's not about the pizza - it's about how we treat each other and the kind of community we create together.

The last slice dilemma might seem like a trivial thing, but it's actually a powerful tool for understanding ourselves and each other better. So let's not just savor that last piece of pizza - let's use it as a chance to build a world where everyone gets a fair share, and where kindness is always on the menu.

CHAPTER 42
THE ULTIMATE ENIGMA: UNDERSTANDING THE MEANING OF THE LIFE, THE UNIVERSE AND EVERYTHING

"The unexamined life is not worth living." — Socrates

In a universe as vast and enigmatic as Douglas Adams' imagination, what if 42 isn't just an answer but a mosaic of all life's questions and experiences? What if the actual power lies not in finding the ultimate answer but in discovering your own ultimate question?

The quest for meaning is as old as humanity itself. Our brains are wired for curiosity, seeking understanding and purpose. Crafting our ultimate question is a deep dive into our psyche, a chance to confront, challenge, and ultimately embrace our place in the universe.

Picture each chapter, each problem we've explored, as a unique star in the galaxy of our existence. Chapter 42 is where we step back to admire the constellation we've created, seeing how each star, each challenge, illuminates our path.

This final chapter isn't a solitary question but an ensemble of every inquiry we've posed, a symphony of our collective curiosity.

It's where procrastination meets purpose, solitude dances with social connection, and the burnout of passion reignites in the flames of resilience.

Every question we've explored is a hue in the spectrum of our lives. From navigating the digital age to rekindling creativity, each color adds depth and richness, painting a portrait of our shared human journey.

Reflect on the lessons learned. Each chapter has been a stepping stone, a lesson in balancing life's intricacies with humor, boldness, and insight. Use these lessons as tools to craft a life of fulfillment and meaning.

Encourage continuous exploration. The end of this book is merely the beginning of your journey. Keep asking questions, keep seeking answers, and keep exploring the uncharted territories of your life.

Create your life's masterpiece. Each chapter, each problem, and each solution are a brushstroke in the art of your existence. Be bold in your choices, be vibrant in your actions, and be profound in your thoughts.

Reflect on your passions and fears. What drives you, and what holds you back? Your ultimate question often lies at the intersection of these two forces.

Explore different philosophies and perspectives. Broadening your intellectual horizons can help crystallize your thoughts and bring you closer to your question.

Write a personal manifesto. This will guide you to distill your beliefs, values, and aspirations, paving the way to your ultimate question.

Travel, both physically and through literature. Experiencing diverse cultures and ideas can provide the backdrop against which your ultimate question can take shape.

Seek conversations that challenge you. Discussions with people who think differently can spark insights and refine your understanding of what truly matters to you.

Document your journey. Just as this book has been a narrative of solutions, let your life be a story of exploration, growth, and discovery. Journal, create, express—let your journey inspire others.

See the interconnectedness of each challenge. Understand how overcoming fear intertwines with embracing change, how solitude enriches social bonds, and how the quest for perfection finds harmony in imperfection.

Cherish the wisdom of the collective. Each chapter has been about individual growth and our shared human experience. Remember, in our stories lie the universal truths of life.

Welcome to Your Grand Finale (Or Is It Just the Overture?)

Welcome to our final page, the closing chapter, where we tie all the strings, and yet, we stand at the beginning of everything else. Picture yourself as both the artist and the canvas, the playwright and the stage. Every single challenge you've overcome, every problem you've solved - those are the brushstrokes on the masterpiece that is uniquely YOU.

In the spirit of Douglas Adams' iconic "42," the answer lies in the questions we have the courage to ask and the paths we choose to explore. Your story is a testament to this never-ending quest, a narrative written in the stars themselves.

As we wrap up, remember that the galaxy of your life is ever-expanding, filled with stars yet to be discovered and constellations yet to be named. Your journey through life is a canvas, and you are the artist. Paint boldly, live fully, and remember that in the tapestry of the cosmos, your thread is irreplaceable.

So here's my challenge to you: embrace the unknown, ask the big questions, and paint your own damn masterpiece! Because at the end of the day, that's what life is all about - creating something extraordinary out of the chaos, one bold stroke at a time.

It's time to stop practicing and start living. The world is waiting for you to make your mark!

What are you waiting for?

Let's do this!

ABOUT THE AUTHOR

Gizem Şahan, an engineer turned career and life coach, brings a unique blend of analytical precision and compassionate guidance to the world of personal development. Starting her career in engineering, Gizem mastered the art of solving complex problems with innovative solutions. However, her passion for understanding human behavior led her to transition into coaching, where she earned her certification from the International Coaching Federation.

Gizem's coaching approach is distinctive, combining the logical rigor of engineering with the empathetic, personalized touch of a life coach. Her global perspective and relentless pursuit of personal growth have empowered thousands to overcome obstacles and achieve their full potential.

In "Creative Solutions for Ordinary Problems," Gizem shares her unique insights and strategies, offering readers practical and creative ways to tackle everyday challenges. Her book reflects her journey from engineering to coaching, and her dedication to helping others navigate their paths with clarity and ingenuity.

Gizem Şahan continues to inspire and empower individuals, making a profound impact in the field of self-improvement and communication.

Email: gizemsahan@gizemsahan.com
Website: http://www.gizemsahan.com

linkedin.com/in/gizemsahan
amazon.com/author/gizemsahan